the WILD LAWN handbook

Alternatives to the Traditional Front Lawn

Stevie Daniels

Macmillan • USA

Macmillan General Reference
A Simon & Schuster Macmillan Company
1633 Broadway
New York, NY 10019-6785

Map illustration by Patti Rutman

Library of Congress Cataloging-in-Publication Data
Daniels, Stevie.
    The wild lawn handbook : alternatives to the traditional front lawn / Stevie Daniels.
        p.   cm.
    Includes bibliographical references (p.   ) and index.
    ISBN: 0-02-529445-8
        1. Natural landscaping.   2. Native plant gardening.   3. Ground cover plants.   4. Native plants
for cultivation.   I. Title.
    SB439.D36   1995
    635.9'5173—dc20   94-5369
                                        CIP

Manufactured in the United States of America
10 9 8 7 6 5 4 3

Acknowledgments

This book was made possible by the trailblazing, inventive homeowners across the country who have transformed their front lawns into gardens of native grasses, wildflowers, moss, heathers, or other plants adapted to their particular region. I thank those who are featured here for their time and for sharing their knowledge in order to help others. I particularly thank Will Corley, Vicki Nowicki, Gianna Walker, Lorrie Otto, Chuck Sims, Reed Lewis, Lee Stone, Charles Mann, John Krouse, Art Gover, Craig Tufts, Nancy McLeod, and Bret Rappaport who spent hours taking me to visit "wild lawns" or who provided numerous contacts and information in my search. I am grateful to the staff of Skillman Library, Lafayette College, for tracking down numerous articles and books for me and to Lynda Miller, who typed the charts at the eleventh hour. I also thank William Niering, Terry Riordan, and Pam Hoenig for helpful comments on earlier versions. For their patience during the last few months when I spent early morning hours before going to work, late evening hours, and most of my weekends at the computer, I thank my son, Jonathan, and my partner, Chuck McCullagh, who encouraged me from the day I first began talking about the transformation of American suburbia into a landscape of native plants that would provide food and shelter for wildlife, conserve water, and help restore the unique natural heritage of the many distinctive regions of this country.

Contents

Introduction

We want shaven carpets of grass here and there, but what nonsense it is to shave it as often as foolish men shave their faces! There are indeed places where they boast of mowing forty acres! Who would not rather see the waving grass with countless flowers than a close surface without a blossom? Think of the labour wasted in this ridiculous work of cutting the heads off flowers and grass. Let much of the grass grow till fit to cut for hay, and we may enjoy in it a world of lovely flowers that will blossom and perfect their growth before hay time; some have waving lawns of feathery grass where they used to shave the grass every ten days; a cloud of flowers where a daisy was not let peep.

William Robinson
The Wild Garden
1894

The intensively managed, monotonous single-species turfgrass lawn is gradually giving way across the United States to, at least, a more relaxed approach that allows other plants to mingle, and at most, to a complete substitution with native grasses, wildflowers, ground covers, or moss. Eighty-one percent of the 30 million acres that comprise the landscapes around single-family homes is lawn, according to the Lawn Institute, and in 1992, 52 million homeowners who tended their own lawns spent $7.5 billion on their care, according to the National Gardening Survey. Even though this is about an 8 percent increase since 1988, the rising sales of native grass and wildflower seed and increased participation in national wildlife habitat programs indicate that the nearly 24 million acres of home lawns is declining. Even those who still love their lawns and enjoy their care are reducing the size by enlarging garden beds or by replacing turfgrass with ground covers.

During my travels this past year to visit some of the thousands of homeowners who have created "wild lawns" that reflect the distinctive vegetation of their region, I was struck by the diversity of this country's native habitats and the beauty of our native grasses and wildflowers. As a child, I remember gathering the seed heads of grasses; I thought they were as pretty as flowers and I took them to my mother as a bouquet. Looking back, I realize how important it was that she marveled at my gift and did not say, "Oh, those are just weeds." She talked with me about the subtle colors and fine textures of the grass flowers. All of that wonderful childhood excitement came back when I stepped into the Schulenberg Prairie at the Morton Arboretum in Illinois and saw big bluestem, little bluestem, rattlesnake master, and hundreds of other prairie plants that I had known only through the books that I studied.

When you discover the vast choice of native grasses and flowers available for your specific region, and realize that because they are adapted to your particular soil and climate they do not need additional water or fertilizer once planted properly and well-established, you'll join the ranks of those who have chosen their region's local plant heritage over imported Kentucky bluegrass, Bermuda grass, or St. Augustine lawns. If you have thought about making a change, but are uncertain about what alternatives are available for your yard and what they would look like, this book is for you.

The four main lawn alternatives are a prairie planting, a meadow, moss, and ground covers. Depending on the size of your front lawn, you may choose one of these options or a combination of them. The detailed discussion of each alternative in individual chapters is interspersed with experiences of homeowners who have exchanged their lawns for these diverse, ecologically sound "wild" lawns. You'll learn how to choose the right alternative for your region and how to make the change.

The first step is to determine the ecological region in which you live (see the map on page 21) and then consider the particular soil and climatic conditions of your site. Of most importance in choosing alternative plants for your lawn is to use natives. A native plant is one that is indigenous to a specific location, which could be as small as a county or as large as a country. Some plants may be native to Kansas but at some point were introduced to Virginia and now grow well there. Technically, they are exotics in Virginia; in some cases, native plants that are introduced into another part of the United States become too vigorous and actually pose a threat to the native species of that region. If a native plant evolved in a certain geographical area but your home is built in a suburban development in which all of the topsoil has been removed and the native shrubs and trees cut down, you will have to consider which natives will be able to become established in those trying conditions.

There are hundreds of nonnative, nonaggressive, low-growing ornamentals that can be used along with natives. A controversy exists among natural landscapers about the use of natives versus nonnatives; some feel very strongly that if you are trying to establish a natural plant community, then only plants native to that particular region should be used. This opinion is held due to the complex interrelationship of soil, climate, plants, insects, and animals that makes up a true native plant community. According to the purists, any nonnative plant breaks the web and makes it impossible for the community to truly establish itself. As naturalist and native plant enthusiast Lorrie Otto, of Wisconsin, puts it, "the nonnative plants confuse the landscape."

The continuance of a native species without the constant manipulation of humans depends on it being in the habitat or community of plants in which it originated. The resiliency of the community depends upon genetic diversity.

You will have to decide where you stand on this issue. Whatever your decision, use as many native plants as possible. The tables on pages 35 and 47 are selected lists of the best native grasses and well-adapted and native ground covers for use as alternatives to turfgrass. If you wish your yard to be a reflection of the regional landscape in which you live, then you will need to closely match the plant species that you select with the habitat in which they are planted—that is, if you have a wooded site, plant woodland wildflowers and other shade-loving native plants beneath the trees; if you have a desert location, plant dryland grasses, cactus, desert marigold, fringed sage, penstemons, and so forth.

In parts of the country where rainfall is sufficient for one of the turfgrasses, you may want to keep some part of your yard area as a mown lawn. Even so, consider allowing the lawn to be more relaxed than a pure stand of one species which requires intensive management to eliminate unwanted plants, maintain fertility, and keep it green. A more relaxed or biodiverse lawn may include dandelions, violets, Dutch white clover, and yarrow. These alternative lawns require no fertilizer, no additional water, and mowing only every third week or so.

This book is not a treatise against lawns; it is a handbook for homeowners who want to reduce or stop using chemical fertilizers and pesticides, conserve water, turn their yard into a collection of plants that attracts birds, butterflies, and other wildlife, or want to use their small piece of land to restore one of the natural habitats of our country. Indeed, stepping away from a traditional close-cropped front yard turf to a diverse, ever-changing landscape marks a change from just mowing the grass to becoming a gardener.

Gardens, unlike lawns, create experiences that uplift our spirits, expand our visions, and invigorate our lives. The efforts expended to maintain a lawn can be used instead to plant and restore the native vegetation of your part of the country. Your "wild lawn" becomes an extension of the natural world rather than a constant battle to maintain a crop where it does not want to be. Instead of traveling to see the last protected wilderness areas in our country, you can make your yard a small spot of wilderness where the butterflies, hawks, rabbits, turtles, and, in some areas still, foxes, will come to you.

Many species of plants and animals need large expanses of natural areas and connections between those areas to survive. Throughout our country exist parks, forests, and wildlife and nature preserves where natural plant communities are protected and efforts are underway to eradicate the exotic species that have invaded them. Some states have begun to restore native vegetation along major roads and highways. Research has shown that powerline corridors through forests must be a little more than sixty yards wide before animals will migrate through and birds will use the area as habitat; forest corridors through agricultural land need to be more than 100 yards wide to retain the native tree species.

Three major efforts to conserve and restore native ecosystems in our country are: the Gap Analysis Project of the United States Fish and Wildlife Service, the Wildlands Project, and a proposed Native Ecosystems Act still in the formative stages. Although the Gap Project uses vegetation maps to highlight gaps in the protection of certain ecosystem types, it does not include specific plans for protection of entire ecosystems. The Wildlands Project, on the other hand, is meant to establish comprehensive networks of reserves, buffer zones, and connections in every region of North America.

The more natural landscapes that homeowners create by converting their yards, the more corridors will be opened up to connect what remaining large natural acreages we have left. You will see and experience the difference it makes when you change your own yard; the more landowners around you who do the same, the more species will thrive and the greater the range of wildlife that will pass through and be supported by the increased natural land area and diversity of plants. "In the big picture, connectivity is directly related to long-term biodiversity," says Joan Nassauer, head of the University of Minnesota's Department of Landscape Architecture. She has researched how aesthetics affect the acceptance (or nonacceptance) of ecologically sustainable landscapes.

Why should our homes be circumscribed by nonnative plants and sit in a moat of nonnative grass that requires constant watering, fertilizing, and mowing to meet the conventional standards? Somehow we have arrived at the point in which homogenization and monotony are called "aesthetically pleasing" and not cutting the lawn is called "un-American." Some have referred to the lawn as an "American tradition" but it is hardly so. Only extensively implemented since World War II, it is a monocrop of species that are not indigenous to the United States; they are not "American" plants. They are not part of any of our native plant heritage, they do not thrive well without constant care, and they do not feed wildlife.

Warren Kenfield, author of *The Wild Gardener in the Wild Landscape*, said it best: "The lawn is one of the most interesting sociological and psychological phenomena of our times....It is a sort of a living fossil, having evolved several thousand years ago in the history of our West European culture....Lawns are kept alive only by an exorbitant amount of nursing and babying, otherwise they would disappear, to be as extinct as the dodo....I prefer a bed of moss, the subtle satisfaction of a stretch of periwinkle, or the inviting expanses of an unmowed grassland rippling in the breeze."

Kenfield's unique book was based on his twenty-one years of experience managing the meadow, hedgerows, and forests of a farm in New England by encouraging native species and getting rid of invasive and weedy plants. He describes naturalistic landscaping as "a practical art involving the aesthetic manipulation of plants and plant-communities to form a pleasing whole." His voice was the earliest (the book was published in 1966) to question our attachment to lawns and to offer practical advice for an alternative. Nearly half the book is a list of plant families, including their role in a naturalistic plant community, problems of introducing them, and how they behave after introduction.

In a country whose people are known for their penchant for "making a statement," it is ironic that we have created and participated for so long in this ritual of lawn mowing that calls for consensus and conformity. So deeply entrenched as a way of showing that one cares and has pride in one's home grounds, it makes it difficult for people to break through and use their land as a means of self-expression. Our society proscribes so much of our lives that our homes and yards are the only quiet, personal refuge left.

Many Americans are emerging from this fifty-year coma of landscape monotony and are reclaiming their yards—front and back. They are beginning a *true* American tradition by growing native plants in a managed landscape, creating unique, personalized expressions based on the native plant communities that existed on the site before it was developed. As they take responsibility for working with nature, releasing the landscape from the encroachment and demise caused by invasive exotic species, they find that their own artistic and aesthetic capabilities are released. Our native vegetation is our American tradition, not mowing lawns.

As these issues inevitably get played out again and again in the many neighbor-to-neighbor conflicts, more people are made aware of the environmental costs of the lawn and are educated about their region's native plants. Too often, those who object think that the native plants are "weeds" because they have seen them along the roadsides or in country areas all of their lives. But as they soon discover, those plants are not "weeds" at all and in fact are endangered because the natural areas have been invaded by actual "weeds" that crowd out the natives. The health and survival of the complex interrelated web of life which includes the air, soil, water, plants, insects, animals— and, yes, us—depends on biodiversity and the balance of all the elements.

This book reports the efforts that have already begun and gives in formation for you to act on as well. Despite the many years and millions of dollars spent on research and development of turfgrass species, they are still nonnative plants and are considered by many to be inherently incompatible with an ecological, native landscape. This notion of natural landscapes has caught the imagination and commitment of thousands of gardeners, homeowners, and professional horticulturalists—even the United States Golf Association, which recently helped fund a landmark book on restoring native landscapes. These individuals have created landscapes that are beautiful, self-sustaining, and demonstrate their care and pride in not only their own yard but the entire ecosystem in their region. You will discover, as they have, the constantly changing display that a diverse landscape with many native plants provides.

the WILD LAWN

handbook

1

Choosing a Wild Lawn for Your Yard

Lawns have been called "an institution of democracy." Driving through the suburbs of the United States today, seeing street after street lined with uninterrupted green expanses, makes it easy to understand the reason for this label. Since the practice began in this country, a little more than 100 years ago, it has spread as the population has. Wherever single-family homes have been built, the lawns have surely followed.

With the development of the electric trolley and an extensive railway system after the Civil War, suburbs became widespread. In 1868, when Frederick Law Olmsted designed Riverside, an influential suburb of Chicago, he eliminated fences in the front yards where lawns were to be maintained and set a distance of at least thirty feet between the house and the street. Andrew Jackson Downing, a landscape architect, and one of his students, Frank Scott, both wrote books in the mid-1800s that promoted the lawn as an essential foil or foreground for clusters of trees and shrubs. They both decried tall, meadow grasses as unruly and coarse; Scott went so far as to claim that every person had a "moral obligation" to maintain a neat, well-kept lawn. He wrote, "It is unchristian to hedge from the sight of others the beauties of nature which it has been our good fortune to create or secure....The beauty obtained by throwing front grounds open together, is that of excellent quality which enriches all who take part in the exchange, and makes no man poorer."

Since several generations of homeowners have dutifully spent their weekends cutting and watering the lawn, it seems that these notions do run deep in the American psyche. In 1910, only 23 percent of the American population lived in suburbs. The Interstate Highway Act passed in 1956 sent millions outward from the cities. By 1980 the number of suburb-dwellers had risen to 60 percent, and nearly two-thirds of the 86.4 million residences—about 57 million—were single-family homes, most having front and back yards. By this time, the lawn had become entrenched as part of the social fabric of suburban culture.

Reasons for Lawns

Other theories have been proposed about why we keep lawns. John Falk, an ecologist who has studied lawns for nearly twenty years, believes that humans have a preference for a terrain that is like the savannah in East Africa where there are trees for protection, available water, and open grassland to forage. He thinks that because for nearly 90 percent of human history the savannah was home and it provided safety, the predilection for that environment could be genetic. Research by Gordon H. Orians, professor of zoology and environmental studies at University of Washington, brought him to the same conclusion. He has shown that people work hard to create savannahlike environments because they feel at home in them.

Another explanation is that during the Middle Ages, feudal lords kept open fields around their castles to prevent sneak attacks and to provide forage for sheep and cattle. Manor lords later kept green open areas around their large mansions. These "lawns" become a mark of prestige. The cultural theory is that upper-class Americans copied what they saw in Britain and the practice sifted down to the middle class and eventually to the working class. Thorstein Veblen pointed to the lawn as an example of "conspicuous consumption" in 1899. By keeping a large portion of their ground in cropped grass, homeowners demonstrated that their economic success had reached such a level that they did not have to put that land to practical use; they could afford the luxury of maintaining it for appearance's sake.

The spread of the suburbs and their accompanying lawns came at the same time that vast numbers of Americans were leaving farms and taking jobs in factories or other businesses close to cities. This population shift from farms to urban areas was most dramatic between 1950 and 1970; the farm population declined from 24 to 9 million. The intense involvement with lawn chores—seeding, cutting, raking, fertilizing—may have been a way for people who missed taking care of their meadows, pastures, and crops to remain close to the land.

Finally, there are the more obvious reasons that continue today: the pleasure of walking on a lawn in bare feet, playing games on the lawn, lying on the grass to look up at the stars, and the fact that it covers the ground, preventing erosion, absorbing dust, noise, and glare, releasing oxygen, and cooling the temperatures near the house. A lawn is also relatively quick and easy to install, providing a green cover in a short time, and stands up to heavy people traffic.

Whatever the reasons, along with the increase of lawns in the country came research to improve the grasses and new products—chemical bug and weed killers and gasoline-powered mowers, blowers, and trimmers—for maintaining the lawn. As breeding improved turfgrasses, the standards for lawn appearance rose, and the goal eventually became to have a monoculture of one grass with no weeds. In 1901, Congress approved $17,000 for the study of native and foreign grass species that would be most suitable for turf use; but a much larger impetus came in 1920 when the United States Department of Agriculture, under heavy lobby from the United States Golf Association, adopted a program to research grass species for golf greens and fairways. Today, most state agricultural universities have a turf research program, and the Lawn Institute estimates that about $15 million is spent annually on turfgrass research for an industry that is now a $30-billion-a-year business.

Lawns and Chemical Use

Herbicides, such as 2,4,5-T and 2,4-D, introduced in the 1950s, made it easy for homeowners to zap the most stubborn weeds in their lawns—dandelions, chickweed, plantain, crabgrass, and sorrel. The insecticide DDT was introduced shortly after World War II and was highly effective on a wide range of pests, from Colorado potato beetles and gypsy moth larvae to mosquitos, sod webworms, and chinch bugs. By the 1960s the severe environmental consequences were obvious—dying wildlife and contaminated water supplies. DDT was banned in 1972. A few years later, 2,4,5-T was banned and now 2,4-D is under suspicion as a carcinogen.

"Improved" pesticides—diazinon and carbaryl—were introduced later. But in 1986 diazinon was banned for use on golf courses and sod farms because its use has resulted in the death of songbirds, waterfowl, eagles, and other birds of prey. It is, however, still widely used by homeowners on lawns despite the known health effects—neurotoxicity, kidney and/or liver damage, and being an irritant—reported in Environmental Protection Agency (EPA) documents and standard toxicology references. Buried in these "improvements" were some of the problems that would begin the erosion of Americans' long romance with the lawn.

Approximately 67 million pounds of pesticides are used on lawns each year, about five to nine pounds per treated acre. In 1972, Congress mandated that thirty-two of the thirty-four pesticides most widely used in lawn care be reregistered since evaluations for health and environmental risks were incomplete. New tests have not been done but the products continue to be used. Insecticides are designed to kill or control living organisms; they also have detrimental effects on human health and the environment. It is known from studies already done that these effects include causing cancer; damage to the liver, kidney, or nervous system; birth defects; reproductive system damage; irritation to the lungs and eyes; skin rashes; and toxic chemical sensitization. In addition, twelve of these pesticides have been found in the groundwater of dozens of states, according to an EPA groundwater survey in 1990.

Medical authorities told a subcommittee of the Senate Committee on Environment and Public Works in 1991 that as the number of Americans using these products increases, so does the incidence of people who become sick or injured from exposures.

Besides the environmental problems, the 1970s brought severe drought to California and parts of the Southwest, Midwest, and South, with long dry spells being experienced even in the mid-Atlantic states. Those who live in places where water supplies are limited and costly have been switching to drought-tolerant alternatives (native grasses, low-growing perennials, and/or ground covers). The trend toward using native plants to create more naturalistic landscapes has now spread, though more slowly, where the pressure on water supplies is not as intense.

Changing Attitudes about the Lawn

In addition, many homeowners in this generation say they are tired of spending their leisure time cutting the grass, and they find the unending expanse of green uninteresting. Besides the feeling that taking care of a lawn is just too much work for little return, many homeowners want to be able to use their front yards as places to enjoy the outdoors, to be closer to nature; they want to turn their yards into places where birds and other wildlife feel welcome and safe.

"I'm a bird-watcher," Milt Ettenheim of Milwaukee said as Lorrie Otto and I stood chest-high in grasses and wildflowers in his front-yard prairie, "and one of my favorite things when I used to go out in the fields away from the city was watching the tall grasses and wildflowers swaying in the breeze. I knew that I wanted those same plants in my own yard." When he and his wife, Toni, built their house in 1976, they planted some seeds and some plants of prairie wildflowers. The fact that they hand-pulled and dug out the Canadian thistle and reed canary grass so that the natives could get established speaks worlds about their determination and devotion. Now, Milt starts plants every spring from seed that he gathers from his plants or purchases from native nurseries. He grows the plants in a protected area until they have strong root systems and have reached a good size—usually one growing season, sometimes two—and gives them away in the fall to people who are starting new prairie plantings.

When my dental hygienist heard me discussing the topic of my book, she excitedly told me about her plans for a wildflower meadow. "There is a narrow, sloped area along the side of the house that is sort of an odd shape," she said. "We are going to plant it all with wildflowers. I just want to be able to lie down in them and look up at the sky." This feeling is widely held, according to the staff of the National Wildflower Research Center, Austin, Texas. They told me that nearly everyone who visits wants to know if they can go lie down in the fields of wildflowers around the center.

Sara Stein has told the most eloquent story of why and how she converted most of her landscape back to native plants in her book *Noah's Garden*. She spent ten years clearing brush, pulling vines, hauling rocks, putting in new beds, and mowing, then realized that she had created a barren ground—the abundance of wildlife that had been there when they first arrived was gone. So she and her husband began reversing the process, which, she writes, is ongoing. They have added native fruiting shrubs to island beds and outcrops close to the house, connected them with more plantings in groves and hedgerows, replanted the area around the pond, and joined it all together with native grasses and wildflowers in a meadow. Bluebirds, meadowlarks, frogs, and butterflies have returned.

Another author who has told his gardening story is Michael Pollan. He argues in his book *Second Nature* that "Lawns are a symptom of, and a metaphor for, our skewed relationship to the land. They teach us that, with the help of petrochemicals and technology, we can bend nature to our will." The alternative is to turn them into gardens not necessarily "to exclude lawns altogether or that just by gardening that we will right our relationship to the land," but that the "habits of thought that they [gardens] foster can take us some way in that direction."

The perspective on lawns is moving away from ceremonial—keeping an open mown expanse in the front to match the neighbors—to functional—using turfgrass or a mown area only as large as necessary for children to play, as an extension of the home for entertaining, or as a low plane to contrast harmoniously with perennials, shrubs, and trees. This changing attitude about home grounds is reflected in various movements that have grown steadily in the last ten years—natural landscaping, including the use of native plants, ornamental grasses, and ground covers; Xeriscaping or low-water landscaping; backyard wildlife habitat programs; wildflowers in home landscapes and roadside plantings as part of civic beautification efforts; and restoration of native plant communities such as meadows, prairies, woodlands, wetlands, desert, alpine meadows, savannah, hammocks, and marshes.

In many ways, the directions that homeowners are taking to avoid the environmentally unsound practices that are required to maintain lawns are leading them back to the "ancestor" of lawns: mown meadows. The word "lawn" derives from the old French word *launд*, which in its earliest form referred to an open space between woods, and later, by about the sixteenth century, to a portion of garden or pleasure ground covered with grass and kept closely cropped. That earliest form of the lawn was planted with large patches of sod that had been dug up from naturally occurring meadows and thus included some herbs and wildflowers as well. Some old documents refer to them as "flowery medes." These grassy plots were usually grazed by sheep—the first lawn mowers.

Even by the mid-1800s, when areas were sometimes seeded with specific grass varieties, the "lawn" was still not an evenly cut smooth surface of one species. Mowed by teams of men using scythes, these areas of grass still contained numerous types of plants, some bearing flowers, and the height ranged from five to eight inches. Here's an example of a seed mix used in England in the 1870s, from *The Art and Craft of Garden Making* by Thomas Mawson:

Cynosurus crustatus (Crested dogtail), 4 pounds
Festuca duriuscula (Hard fescue), 3 pounds
F. ovina tenuifolia (Sheep fescue), 2 pounds
Lolium perenne (Dwarf perennial ryegrass), 20 pounds
Poa nemoralis (Wood bluegrass), 2 pounds
P. n. sempervirens (Wood bluegrass), 3 pounds
Trifolium minus (Shamrock clover), 2 pounds
T. repens (White Dutch clover), 6 pounds
Trisetum flavescens, 1 pound
Total (per acre), 43 pounds

Mowing and Meadows

If one factor were to be isolated as *the* reason we have lawns, it could be the next development in lawn history: the invention of the lawn mower. In 1830, Edwin Budding, an Englishman who had devised a machine to shear the nap on velvet, invented a machine based on the same principle to shear grass. In 1902, Ransomes introduced a gasoline-powered mower, the precursor to the ones we are familiar with today.

Not everyone in the horticultural world was enamored with this mowing machine. As early as 1894, the demise of the "meadowed lawn" was bemoaned by the well-known British landscape designer William Robinson in his book *The Wild Garden*. He hoped to revive the meadow—rapidly being replaced by grass-only lawns—that was a blend of wildflowers, grasses, and bulbs and was cut, at most, once every four weeks with scythes to a height of about four inches. The word "meadow" derives from the Old English word *medwe*, which means a piece of land covered with grass and cropped for hay or used as pasture. The word "mow" also comes from an Old English word, *mawan*, which means to cut down with a scythe. Both words contain the original Teutonic root "*me-*", which means "mow." The French word for "meadow" is *prairie*: a tract of grassland without trees and usually of great expanse.

The words "meadow" and "prairie" have been used interchangeably, although prairie gradually came to be used mainly to refer to the plains of North America. That distinction, largely held today, is also used in this book. Neil Diboll, prairie ecologist and owner of Prairie Nursery in Wisconsin, provides a helpful explanation:

> Native Midwestern grasslands are typically referred to as meadows. The primary distinction between these two grassland communities is that the prairie tends to be dominated by heat-loving "warm-season" grasses and flowers, while the Eastern meadow has a higher contingent of "cool-season" grasses and flowers. Midwestern prairie is subjected to severe heat and drought while the Eastern meadow has higher average rainfall, higher humidities, and less extreme summer temperatures. But many species are found in both. "Natural" Eastern meadows are nearly always the result of recolonization of old fields by both native species and naturalized exotic species. For this reason, "nonnative" plants are commonly included in the meadow mixes. Prairies are typically thought of as strictly native, original grasslands. Nonnative species are not usually considered acceptable in prairie plantings.

New Garden Style

A specific date and place cannot be given for the beginning of this present movement away from traditional landscapes comprised of green expanses of lawn, foundation plantings near the house, annual flowers, and a few specimen trees. Individuals' decisions, climatic shifts, and environmental concerns have come together slowly over the past ten or fifteen years to create a major change in the appearance of American gardens and landscapes and the plants used in them.

Drought and water shortages in the 1970s led to the development of a set of landscaping design principles to reduce the use of water — Xeriscaping. The Denver Water Department and area nurserymen and landscapers created this technique based on the central practice of grouping plants together according to their water requirements. Turf area is reduced as much as possible by using ground covers and masses of perennials, shrubs, and trees instead. The emphasis is on choosing native and well-adapted plants that normally thrive in the soil and weather fluctuations of a region's climate. Ken Ball, one of the creators, is currently overseeing the redesign of the Denver Water Department property into Xeriscapes.

Most Xeriscape literature and programs do not mandate substituting the traditional turfgrasses with native grasses, nor do they call for removing the lawn altogether. Instead, they suggest using the most drought-tolerant conventional variety, reducing the area as much as is practical, and arranging the landscape so that any turf that remains is in the regular water use zone. It is crucial to keep in mind that the primary reason for the success of the British lawn is climate. That consistently mild temperature and sufficiency of moisture through the year is duplicated in the United States only in some parts of the Pacific Northwest and a few areas of the Eastern states. Standard lawn grasses require one inch of water per week; for a 1,000-square-foot lawn, that means 626 gallons a week and 10,000 gallons over a summer. This must come from irrigation or rainfall. Rainfall throughout the West and in many parts of the rest of the country is insufficient to provide this amount. From May through October, major cities in the West receive from only one to ten inches. Although major cities in the East receive twenty to thirty inches during the same time period, it does not fall on a consistent basis and irrigation is required during the long dry periods.

Typical Lawn Grasses

So, for most of the country, that manicured, single-species turf depends on overcoming local conditions in order to thrive. The soils and climate of most parts of the United States are not suited to the nonnative turfgrasses. The cool-season types include Kentucky bluegrass (genus *Poa*) from France or Germany; fescue (*Festuca*) from Europe (though there are some native species); rye (*Lolium*) from England; and bentgrass (*Agrostis*) from England. The warm-season types include St. Augustine (*Stenotaphrum secundatum*) from the West Indies; Bermuda (*Cynodon dactylon*) from Africa; bahia (*Paspalum notatum*) from South America; and zoysia (*Zoysia*) from Southeast Asia. The success of these grasses as turf depends on modern technological intervention—chemical fertilizer, pesticides, automated irrigation, and mechanical mowers and trimmers. Turfgrass research has turned toward finding species that grow slower and require less fertilizer and less water. That search has been focused primarily on species in the fine fescue group. Only one of our native species has been given any attention—buffalo grass (*Buchloë dactyloides*)—which is not a fescue but shares some similar characteristics such as requiring minimal water once established and almost no fertilizer. It is also slow-growing like fescue.

The grass family (Gramineae) includes 600 genera and 10,000 species. In the United States 1,400 species of 170 genera are found indigenously. The Lawn Institute says only fourteen species of four genera are suitable as lawn grasses. By accepting a broader definition of "lawn" and a diversity of species in a low-growing planting that can be mown or left unmown, the range of choices from the hundreds of native grass species becomes much larger. Grasses are divided into two groups based on their growth habit—clump-forming or spreading (by way of stolons over the surface of the ground or rhizomes below the surface). Most prairie and meadow grasses are the clump-forming types. Because their growth habit leaves spaces between the plants, they combine well with wildflowers in massed plantings. (For more on native grasses, see Chapter 3, page 89.)

A demonstration of this new perspective on home landscapes was created at the United States National Arboretum. When Dr. Henry M. Cathey was director, he wanted to show visitors how American front yards could be turned into places to enjoy the sensual pleasures of the natural world. He asked the landscape team of Wolfgang Oehme and James A. van Sweden, of Washington, D.C., who had already become known for their dramatically different landscapes of ornamental grasses and long-blooming perennials, to design the "New American Garden." Installed around a typical ranch house on site at the arboretum in 1987, it includes shrubs such as bird's nest spruce (*Picea abies* 'Nidiformis'), buttercup winterhazel (*Corylopsis pauciflora*), heavenly bamboo (*Nandina domestica*), and slender deutzia (*Deutzia gracilis* 'Nikko'); ornamental grasses like feather reed grass (*Calamagrostis × acutiflora* 'Stricta'), three cultivars of silver grass (*Miscanthus sinensis*) including 'Condensatus', 'Silberfeder', and 'Floridulus', purple silver grass (*M. sinensis purpurascens*), Japanese blood grass (*Imperata cylindrica* 'Red Baron'); and perennials such as black-eyed Susan (*Rudbeckia fulgida* 'Goldsturm'), gayfeather (*Liatris spicata*), threadleaf coreopsis (*Coreopsis verticillata* 'Moonbeam'), Russian sage (*Perovskia atriplicifolia*), and blue leadwort (*Ceratostigma plumbaginoides*). Small lawn areas are used for function, not just for ceremony, as Cathey described them. Two green "ribbons" of lawn wind through the plantings—for play, for guests during a party, and for benches.

Oehme and van Sweden's designs turn yards into gardens filled with a naturalistic balance of shrubs, hardy perennials, and grasses selected for the site that will thrive with minimal care. The plants are chosen and spaced to provide beauty and interest through all the seasons without pruning, staking, or deadheading. In the early spring, those that require it are cut back to allow new spring growth to begin again. The plants are grouped together away from the house and walkways provide views of all sides of the plants. Adjacent to the house are planting beds with low-growing ground-cover plants that lead out toward the garden. Broad masses of plants blend into the next. Although the plants that this team uses have their origins in Europe, Asia, and North America, their look is naturalistic and even evokes what some have called "prairie imagery." As they have said themselves, "We would define [our work] as a kind of 'melting pot' of international plants and ideas, producing an alloy of naturalism and free spirit," and "the ideal is the freedom and ease of the meadow."

Oehme and van Sweden trace this style of naturalism back to two designers who inspired them: Jens Jensen, who was born in Denmark, but developed his "prairie style" of landscaping in the American Midwest in the mid-1900s; and Karl Foerster, a German designer who selects wild grasses with garden characteristics to use in landscapes in order to provide interest throughout the year.

Some other American garden designers whose styles are consistent with this theme of naturalism or natural landscaping are Darrel Morrison, who was key in Wisconsin prairie restorations in the Midwest and now teaches in the environmental design program at the University of Georgia and is designing landscapes with southeastern natives; A. E. Bye, a Connecticut landscape architect whose designs are so harmonized with their native surroundings that it is hard to tell where the natural landscape ends and the "designed" landscape begins; Judith Phillips and Julia Berman of New Mexico, who both use native grasses, perennials, and shrubs blended with nonnative but well-adapted species to create landscapes suited to the Southwestern soil and climate; Steve Martino, Arizona; John Greenlee, an ornamental grass (native and nonnative) expert and designer in Pomona, California; Neil Diboll, Joyce Powers, Don Vorpahl, all of Wisconsin; Sherri and Marc Evans, Frankfort, Kentucky; Sally and Andy Wasowski, Dallas, Texas; and Leslie Sauer of Andropogon, Philadelphia, Pennsylvania. I am sure there are many more whose work I have not seen or who may only be known in their local area.

These professional designers are important as leaders and educators for the rest of us. They inspire homeowners to try something different. However, this handbook is for the majority of Americans who take care of their gardens and yards themselves. Learn from the experts' work and if your particular situation calls for some assistance, find a local designer in your area who uses native plants to help you. A list of sources in Appendix I and II will help you get started.

At the same time that the natural landscaping style was being developed and used, homeowners across the country were turning their backyards and, for many, the front as well, into habitat for wildlife. The National Wildlife Federation started its Backyard Wildlife Habitat Program in 1977. Now including more than 13,000 members, this program offers certification for those participants who provide food, shelter, and water for wildlife in their yards, which means most of the plants must be native. Not surprisingly, once the backyard is done, many start on the front. The Urban Wildlife Institute also certifies private and public landowners in urban areas. Fort Collins, Colorado, started its own certification for its residents.

Native plant societies have been formed all across the country to promote the use of native plants, to support those who are using them, and to educate others. The first were formed in California in the 1970s. In that state alone, there are now thirty chapters. At least twenty other states have started their own native plant groups. In the Midwest, where the prairie used to cover 400,000 square miles, the realization that it was continuing to disappear—about 4 million (scattered) acres remain (roughly 6,200 square miles)—spurred one of the most active native restoration efforts in the country. Those involved started a group called The Wild Ones. They publish a newsletter and the members share plants and seeds and help each other with their native landscapes. "In the United States," estimates Brien Meilleur, director of the Center for Plant Conservation in St. Louis, Missouri, "we have around twenty thousand kinds of native plants. And one of every five is presently in trouble." Meilleur says the group's goal is to protect threatened and endangered species. Gardeners can help prevent more plants from being added to the list by using their yards to grow species that are native to their area.

Other organizations that started or have grown from the rising interest in native plants and natural landscaping are: National Wildflower Research Center, Austin, Texas; New England Wild Flower Society, Framingham, Massachusetts; The American Floral Meadow Society, Silver Spring, Maryland; the Natural Areas Association, Mukwonago, Wisconsin; Association for the Use of Native Vegetation in the Landscape (ANVIL), Lafayette, Indiana; Native Prairies Association of Texas, Austin; and the California Native Grass Association.

Some interesting changes have even occurred in the lawn mower industry. Several companies have introduced or are promoting more widely a heavy-duty mower for people who do not own large enough acreages to justify purchasing a tractor, but have meadows or natural areas that need to be mowed once or twice a year. Unlike the riding mowers and "garden tractors" which cannot take constant use on uneven ground, the walk-behind field mowers are designed to handle a mixture of plant material (even small tree seedlings) and rough terrain. Some have large wheels and brush-hog type rotary blades that cut and chop the vegetation.

Choosing an Alternative

When you decide to reduce the size of your lawn or get rid of it altogether, the first step is to envision what you would rather see. If you are like the numerous homeowners that I visited, your vision may embody three common aspects: diversity in place of monotony, changing color and height through the seasons, and a private oasis with birds, butterflies, and other wildlife as regular visitors.

The *reason* you want to make this change could be one or a combination of many. The reasons I heard again and again were:

- To conserve water
- To stop mowing
- To have a garden and yard that did not need pesticides
- To attract butterflies
- To feed and provide habitat for birds and other wildlife
- To use the yard as a site to restore native plantings for the region
- To increase the home's energy efficiency
- To prevent rain from running off into storm drains.

The key to creating a "lawn" that is low maintenance and has few disease and pest problems is native plants. Because they are adapted to the climate and soil of the area in which you live, they will survive temperature and moisture fluctations and they will serve as sources of food for wildlife. With some exceptions, exotic (imported from another country) species do not provide fruit or foliage to feed wildlife.

The choice you make is partly determined by what is growing on your site now. For example, if you have a front lawn of Kentucky bluegrass that is mostly sunny and you live in the Midwest, you could install a prairie planting. But if you are in Arizona, your environment is too dry and hot for those plants; your choice would be desert ground covers. Your decision needs to be a blend of what you want and what ecological region you live in (see the map on page 21). If the idea of an emerald-green moss lawn appeals to you, then you need to live on a site with large, mature shade trees, have plenty of moisture during the growing season, and acid soil. Residents in the West have the great advantage of living where the soil and climate favor our two lowest-growing native grasses — buffalo grass (*Buchloë dactyloides*) and blue grama (*Bouteloua gracilis*).

Creating a meadow does not mean just discontinuing to mow, nor does it mean that yard chores will end. And, as so many Americans have frustatingly discovered, you cannot create a meadow by sowing an area with a mixture of wildflowers alone. For the long-term, perennial planting that most people have in mind when they plant a meadow, you must include three to four species of native grasses along with the wildflowers. The grasses provide support and protection for the flowers, dense cover that resists invasion by unwanted nonnative plants, and the beauty of their own foliage and flower heads. If you plant a mix that contains only wildflowers, you will do constant battle with weeds and nonnative grasses, and you will need to overseed at least every other year.

So many foreign species have become established in our natural areas and along our roadsides that, sadly, there are few open spaces left in the United States that have not been invaded. Some of these invaders are so aggressive that native plants do not have a fighting chance. The invaders produce great quantities of seed and plant themselves so thickly, or at a time that gives them a headstart on the natives, that they become dominant. The best example, which nearly everyone has seen or heard about, is kudzu, a vine from Japan brought into this country to help with erosion, but, in the warmer climate in the American South, proliferated beyond control.

Learn to recognize these plants, pull them out when you see them, and educate others about why they are destructive. Some primary examples are bittersweet, Russian olive, multiflora rose, white and yellow clover, Canada thistle, bull thistle, honeysuckle, buckthorn, Norway maple, reed canary grass, and purple loosestrife. For a more complete list, see pages 84–87.

To repopulate your land with native plants requires destroying the mostly European (and some Asian) invaders and keeping a vigilant watch so that new seedlings, if they sprout, can be removed before they get tough and difficult to pull up. As Jane Scott put it so well in her very helpful book *Field and Forest*, you are truly "*releasing* the native landscape."

First Steps

Before you begin you will need to determine some specific information about your property:

1. Soil type (sandy, clay, loam)
2. Soil pH (acid, neutral, or alkaline)
3. Unusually wet or dry areas
4. Areas of sun, shade, mixed light
5. Names of plants on the site (indicate which are native)

Then you will need to create:

1. A scale drawing of the entire property
2. A plan of what plants to keep, to replace, and to add

Finally, gather together the following resources:

1. Native plant identification books
2. Seed and nursery catalogs for plants you are interested in using
3. Information on your region's native plants from a local native plant society, the extension or soil conservation service, a chapter of the Nature Conservancy, or botanists at public gardens, universities, or museums in your area.

Native Plant Communities

Determine in which of the following ecological regions you live by looking at the map on page 21: (1) Northern Conifer Forest, (2) Eastern Woodlands, (3) Coastal Plain, (4) Tropical Forest, (5) Prairie, (6) Rocky Mountain Forest, (7) Western Desert/Great Basin, (8) Sonoran Desert Area, (9) Pacific Forest, (10) Chaparral. The numbers assigned to these regions are also used in Tables 1 and 2 to identify the regions for which the listed plants are suitable.

The map is a general presentation of the major native plant communities which gives you a starting point in determining the appropriate plants for the "wild lawn" alternative that you select. Pockets of vegetation types exist within each large area. For example, although the whole state of Alaska is included in Region 1 because a large part of it is northern conifer forest, the west coast and a vast area in the interior are tundra. A small pocket of tall grass prairie exists along the western boundary of Region 6 in the state of Washington. The number of openings, which are meadows, in all of the forested regions are too numerous to show on this map. Another area that is distinctive from the overall charactertistics of Region 3 begins on the lower eastern side of Louisiana and extends along the Mississippi River up to southern Illinois for about 100 miles on either side of the river. It contains a forest of bald cypress (*Taxodium distichum*), tupelo (*Nyssa aquatica*), and sweetgum (*Liquidambar styraciflua*).

Both Alaska and Hawaii have distinctive native plant communities and sufficient detail could not be shown on the map. Most of the state of Alaska is in hardiness zone 1 or 2, which means winter temperatures drop below -50°F. This is the interior region which is blocked from the warming influence of the ocean by the Alaska and Aleutian mountain ranges. At the other extreme, during the long summer days, the temperature may, on occasion, reach 100°F. The eastern coast is in zones 3 and 4 (winter low -30°F) and the southern coast is even milder.

The major vegetation consists of scattered forests of white spruce, aspen, and poplar with tundra in between. Tundra is a treeless plain that supports mosses, lichens, grasses, and hardy low-growing perennials such as moss campion (*Silene acaulis*), mountain heath (*Phyllodoce* spp.), and mountain heather (*Cassiope* spp.).

Most of the state of Hawaii is in zone 11 where temperatures never fall below 40°F. In fact, the variation in seasonal temperatures is minimal; the difference between the average temperatures of the warmest and coolest months in Honolulu, for example, is about six degrees. By comparison, the temperature fluctation in Miami is more than fifteen degrees.

The northeastern sides of the islands receive copious rainfall, more than 100 inches per year in some sites; on the southwestern side, however, the islands are much drier, with annual rainfall as low as twenty inches in some parts. The islands have 900 different plant types that are unique and more than 2,000 species that have been introduced, permanently altering the islands' original vegetation. Intensive agriculture, forest exploitation, and development (mainly for tourism) have also altered the natural landscape.

The low coastal plains on the dry sides of the islands are mostly covered with shrubs and grasses. Mangroves cover the coastal lagoons and estuaries. Forests occur on western mountain slopes above the shrubline; on the eastern slopes, where there is more moisture, they extend down to sea level. On the highest peaks ice may exist throughout the year, and the ground is barren or covered with mosses and lichens.

Like Hawaii, the natural vegetation of most of our country has been altered by human activities such as the introduction of exotic plants which have become dominant over large areas, the drainage of swamps and wetlands, the plowing of large acreages of grassland to grow agricultural crops, and the clearing of forests. However, this map and others like it are constructed by ecologists and plant specialists based on historical records and on the existing natural vegetation.

The lists of representative species—including trees, shrubs, and understory plants (wildflowers, low shrubs, ground covers, ferns, and grasses)—barely scratch the surface of the numerous indigenous plants for each region. Obtain detailed information on your region from local sources and native plant identification manuals. For species that you would like to use, find out their relative importance, how they behave together, and if they are (were) indigenous to your locale. The map is the result of studying many different natural vegetation maps, most of which provided more detail than is possible to present in this book of nationwide scope. Seek out the ones on which it is based (see Appendix IV) to find out more about your specific location.

1. Northern Conifer Forest

Trees

    Abies balsamea (Balsam fir)
    Acer pensylvanicum (Striped maple)
    Betula lutea (Yellow birch)
    Larix laricina (Tamarack)
    Picea mariana (Black spruce)
    Pinus resinosa (Red pine)
    P. strobus (White pine)
    Sorbus americana (American mountain ash)
    Tsuga canadensis (Hemlock)

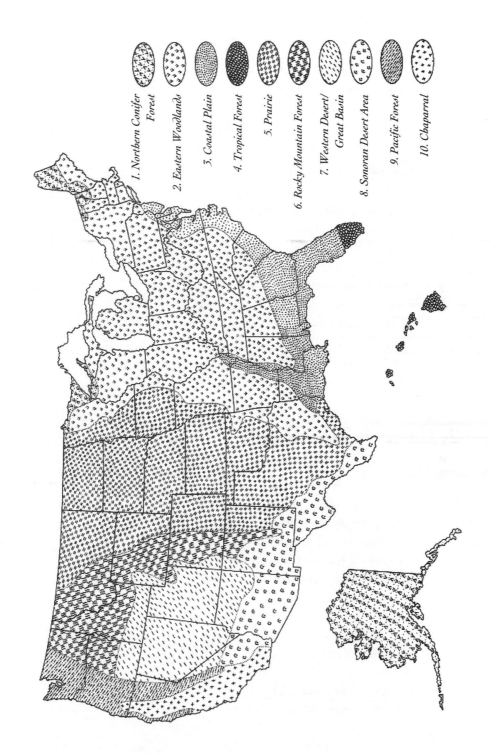

1. Northern Conifer Forest
2. Eastern Woodlands
3. Coastal Plain
4. Tropical Forest
5. Prairie
6. Rocky Mountain Forest
7. Western Desert/ Great Basin
8. Sonoran Desert Area
9. Pacific Forest
10. Chaparral

Shrubs

Amelanchier spp. (Shadbush)
Cornus rugosa (Round-leaved dogwood)
Rhododendron roseum (Rose azalea)
Viburnum alnifolium (Hobblebush)
V. nudum (Possumhaw)

Wildflowers/Ground Covers/Ferns

Aralia nudicaulis (Wild sarsaparilla)
Aster macrophyllus (Largeleaf aster)
Carex debilis (Sedge)
Cornus canadensis (Bunchberry)
Dryopteris campyloptera (Mountain wood fern)
Hepatica americana (Round-leaved hepatica)
Lycopodium clavatum (Running ground pine)
Maianthemum canadense (False lily-of-the-valley)
Mitchella repens (Partridgeberry)
Oxalis montana (Sleeping beauty)
Viola rotundifolia (Round-leaved yellow violet)

2. Eastern Woodlands

Trees

Acer nigrum (Black maple)
A. saccharum (Sugar maple)
Asimina triloba (Pawpaw)
Betula lutea (Yellow birch)
Carya ovata (Shagbark hickory)
Cercis canadensis (Redbud)
Cornus florida (Flowering dogwood)
Fagus grandifolia (Beech)
Quercus alba (White oak)
Q. rubra (Northern red oak)
Q. velutina (Black oak)
Q. prinus (Chestnut oak)
Tilia americana (Basswood)

Shrubs

Amelanchier canadensis (Serviceberry)
Hamamelis virginiana (Witch hazel)
Lindera benzoin (Spicebush)
Sambucus canadensis (Elderberry)
Stewartia ovata (Mountain camellia)
Taxus canadensis (American yew)
Vaccinum angustifolium (Blueberry)
Viburnum acerifolium (Mapleleaf viburnum)
V. lentago (Nannyberry)

Wildflowers/Ground Covers/Ferns/Grasses

Carex pensylvanica (Pennsylvania sedge)
Cornus canadensis (Bunchberry)
Gaultheria procumbens (Wintergreen)
Maianthemum canadense (False lily-of-the-valley)
Mitchella repens (Partridgeberry)
Polystichum acrostichoides (Christmas fern)
Tiarella cordifolia (Heartleaf foamflower)
Trillium undulatum (Painted wakerobin)
Viola rotundifolia (Yellow violet)

3. Coastal Plain

Trees

Cercis canadensis (Redbud)
Magnolia grandiflora (Magnolia)
Pinus elliottii (Slash pine)
P. palustris (Longleaf pine)
P. taeda (Loblolly pine)
Quercus virginiana (Live oak)
Taxodium distichum (Bald cypress)

Shrubs

Aesculus sylvatica (Painted buckeye)
Amelanchier canadensis (Serviceberry)

Asimina parviflora (Small-flower pawpaw)
Calycanthus floridus (Eastern sweetshrub)
Chionanthus virginicus (White fringetree)

Wildflowers/Grasses/Ferns

Actaea pachypoda (Baneberry)
Andropogon virginicus (Broomsedge)
Aster paternus (Toothed white-top aster)
Coreopsis major (Greater tickseed)
Cypripedium acaule (Pink lady's slipper)
Desmodium spp. (Tick-trefoil)
Lespedeza repens (Creeping bush clover)
Polygonatum biflorum (Solomon's seal)
Sanguinaria canadensis (Bloodroot)

4. Tropical Forest

Trees

Asimina spp. (Pawpaw)
Avicennia germinans (Black mangrove)
Bursera simaruba (Gumbo-limbo)
Conocarpus erectus (Button mangrove)
Laguncularia racemosa (White mangrove)
Magnolia grandiflora (Magnolia)
Persea borbonia (Red bay)
P. palustris (Swamp bay)
Quercus geminata (Sand live oak)
Q. nigra (Water oak)
Q. virginiana (Live oak)
Rhizophora mangle (Red mangrove)
Taxodium distichum (Bald cypress)
Thrinax radiata (Florida thatch palm)

Shrubs

Ilex glabra (Inkberry)
I. vomitoria (Yaupon)

Myrica cerifera (Southern wax myrtle)
Prunus caroliniana (Laurel cherry)
Quercus pumila (Running oak)
Serenoa repens (Saw palmetto)

Wildflowers/Grasses

Andropogon floridanus (Florida bluestem)
A. virginicus (Broomsedge)
Aristida spp. (Three-awn)
Cladium mariscus (Saw grass)
Eragrostis spp. (Love grass)
Helianthus spp. (Sunflowers)
Helenium spp. (Sneezeweed)
Liatris spp. (Gayfeather)
Licania michauxii (Gopher apple)
Nephrolepis exaltata (Sword fern)
Sorghastrum nutans (Indian grass)
Zamia floridana or *Z. pumila* (Coontie)

5. Prairie

Trees (only in a savannah)

Acer negundo (Box elder)
Populus deltoides (Cottonwood)
Prosopis glandulosa (Mesquite)
Quercus macrocarpa (Bur oak)

Wildflowers/Grasses

Agropyron smithii (Western wheat grass)
Amorpha canescens (Leadplant)
Andropogon gerardii (Big bluestem)
Antennaria neglecta (Field pussytoes)
Arenaria hookeri (Hooker's sandwort)
Aristida purpurea (Purple three-awn)
Artemisia spp. (Sagebrush)
Aster laevis (Smooth blue aster)

Bouteloua curtipendula (Sideoats grama)

B. gracilis (Blue grama grass)

Buchloë dactyloides (Buffalo grass)

Dalea purpurea (Purple prairie clover)

Eriogonum ovalifolium (Cushion wild buckwheat)

Eryngium yuccifolium (Rattlesnake master)

Helianthus occidentalis (Western sunflower)

Lespedeza capitata (Round-head bush clover)

Lithospermum caroliniense (Hairy puccoon)

Opuntia polyacantha (Hair-spine prickly-pear)

Panicum virgatum (Switchgrass)

Schizachyrium scoparium (Little bluestem)

Silphium laciniatum (Compassplant)

Sorghastrum spp. (Indian grass)

Spartina pectinata (Prairie cordgrass)

Sporobolus cryptandrus (Sand dropseed)

Stipa comata (Needle-and-thread)

S. spartea (Porcupine grass)

Zinnia grandiflora (Little golden zinnia)

6. Rocky Mountain Forest

ABOVE THE TIMBERLINE (ALPINE TUNDRA)

Shrubs, Wildflowers, Grasses

Carex spp. (Sedges)

Deschampsia caespitosa (Tufted hair grass)

Lewisia rediviva (Bitterroot)

Penstemon spp. (Penstemon)

Phlox pulvinata (Tundra phlox)

Salix anglorum (Dwarf willow)

Satureja douglasii (Yerba Buena)

Sedum lanceolatum (Stonecrop)

Silene acaulis (Moss campion)

Sisyrinchium bellum (Blue-eyed grass)

Townsendia hookeri (Easter daisy)

At the Timberline (11,500 Feet)

Trees

Abies lasiocarpa (Subalpine fir)
Larix occidentalis (Western larch)
Picea engelmannii (Engelmann's spruce)
Picea pungens (Blue spruce)
Pinus flexilis (Limber pine)
Populus tremuloides (Quaking aspen)

Shrubs

Acer glabrum (Rocky Mountain maple)
Chamaebatiaria millefolium (Fernbush)
Juniperus communis (Common juniper)
Prunus emarginata (Bitter cherry)

Wildflowers/Grasses

Arnica cordifolia (Heartleaf leopard bane)
Blepharoneuron tricholepsis (Pine dropseed)
Calamagrostis rubescens (Pine grass)
Carex grayi (Gray's sedge)
Maianthemum stellatum (Starry Solomon's-seal)
Stipa occidentalis (Western needle grass)
Thalictrum occidentale (Western meadow rue)
Viola glabella (Pioneer violet)

Below the Timberline (9,000–6,000 Feet)

Trees

Amelanchier alnifolia (Saskatoon serviceberry)
Crataegus douglasii (Black hawthorn)
Pinus contorta (Lodgepole pine)
P. ponderosa (Ponderosa pine)
Populus tremuloides (Aspen)
Pseudotsuga menziesii (Douglas fir)

Shrubs, Wildflowers, Grasses

Arctostaphylos patula (Greenleaf manzanita)
A. uva-ursi (Red bearberry)
Asarum caudatum (Wild ginger)

Carex grayi (Gray's sedge)
Ceanothus velutinus (Tobacco brush)
Linnaea borealis (American twinflower)
Pachystima myrsinites (Myrtle boxleaf)
Rosa woodsii (Wood's rose)
Symphoricarpos albus (Snowberry)

LOWEST ELEVATIONS (4,000–2,000 FEET)

Trees

Pinus edulis (Pinyon pine)

Shrubs

Artemisia arbuscula (Dwarf sagebrush)
A. tridentata (Big sagebrush)
Chrysothamnus nauseosus (Rubber rabbitbrush)
Juniperus communis (Common juniper)
Philadelphus lewisii (Native mock orange)
Physocarpus spp. (Nine-bark)
Ribes sanguineum (Flowering currant)

Wildflowers/Grasses

Aquilegia caerulea (Rocky Mountain columbine)
Aster occidentalis (Western mountain aster)
Bouteloua gracilis (Blue grama)
Campanula rotundifolia (Harebell)
Carex filifolia (Threadleaf sedge)
Elymus elymoides (Western bottle-brush grass)
Eriogonum umbellatum (Sulphur flower)
Geum triflorum (Prairie smoke)
Grayia spinosa (Spiny hop-sage)
Lupinus polyphyllus (Washington lupine)
Oryzopsis hymenoides (Indian mountain ricegrass)
Penstemon barbatus (Scarlet bugler)
P. virens (Blue-mist penstemon)
Phlox longifolia (Longleaf phlox)
Poa secunda (Curly blue grass)
Polygonum bistortoides (American bistort)

Senecio longilobus (Threadleaf groundsel)
Stellaria nitens (Shiny starwort)
Stipa comata (Needle-and-thread grass)

7. Western Desert/Great Basin

Trees

Forestiera neomexicana (Desert olive)
Pinus aristata (Bristle-cone pine)
P. edulis (Pinyon pine)
P. flexilis (Limber pine)
Prosopis glandulosa (Mesquite)
Juniperus monosperma (One-seed juniper)
Quercus gambelii (Gambel's oak)
Q. grisea (Gray oak)

Shrubs/Cactus

Artemisia arbuscula (Dwarf sagebrush)
A. tridentata (Big sagebrush)
Atriplex canescens (Saltbush)
Ceanothus velutinus (Tobacco brush)
Chrysothamnus nauseosus (Chamisa)
Encelia farinosa (Brittlebush)
Ephedra spp. (Joint fir)
Fallugia paradoxa (Apache plume)
Opuntia bigelovii (Teddy-bear cholla)
Sarcobatus vermiculatus (Greasewood)
Yucca schidigera (Yucca)
Y. brevifolia (Joshua tree)

Wildflowers/Grasses

Bouteloua curtipendula (Sideoats grama)
B. gracilis (Blue grama)
Claytonia lanceolata (Lanceleaf spring beauty)
Delphinium nuttallianum (Two-lobe larkspur)
Erigeron flagellaris (Trailing fleabane)

Eriogonum heracleoides (Parsnip flower)

E. umbellatum (Sulphur flower)

Ipomopsis aggregata (Scarlet skyrocket)

Lithospermum ruderale (Columbian puccoon)

Poa secunda (Curly blue grass)

Pseudoroegneria spicata (Bluebunch wheat grass)

Sporobolus cryptandrus (Sand dropseed)

Stipa comata (Needle-and-thread grass)

8. Sonoran Desert Area

Trees

Cercidium floridum (Palo verde)

Chilopsis linearis (Desert willow)

Olneya tesota (Ironwood)

Prosopis glandulosa (Honey mesquite)

Shrubs

Artemisia filifolia (Threadleaf sage)

Calliandra eriophylla (Fairy duster)

Encelia farinosa (Brittlebush)

Fouquieria spendens (Ocotillo)

Larrea tridentata (Creosotebush)

Leucophyllum frutescens (Texas sage)

Wildflowers/Grasses

Abronia spp.(Sand verbena)

Dasylirion wheeleri (Sotol)

Eragrostis trichoides (Sand lovegrass)

Eschscholzia mexicana (Gold poppy)

Melampodium leucanthum (Blackfoot daisy)

Oenothera spp.(Evening primrose)

Oryzopsis hymenoides (Indian ricegrass)

Penstemon ambiguus (Bush penstemon)

Salvia greggii (Cherry sage)

Sphaeralcea ambigua (Mallow)

S. coccinea (Prairie mallow)

Sporobolus wrightii (Sacaton)
Yucca elata (Palmilla)
Zinnia grandiflora (Desert zinnia)

Cactus/Agave

Agave palmeri (Palmer century plant)
A. parryi (Parry century plant)
A. parviflora (Century plant)
Carnegiea gigantea (Saguaro)
Ferocactus acanthodes (Barrel)
Ferocactus covillei (Barrel)
Lemaireocereus thurberi (Organ pipe)
Mammillaria spp. (Pincushion)
Opuntia spp. (Prickly pear)

9. Pacific Forest

Trees

Picea sitchensis (Sitka spruce)
Pinus ponderosa (Ponderosa pine)
P. contorta (Lodgepole pine)
Pseudotsuga menziesii (Douglas fir)
Sequoia sempervirens (Redwood)
Thuja plicata (Western red cedar)
Tsuga heterophylla (Western hemlock)

Shrubs

Amelanchier alnifolia (Serviceberry)
Arctostaphylos nevadensis (Pinemat manzanita)
A. patula (Greenleaf manzanita)
Mahonia aquifolium (Oregon grape holly)
M. repens (Creeping Oregon grape)
Myrica californica (Pacific bayberry)
Physocarpus capitatus (Nine-bark)
Shepherdia argentea (Silver buffaloberry)
Vaccinium ovatum (Evergreen blueberry)

Wildflowers/Grasses/Ferns

Aconitum columbianum (Monkshood)
Aquilegia formosa (Western columbine)
Asarum caudatum (Wild ginger)
Athyrium filix-feminia (Subarctic lady fern)
Blechnum spicant (Deerfern)
Chimaphila umbellata (Pipsissewa)
Claytonia sibirica (Siberian spring beauty)
Dicentra formosa (Western bleeding heart)
Disporum smithii (Large flower fairybells)
Dryopteris campylpotera (Mountain wood fern)
Linnaea borealis (Twinflower)
Oxalis oregana (Redwood sorrel)
Polystichum munitum (Pineland sword fern)
Smilacina racemosa (False Solomon's-seal)
Trillium spp. (Trillium)
Vancouveria spp. (Inside-out flower)

10. Chaparral

Trees

Pinus jeffreyi (Jeffrey pine)
P. ponderosa (Ponderosa pine)
P. sabiniana (Digger pine)
Quercus chrysolepsis (Canyon live oak)
Q. douglasii (Blue oak)
Q. kelloggii (California black oak)
Q. lobata (Valley oak)

Shrubs

Adenostoma fasciculatum (Common chamisa)
Arctostaphylos spp. (Manzanita)
Baccharis pilularis (Coyote brush)
Ceanothus spp. (Red root or Mountain sweet)
Cercocarpus montanus (Mountain mahogany)
Eriogonum fasciculatum (Wild buckwheat)

Rhamnus crocea (Hollyleaf buckthorn or Redberry)
Ribes indecorum (White-flower currant)
Salvia mellifera (California black sage)

Wildflowers/Grasses

Aristida oligantha (Prairie three-awn)
Corydalis aurea (Golden smoke)
Deschampsia danthonioides (Annual hair grass)
Elymus glaucus (Blue wild rye)
Gilia aggregata (Fairy trumpet)
G. clivorum (Purple-spot gillyflower)
Hymenoxys argentea (Rubberweed)
Lupinus luteolus (Butter lupine)
Nasella cernus (Tussock grass)
Orthocarpus purpurascens (Red owl-clover)
Phlox nana (Canyon phlox)
Trifolium olivaceum (Olive clover)
Thermopsis montana (Golden banner)

Grasses or Meadows

If you are considering using low-growing native or ornamental grasses as an alternative, look through those listed in the following table to find species that would be suitable to your location.

Grasses

This table includes selections from the grass family (Gramineae) with a few from the sedge family (Cyperaceae). They can all be used in meadow plantings, that is, mixed with other native bunch-type grasses or wildflowers, unless otherwise noted. Species marked with an asterisk may be used literally as a substitute for lawn grass and mowed one to three times a year, or, for a less manicured, billowy look, not at all.

The native plants are indicated by an "X" in the column labeled "N," and those that are evergreen are indicated by a mark in the "E" column. All of these plants are used by wildlife either as food or shelter. The "Regions" column corresponds to the Native Plant Communities Map (page 21) and the "Zone" column refers to U.S.D.A. Hardiness Zones, which are based on average minimum winter temperatures.

Since the number of wildflower species suitable for a meadow or prairie are in the thousands, I have not provided a list in this book. Some of the most common species and ones for which seed is readily available are discussed in the personal stories of individuals who have created prairies or meadows in their front yards (Chapters 3 and 4). If you are considering a meadow or prairie, obtain catalogs from the companies that provide seed for individual species or in mixes customized for particular soils in particular parts of the country. The catalogs provide excellent descriptions and guidelines (see Appendix I).

TABLE 1. GRASSES

PLANT NAME	N	REGIONS	LIGHT REQ.	SOIL	HEIGHT	ZONE	E	BLOOM TIME & COLOR	COMMENT
Agropyron smithii (Western wheatgrass)	X	6,7,8	Sun	Dry; may need to water once or twice in a dry summer to keep green, or let it go beige and it will revive when rains come	12–18"	4–8		June, green spikes turn to beige in summer and arch over	Blue foliage, cool-season grass, clumping type. Can be mowed to 4" during season, or let grow to mature height and mow in late winter or spring. Some gardeners have reported it taking over prairie planting on sites where it receives regular water. Use alone or sparingly in a prairie mix.
Andropogon gerardii (Big bluestem)	X	2,3,5	Sun	Moist, well-drained soil but will tolerate some drought, just be more compact, in arid Southwest climates will need water in summer	3–8'	3–9		Aug.–Sept., purplish	Clumping, warm-season type, blue-green, narrow foilage turns bronze in fall. Three-forked seed heads occur along the flower spike that rises above the foliage. Was the primary grass in the tallgrass prairie.
A. glomeratus (Bushy bluestem)	X	3	Sun	Moist loam, at its best near water along streams; tolerates hot climates and coastal conditions	1–2'	5–10		Aug.–Sept., cottony white	Clumping, warm-season type with glossy green foliage. The flower spikes turn orange in fall and the leaves reddish purple.

PLANT NAME	N	REGIONS	LIGHT REQ.	SOIL	HEIGHT	ZONE	E	BLOOM TIME & COLOR	COMMENT
Andropogon ternarius (Split-beard bluestem)	X	2,3	Sun	Dry, widely adaptable; can tolerate coastal conditions	1', though flower stems may reach 4'	6–9		August, white	Clumping, warm-season type with green foliage; most of plant is flower stems with fluffy seed heads all along them. Reseeds readily.
A. virginicus (Broomsedge)	X	2,3,4	Sun	Dry to moist; tolerates poor soil	1' flower stems to 2'	4–9		Aug.–Sept., white	Clumping, warm-season type with light green foliage turning russet in fall. Fluffy seed heads tucked in folds of leaves along stem.
Anthoxanthum odoratum (Sweet vernal grass)		1,2,3, 9,10; Eurasian but has naturalized in pastures in these areas	Sun, tolerates light shade	Prefers moist, acid loam but will adapt to other conditions	6–8"	5–10	X	May–June, green with yellow stamens 10–12" above foliage	Clumping, cool-season type with medium green foliage that is fragrant when crushed. Seed heads turn golden in late summer to early fall. Tolerates foot traffic. Can be planted closely and mowed on occasion for a lawn.
Aristida purpurea (Purple three-awn)	X	2,5,7,8	Sun	Well-drained but is drought tolerant	6–12"; flower stems to 2'	6–9	X	August, purple	Clumping, warm-season type, with fine-textured sage green foliage. Flower heads eventually turn light brown and will stick to clothing and pets' coats. Self-sows readily.

Species		Region	Exposure	Soil	Height	Zone		Bloom	Description
A. stricta (Pineland three-awn, Wiregrass)		lower part of 3,4	Sun	Sandy, dry	1–2'	8–10	X semi	July–August	Clumping, warm-season type; fine-textured, thin, wirey foliage. The needle-like awns protrude all along the flower stem, turn light brown before they fall or are blown away.
Bouteloua curtipendula (Sideoats grama)	X	2,5,7,8	Sun to part shade	Dry; drought tolerant; pH adaptable	1½–3'	4–10		June–July, purplish tint	Clumping, warm-season type, blue-green fine foliage, stems have purple-tinted seed spikelets along one side which mature to a gold color; whole plant is straw color in winter.
*B. gracilis (Blue grama)	X	5,7,8 possible use in 2 & 3 largely untested	Sun	Dry; pH adaptable can grow in sandy or loamy soil; drought tolerant	8–14" but can be mowed to 2"	3–10		June, tan	Low-growing bunch grass that can be mowed to encourage thick sod development (best to mix with buffalo grass in a ratio of 40:60). Tolerates foot traffic. Light grey-green, fine-textured foliage. Light tan flowers rise above the foliage and look like combs attached at an almost 45-degree angle. The flowers and plant turn purple at first frost, then beige in winter.

PLANT NAME	N	REGIONS	LIGHT REQ.	SOIL	HEIGHT	ZONE	E	BLOOM TIME & COLOR	COMMENT
Buchloë dactyloides (Buffalo grass)	X	5,7,8 currently being tested in 2,3	Sun	Dry; widely adaptable but prefers slightly clayey soil; tests in sandy soil of Florida underway now; tolerates drought, cold, and poor soil.	3–5"; do not need to mow but can if prefer a smoother look—will also be softer on the feet if mowed 2 or 3 times a year.	5–10		June–July, small, barely rise above foliage	Warm-season type, low-growing with blue-green, fine-textured foliage that has purplish tinge at frost and turns beige for winter, greening up in late spring. Tolerates foot traffic. Resents fertilization and overwatering which will lead to pest and disease problems. Slow to establish, spreads by stolons that run along the surface and root as they grow. Use alone or with blue grama. Can blend with some low-growing wildflowers.
Carex pansa (California meadow sedge)	X	3,4, some parts of 8, 9,10	Sun or shade	Moist, well-drained soil but tolerates range of conditions, including coastal; will go dormant without water in hot, arid climate.	3–4"	8–10	X in mild climate	Early spring, fuzzy, cream color	Perennial, creeping with dark green curling leaves; spreads by rhizomes. Tolerant of occasional mowing but can be left unmowed; tolerates moderate foot traffic.

C. pensylvanica (Pennsylvania sedge)	X	2,3,5,6,10	Moderate shade to full sun	Dry, especially oak woods	4–6"	4–8	X	Early spring, semi brown to reddish purple	Perennial with tufting habit, spreads by stolons; will form a soft, low turf in full sun on dry soil. Dark green grass-like leaves.
C. texensis 'Catlin' (Texas sedge)	X	2,3,4,9,10; perhaps 1, needs to be tested there	Sun to part shade	Moist, fertile soil but tolerates wide range of conditions	3–4"	4–10	X	Early spring, inconspicuous	Perennial, clumping type; medium green foliage; tolerates foot traffic. Space closely for use as lawn—mow occasionally or not at all. John Greenlee recommends planting with dwarf grassy sweet flag *Acorus gramineus* 'Pusillus' for a fragrant lawn.
C. × 'The Beatles' (Mop-headed sedge)	X	2,3, some parts of 8, 9,10	Light shade	Moist, rich	3–4"	5–9	X	Early spring, inconspicuous	Perennial, slow-creeping with fine-textured, soft, green foliage. Tolerates light foot traffic.

PLANT NAME	N	REGIONS	LIGHT REQ.	SOIL	HEIGHT	ZONE	E	BLOOM TIME & COLOR	COMMENT
Chasmanthium latifolium (River oats, Northern sea oats) (See closely related coastal version, *Uniola*, below)	X	2,3, woods in 5	Part shade but will tolerate sun if given enough moisture	Moist, deep, rich; salt tolerant	1½–3'	5–9		June–July, green	Clumping, warm-season type, light green bamboolike foliage, flat flower spikes ³/₄–1" long are clustered in panicles that droop. Foliage and seed heads turn from green to bronze in fall, to light brown in winter and persist.
Deschampsia caespitosa (Tufted hair grass, native Calif. strain)	X	2,9,10	Sun or shade	Tolerates drought once established but will respond with richer foliage if receives regular water	18"	5–10	X	Spring, golden yellow, turning soft gray by late summer	Clumping, medium green foliage. Useful as ground cover under oaks or in a massed planting for a meadow-type look.
Eragrostis trichoides (Sand lovegrass)	X	2,3,5,7,8	Sun	Prefers moist, sandy soil but will handle dry, poor soil	2'; flower clusters held 2' above foliage	5–9	X	July, semi pink	Clumping, warm-season type with dark green, fine-textured foliage. Flower panicles are 6–8" across and nodding. Rusty tan in winter.

Name			Exposure	Soil	Height			Bloom	Description
E. spectabilis (Purple lovegrass)	X	2,3,5,7,8	Sun	Prefers moist, sandy soil but will handle heat and drought; water will be needed in arid Southwest in summer.	12–18"; flowers 1–2' above foliage	5–9	X	June–Aug., reddish purple	Clumping, warm-season type with light green foliage. Flowers in airy panicles that cover the foliage; eventually turn creamy white and break off.
Eriophorum vaginatum (Cotton grass)	X	1,2,6	Sun	Wet or moist, peaty soil	1'; flowers 1' above foliage	4–7	X	April–May, white cotton heads	Perennial, clumping sedge with gray-green foliage.
Festuca californica (California fescue)	X	10	Part shade to sun	Adaptable but requires shade in hot interior areas of Calif.	18"	8–9	X	May, silvery green fading to tawny yellow to 3'	Bright green to steely blue-gray fine-textured foliage. Cool-season, bunching grass.
F. cinerea (also known as *F. ovina* and *F. glauca*; Blue fescue)	X	2,3,5,6, 9 (6,7,10 will need part shade)	Sun	Moist, well-drained; does not like hot, humid summers	Ranges from 4–16"	4–9	X	May–June, straw color	Clumping, cool-season type with densely tufted, fine-textured foliage. Many cultivars available ranging in size and color from blue to dark green. Try a mass planting of one cultivar or a mixture. To keep neat, trim in late fall or early spring, but no shorter than 3".

PLANT NAME	N	REGIONS	LIGHT REQ.	SOIL	HEIGHT	ZONE	E	BLOOM TIME & COLOR	COMMENT
Festuca muelleri (Mueller's fescue) *F. tenuifolia* (Fine-leaved fescue)		2,3, some parts of 5	Sun	Moist, well-drained, fertile soil	4–6"	5–9	X	June, bluish green fading to buff	Perennial, clumping, cool-season type with fine-textured shiny green foliage. Creates hummocks; does not like hot, inland climates.
Koeleria cristata (Junegrass)	X	2,3,5,6,7, 8,10	Sun	Dry, drought tolerant	2'	4–9		June, silver-green narrow flower head at top of stem	Perennial, cool-season bunching type with green foliage. The seed heads turn a golden color and begin to fall apart in July.
Muhlenbergia filipes (Purple muhly); close cousin to *M. capillaris* (Hairy awn muhly)	X	3,4, lower part of 5,10	Sun	Sandy or rocky soil; tolerates drought and wind, can take coastal conditions	1'; blooms rise 1–2' above foliage	7–9		October, purple	Perennial, warm-season clumping type; open, airy, cloudlike flower ⅓ to ½ the length of the spike (about 2–2½') often covers the foliage. Whole plant turns tan in winter.
Oryzopsis hymenoides (Indian rice grass)	X	7,8,10, arid parts of 5	Sun	Well-drained sandy soil, tolerates heavy soil and alkaline conditions; drought tolerant can survive on 5"/year.	1–2'	8–10		May	Clumping, cool-season type with long, slender bright green leaves. Flowers are open panicles developing small seeds. An important Western grass that was a major food source for Native Americans. Straw color when dormant from late June until early spring rains.

Name		Region	Light	Soil	Height	Zone		Bloom	Description
Panicum virgatum (Prairie switchgrass)	X	2,3,5	Sun	Prefers moist, fertile soil but tolerates sand, clay, dry slopes and boggy areas. Can take wind and salt spray of coast.	3–5'; flower spikes 1–2' above foliage	5–9		July, pink-red	Clumping, warm-season type, foliage ranges from deep green to gray-green; flower panicles turn white, foliage turns yellow, then fades to beige. Another of the major grasses in the tallgrass prairie. Vigorous, it can take over a prairie planting. Should be no more than 10% in a mix or add as plants later.
Schizachyrium scoparium (Little bluestem; formerly *Andropogon scoparius*)	X	2,3,5,7,8	Sun	Dry to moist; pH adaptable	1–2'	3–8		Aug.–Sept., white fluffy seeds along orangish stem	Clumping, warm-season type, blue-green foliage, thin flower spikes rise in late summer, plant turns copper-red in fall with fluffy seed heads along the stem.
Sesleria caerulea (syn. *S. autumnalis*; Blue moor grass)		2,3 (northern European origin)	Sun to light shade	Moist, well-drained loam, cannot tolerate dry sites; prefers limey soils but is pH adaptable	6–12"; flowers 6–8" above foliage	5–9	X	March–June, purple	Clumping, cool-season type with curled foliage that is dark green on top and bluish white underneath. Can be used as a lawn substitute, tolerates limited amount of foot traffic.

PLANT NAME	N	REGIONS	LIGHT REQ.	SOIL	HEIGHT	ZONE	E	BLOOM TIME & COLOR	COMMENT
Sorghastrum nutans (Indian grass)	X	2,3,5,7,8	Sun	Prefers deep, rich loam, will tolerate wide range of soil types and conditions. Drought-tolerant once established. May need water in arid Southwest.	2–3'; flower spikes 2–3' above foliage	4–9		August, tan-yellow	Clumping, warm-season type; ½" wide leaves range from green to almost blue and branch off at an angle from stems. Panicles at top of flower spikes are featherlike; turn bronze in winter. Foliage turns burnt orange. Readily reseeds. Another of the major grasses in the tallgrass prairie.
Sporobolus airoides (Alkali dropseed)	X	5,6,7,8,10	Sun	Prefers moist but tolerates drought; pH adaptable	2–3'	7–9		June–July, pink	Clumping, warm-season type, gray-green foliage; flower heads are pink panicles 5–10" long, turning golden by fall; whole plant is beige in winter. Was a major constituent of Calif. central valley grasslands.
S. heterolepis (Prairie dropseed)	X	2,3,5	Sun	Dry; pH adaptable	1–2'	3–9		August, light green	Upright, arching dense clumps of fine-textured emerald green leaves; warm-season type although emerges sooner than most; airy panicles have sweet scent; whole plant turns

| Uniola paniculata (Coastal sea oats) | 3,4 in coastal areas | Sun | Sand, salt tolerant, coastal areas only | 3–8′ | 7–10 | X | Throughout the season; forms flat oat-like spikes that droop, green turning beige / orangish in fall, then creamy brown. | Coastal dune grass (warm-season type) that is protected in most areas; rhizomatous; arching gray-green foliage; forms dense colonies in sand. Contact local extension agent for legal sources. |

Ground Covers

If you decide that you prefer a more formal look or want to have a garden in front of your house that is low but filled with interesting foliage and blooms at different times during the season, then look through the selected list of ground covers that follows. The table includes low ground covers for sun and shade, many of which are native. Some, such as heaths and heathers, snow-in-summer, mondo grass, and wild strawberry are suitable to use as a mass planting given the right conditions. Others will need to be established in small areas in an overall mixture of low-growing species. Some ground covers are very aggressive. Several gardeners I visited had planted three or four of these together (to "fight it out" as they put it), knowing that they would cover the ground thickly and keep each other in check at the same time.

This table is a very selected group of low-growing herbs, shrubs, perennials, and succulents that have a spreading habit and will cover the ground to form an effective and attractive alternative to turfgrass. All are perennial and many are evergreen, or have an interesting color in winter. Some are best used alone, others can be blended to create different textures and colors in one area. For success with ground covers, select those that match the soil and light conditions of your location.

Native plants are indicated with an "X" in the column labeled "N." The "E" column indicates evergreen; "B" indicates that the plant attracts and feeds butterflies or their larvae; and "W" means that the plant feeds bees, hummingbirds, or other wildlife. The "Regions" column corresponds to the Native Plant Communities Map (page 21), and the "Zone" column refers to U.S. Hardiness Zones, based on average minimum winter temperatures.

TABLE 2. GROUND COVERS

PLANT NAME	N	REGIONS	LIGHT REQ.	SOIL	HEIGHT	ZONE	E	BLOOM TIME & COLOR	B	COMMENT	W
Achillea millefolium (Common yarrow)		2,3,5,6, 9,10	Sun	Well-drained, tolerates poor or dry	6–20"	4–9	X in mild climate	Throughout summer, white	X	Perennial herb with aromatic gray-green foliage; spreads quickly; can be invasive in wet parts of Southwest. Tolerates foot traffic and mowing.	
A. tomentosa (Woolly yarrow)		1,2,3,5, 6,9	Sun	Sandy, well-drained	8"	3–9		Spring, flat-topped, yellow on 6" stems	X	Perennial herb with gray-green ferny foliage that forms a carpet.	
Ajuga reptans (Bugleweed)		2,3	Sun to part shade	Well-drained, needs regular moisture	3–4"	4–9	X semi	Early spring, blue	X	Perennial herb with foliage in rosettes; cultivars with variegated foliage, green or purple; spreads by underground stolons.	
Antennaria dioica (Pussytoes)	X	2,3,5,6, 9,10	Sun	Dry, sandy	4–10"	4–8	X	Early summer, white with pink tips held 2–3" above foliage		Gray-leaved herb that is a mat-forming, aggressive spreader best grown alone. Trim with string trimmer in spring if looks unruly.	X
Anthemis nobile (Roman chamomile)		2,3,5,6,9	Sun	Regular soil, can take sandy conditions	6–12"	6–8	X	Summer, yellow, with white rays	X	Perennial herb that, if sheared off regularly, will form spreading, tight clumps. Has feathery, green, fragrant foliage.	

PLANT NAME	N	REGIONS	LIGHT REQ.	SOIL	HEIGHT	ZONE	E	BLOOM TIME & COLOR	B	COMMENT	W
Arctostaphylos uva-ursi (Bearberry)	X	1,2, parts of 3,5,6,9	Full sun to part shade	Poor, sandy infertile; acid, will adapt to other pH; has salt tolerance	6–12"	2–8	X	Spring, white with pink tinge; red berry in August persists into winter	X	Spreading shrub with glossy bright green leaves that turn bronze to red in fall and winter; excellent in milder climates, especially lower-growing cultivars; can tolerate light foot traffic.	X
A. nevadensis (Pinemat manzanita)	X	6,9,10	Sun to part shade	Well-drained, but will tolerate dry soil and heat	10–18"	5–11	X	Spring, pale pink		Shrub with rich green leaves that spreads to 5'.	X
Arenaria verna (Sandwort, sometimes Irish moss)		1,2,3,5, 6,9	Sun	Well-drained, average soil; likes rock garden setting; cannot withstand cold, hard winters or dryness	1"	4–7	X	March–June, white, star-shaped		Perennial that forms dense, mosslike clumps; light green; can take only very light foot traffic, best to put steppingstones in the area.	
Artemisia frigida (Fringed sage)	X	5,6,7, 8,9	Sun to part shade	Poor, dry soil but can stand occasional watering	18"	3–10	X semi	Inconspicuous		Mat-forming perennial with soft, woolly semi-evergreen foliage; blends well with cerastium, native grasses, or penstemon. Aromatic. Shear flower stalks back to basal foliage in late winter to renew.	

Name		Zones	Light	Soil	Height	Hardiness		Bloom		Notes
Asarum spp. (Wild ginger; consult local sources for species native to your area)	X	1,2,3,5,6,9	Shade	Moist, rich	4–6"	3–8	X	Spring, brownish purple, hidden in foliage		Some evergreen, some deciduous, forms clusters of heart-shaped leaves; spreads by rhizomes.
Baccharis pilularis (Coyote brush, dwarf forms)	X	7,8,10	Sun	Dry but tolerates some watering	1–2'	8–11	X	Spring, insignificant		Shrub with small, thick, gray-green resinous leaves. Shear yearly in late winter before new growth begins to keep low and tidy. Spreads 6' or more.
Calluna vulgaris (Scotch heather; naturalized in northeastern North America)		2,3,6,9	Sun	Acid (pH 6 or less), sandy, organic, moist, well-drained soil	4–20"	4–6	X	July–Sept., rose to purple-pink	X	X	Upright branching, with dense branches that form thick mats; may need shearing after blooms fade to keep tidy. Foliage is medium green, changing to bronze in winter; cultivars may be silver, yellow, or red; increase by cutting, some will self-sow.
Calylophus hartwegii (Sundrops)	X	5,6,7,8,10	Sun to light shade	Well-drained; drought-tolerant	8"	6–10		Spring–summer, yellow		Light green, thin leaves; spreads by underground rhizomes to 2'. Cut back in winter to renew.

PLANT NAME	N	REGIONS	LIGHT REQ.	SOIL	HEIGHT	ZONE	E	BLOOM TIME & COLOR	B	COMMENT	W
Cassiope hypnoides (Mountain Heather)	X	1,2 mountain areas	Part shade	Tundra plant, sandy, peaty soil, needs moisture	3–5"	3–6	X	Summer, white		Prostrate, densely tufted, branches out.	
Cerastium tomentosum (Snow-in-summer)		1,2,5,6, 7,8,9	Sun	Dry, sandy, adaptable but needs well-drained site	6"	3–7	X	Early summer, white		White, woolly-leaved herb, mat-forming, invasive, needs to be grown alone or with other ground covers.	
Chrysogonum virginianum (Green-and-gold)	X	2,3,5	Sun to part shade	Moist, well-drained, can only take full sun if moisture is consistent	4–10"	5–9	X	Mostly in spring but continues until frost except in hot summer areas, yellow		Perennial herb with medium green, triangular-shaped leaves; spreads to form a cover by rhizomes and self-seeding.	
Cornus canadensis (Bunchberry)	X	1,2,3,6,9	Part to full shade	Humus-rich, moist soil, woodland plant, acid	4–10"	2–6 Needs cold climate		May–July, greenish with white bracts, look like miniature dogwood blooms		Creeping rootstock, light green whorled foliage, turns wine color in fall before dropping. Red berries fall to winter; tolerates light foot traffic.	X
Daboecia spp. (Irish heath)		2,3,6,9	Sun	Same as for *Calluna*	10–12"	6–8	X	Summer to fall, purple, white, pink		Erect, spreading stems with flat, tiny, glossy green leaves.	

Plant			Light	Soil	Height	Zone		Bloom		Description
Dalea greggii (Prostrate indigobush)	X	7,8	Sun to part shade	Poor, dry, water until well-established	6–10"	6–10	X	Summer, small, blue-lavender	X	Mat-forming perennial with soft pearly gray foliage; roots along the stem as it creeps, fast growing.
Dianthus gratianopolitanus (Cheddar pink)		2,3,6,9	Sun	Well-drained, will tolerate dry soil	3"	4–8	X	Spring, from white to carmine, held above foliage	X	Herb with gray grasslike leaves, forms a mat covered with blooms in spring.
Dichondra carolinensis or *micrantha* (Penny grass; don't confuse with dollarweed or pennywort)	X	Florida, California	Sun to part shade	Moist	1–2"	9–10	X	Inconspicuous		Creeping prostrate perennial herb with tiny round bright green leaves. Tolerates foot traffic. No need to mow or trim, can grow from seed.
Erica carnea (Winter heath)		2,3,6,9	Sun	Acid (pH 6 or less), sandy, organic, moist but well-drained; somewhat adaptable to nonacid soil	6–12"	5–8	X	Winter to spring, white, pink, purple	X	Spreading leaves, not as compressed as heather; does not seem to be as well-adapted to the United States as heather, according to Michael Dirr.
Eriogonum umbellatum (Dwarf sulfur buckwheat)	X	6,9,10	Sun to part shade	Will tolerate dry soil and heat	4"	7–9	X	June–Sept., yellow, orange or red		Perennial with green leaves (woolly below), forms a low mat, spreads to 2'.

PLANT NAME	N	REGIONS	LIGHT REQ.	SOIL	HEIGHT	ZONE	E	BLOOM TIME & COLOR	B	COMMENT	W
Fragaria chiloensis (Coast strawberry)	X	9,10	Sun	Well-drained	6"	5–10	X	Spring, white; tasty delicate berries follow		An herb with green, glossy leaves, native to the Pacific coast. Do not need to mow, water, or fertilize. Pull out grassy weeds first few years. Tolerates all foot traffic.	X
F. virginiana (Wild strawberry)	X	2,3	Sun to part shade	Well-drained; will need some water in prolonged dry spells	4–10"	5–10	X	Spring, white; small red fruits follow		Green leaves turn red and purple in fall; fruit not very tasty; tolerates foot traffic. Naturalize beneath shrubs and in meadow.	X
Galax urceolata (Galax, Wandflower)	X	2,3	Shade to part shade	Moist, humus rich, acid	6"	5–8	X	Late spring, white spike above foliage		Perennial herb with nearly round dark green glossy leaves that form clumps; spreads by rhizomes; turns purple or bronze in autumn.	
Gaultheria procumbens (Wintergreen)	X	2,3, possibly 9	Part shade	Acid, moist, but will tolerate some drought	4"	3–9	X	May–Sept., white or pinkish scarlet capsules persist through winter		Evergreen woody shrub with dark green glossy leaves; turns purplish with cold.	X

Name		Regions	Light	Soil	Height	Zones		Bloom	Description	
Gaylussacia brachycera (Box huckleberry)	X	2,3,6,9, parts of 10	Part to full shade	Peaty, acid moist, well-drained, such as conditions beneath pine trees	8–16"	5–8	X	May–June, white or pink tiny flowers followed by blue berries	Prostrate creeping shrub; edible berries though not very tasty; smooth, shiny green leaves; spreads by underground rootstocks to form a mat.	X
Gypsophila repens (Creeping baby's-breath)		2,3,5,9	Sun	Well-drained, neutral, likes rock garden setting	6"	4–9		June, white	Perennial herb with small green leaves that forms a mat.	
Helianthemum nummularium (Rock rose)		7,8,10	Sun	Sandy, alkaline, well-drained or rocky soil; will rot if too much moisture in soil	8–9"	5–7	X	Summer, yellow, pink gold, red, orange, white	Low-growing subshrub with gray-green foliage, trailing habit; cut back after blooming to encourage new growth.	
Hepatica americana (Liverleaf)	X	2,3,5	Shade to part shade	Alkaline, woodsy, rich soil	6"	4–8	X	Early spring, blue to white	Lobed, thickish leaves; increase by seeds or division.	
Herniaria glabra (Rupturewort)		Lower part of 2,3,9, parts of 10	Sun	Well-drained soil; may be short-lived in some situations	3"	6–8	X	Inconspicuous	Prostrate, perennial herb with tiny, oblong, green, stalkless leaves and swollen joints.	

PLANT NAME	N	REGIONS	LIGHT REQ.	SOIL	HEIGHT	ZONE	E	BLOOM TIME & COLOR	B	COMMENT	W
Iris cristata (Dwarf crested iris)	X	2,3,5,6,9	Sun to light shade	Well-drained, humus rich; more tolerant of heat and sun if soil is moist	4–7"	3–9		Two weeks in early spring; pale blue to white with yellow on the crests		Long-lived perennial, light green foliage; spreads easily by rhizomes, nice in masses or mixed with low grasses.	X
Lampranthus spp. (Iceplant)		5,6,10	Sun	Dry, good on banks or slopes; drought tolerant	1–1½'	9,10		Year-round, orange, purple, pink, yellow		Low shrub with fleshy, thick, gray-green leaves; trailing habit; select ground-cover species with more delicate appearance than coarse ones used on roadsides.	
Licania michauxii (Gopher-apple)	X	3,4, coastal	Sun	Sandy, dry	3–12"	10	X	Spring, white		Prostrate shrub with shiny, green, stiff leaves; spreads by underground stems. Increase by cuttings or seeds.	
Linnaea borealis (Twinflower)	X	6,9, forests	Shade	Moist, peaty or woodsy soil	1–2"	6–10	X	Fragrant, rose or white; fruit yellow, ⅛"		Evergreen subshrub with trailing habit.	
Lysimachia nummularia (Creeping Jennie)		2,3,5,6,9	Shade to part shade	Moist	2"	4–9	X	Midsummer, golden		Perennial herb with round, green leaves on stems that root at the joints; creeps.	

Species		Regions	Light	Soil	Height	Zone	Bloom		Notes	
Maianthemum canadense (Two-leaved Solomon's-seal, False lily-of-the-valley)	X	1,2,3,6	Shade	Moist, woodsy	8"	3–7	May–June, short spiked tiny, white flowers		Low perennial herb with oval leaves that spreads by creeping rhizomes.	
Melampodium leucanthum (Blackfoot daisy)	X	5,7,8,10	Sun to part shade	Dry, gravelly; thrives in hot situations; does not do well in heavy soil or if over-watered	6–10"	5–10	Spring to fall, white daisylike flowers with yellow centers	X	Reports mixed on short- or long-lived quality but does self-sow. Spreads to 1½'. Small, narrow, gray-green leaves.	
Mimosa strigillosa (Sunshine mimosa)	X	4	Sun	Dry; prefers limey soil but will adapt to others; deep-rooted	4–10"	10	Spring, pink	X	Creeping legume that spreads by stolons and rhizomes; soft, no thorns, will crawl under shrubs and other flowers without crowding them out. Fills in fast. Can be walked on, mowed like grass.	
Mitchella repens (Partridgeberry)	X	1,2,3,6, maybe parts of 9 if conditions right	Shade	Acid, moist, well-drained soil with lots of leafmold; forest floor, sensitive plant	2"	3–9	May–June, white or pinkish fragrant; irregular-shaped red berries persist into winter	X	Prostate ground-hugging shrub with dark green leaves, sometimes with white lines through them. In nature found with mosses and lichens under forest canopy; spreads.	X

PLANT NAME	N	REGIONS	LIGHT REQ.	SOIL	HEIGHT	ZONE	E	BLOOM TIME & COLOR	B	COMMENT	W
Myoporum parvifolium (Creeping myoporum)		7,8,10	Sun	Well-drained; will tolerate alkaline conditions; may need water in height of summer to look good	6–8" (*M.p.* 'Prostratum' 3")	6–9		Spring–summer, white starlike; followed by purple berries		Rich green oval-shaped leaves form a dense fine-textured mat; spreads to 9'. Cut back in winter to renew. Roots where stems touch ground.	
Ophiopogon japonicus 'Nana' (Dwarf mondo grass)		3,4	Sun to shade	Well-drained, sandy	2–3"	7–10	X	Summer, white; blue berries in fall		Dark green grasslike leaves in tufts; spreads by underground stolons to form dense, turflike cover; cut back in spring if needs renewal.	
Opuntia humifusa (Prickly pear)	X	2,3,4	Sun	Dry, sandy, or rocky	12", will spread 3'	4–9	X	May–June, yellow; purple to reddish edible fruit in late summer		Cactus with flat, fleshy green pads, barbed bristles usually have no spines but are troublesome if you touch them.	
O. polyacantha (Plains prickly pear)	X	5,7,8	Sun	Poor; dry tolerates heat	4", will spread 4–5'	3–6	X	June, waxy yellow; edible fruit ripens in August		Cactus with many spines on leafless jointed stems that are flattened, padlike, light green; keep weeded.	X
Osteospermum fruticosum (African trailing daisy)		7,8,10	Sun	Well-drained soil, not heavy clay, prefers dry soil	8–12"	9–10	X	Late winter to early spring, sporadic rest of year, purple, pink, or white		Spreading, shrubby perennial with oval leaves; stems root where they touch ground; spreads to 3'. Cut back old branches to renew.	

Plant		Forest/region zones	Light	Soil	Height	Hardiness zone		Bloom			Notes
Oxalis oregana (Redwood sorrel)	X	6,9, possibly forests in 2	Shade	Cool, moist woodland soil	7"	6–9	X	Spring, rich pink before leaves fully develop	X		Velvety rich green leaves; spreads up to 3'.
Pachysandra procumbens (Alleghany spurge)	X	2,3	Shade to part shade	Rich, woodsy	10–12"	5–8	X in South	Spring, greenish or purplish			Medium green foliage, toothed, stems trailing; increase by cuttings.
Paxistima canbyi (Mountain lover, sometimes called rat-stripper)	X	1,2, cooler parts of 3,5,6	Part shade to full sun, more dense and compact in sun	Moist, well-drained, high organic matter; will tolerate high pH	10–12", spread 3–5'; *P. myrsinites* is taller, 1–12'	3–8	X	Early May, greenish or reddish, not showy	X		Low shrub with dark green, long, narrow leaves that turn bronze in winter; leathery tiny white capsule fruit follow.
Penstemon pinifolius (Pineleaf penstemon)	X	7,8,10	Sun	Well-drained, will tolerate dry soil and heat	8–12"	5–10	X	May–June, again in Sept., orange-red	X	X	Evergreen perennial with fine bright green leaves; forms a cushion, spreading 8–12". Nice blended with fringed sage or cerastium as ground cover.
Phlox divaricata (Wild sweet William)	X	2,3,5	Part shade to shade	Moist, peaty soil, woodland	8–12"	3–9	X	Spring, blue	X		Medium to dark green foliage, spreads to 2' by rhizomes.
P. stolonifera (Creeping phlox)	X	1,2,3,5	Part shade to shade	Moist, peaty soil, woodland	6–10"	2–9	X	Spring, for 2–4 weeks, blue, lavender or white	X		Medium green foliage; plants form mat and will spread by stolons where space is open.

PLANT NAME	N	REGIONS	LIGHT REQ.	SOIL	HEIGHT	ZONE	E	BLOOM TIME & COLOR	B	COMMENT	W
Phlox subulata (Moss phlox)	X	1,2,3,5	Full sun	Well-drained	6"	2–9		Spring, pink but cultivars in blue, white, and red	X	Narrow, linear, stiff green leaves, almost prickly. Spreads up to 16", forming a mat. Layer or divide to increase.	
Phyllodoce empetriformis (Mountain heath)	X	1,2 mountain areas	Sun to part shade	Tundra plant, moist, peaty soil	6"	3–6	X	April and August, pink		Needlelike leaves; spreads to 12", forming small shrublike mound.	
Potentilla tridentata (Three-toothed cinquefoil)	X	1,2, upper part of 5, 6,9	Sun to part shade	Acid, well-drained to dry, sandy, or rocky	6–8"	2–7	X	Summer, white	X	Palmate, leathery green foliage spreads by runners; foliage turns red in autumn.	
Sagina subulata (Pearlwort; 'Aurea' has golden green leaves)		2,3,5,6,9	Sun, part shade in southern and hot summer areas	Fertile, moist, well-drained soil; does not like it dry	2"	5–7	X	Summer, tiny, white, on short stalks		Perennial evergreen herb with tiny, needlelike foliage that forms a moss-like mat, best to put steppingstones through it.	
Salvia chamaedryoides (Mexican blue sage)	X	Parts of 5,7,8	Sun or shade	Poor or dry soil	8–18"	8–10		Summer and fall, blue, aromatic	X	Perennial subshrub with tiny, silver-gray leaves; spreads to 18". Shear off spent flowers.	

Plant		Region	Light	Soil	Height	Zone		Bloom		Description
Saponaria ocymoides (Rock soapwort)		2, parts of 3,5, 6,9	Sun to light shade	Well-drained average soil; does not like humidity and hot summers	8"	4–7		May–June, pink		Perennial herb with small, dark green leaves, with a trailing habit; to restrain growth cut back after flowering.
Sedum lanceolatum (Lance-leaved stonecrop)	X	2,3,5,6,9	Sun	Shallow, gravelly soil, tolerant of dry soil and heat	3–7"	5–8		Spring to summer, yellow	X	Tufted succulent with small linear green leaves that turn bronze in fall. Does not tolerate foot traffic.
S. oreganum	X	2,3,5,6, 9,10	Sun to part shade	Well-drained	2–3"	4–8		Spring to summer, bright yellow in flat-topped clusters	X	Succulent with glossy green spatulate foliage forming rosettes; turns crimson in sun or poor soil.
S. spathulifolium ('Cape Blanco' has silver leaves)	X	2,3,5,6, 9,10	Sun	Likes shallow, gravelly soil, tolerates dry soil but does not like heat and humidity combined	2–6"	4–8		May–June, yellow	X	Succulent with broad, bluish foliage, rosettes; spreads.
S. ternatum (Mountain stonecrop)	X	2,3,5,6,9	Shade to part sun	Well-drained, likes rocky slopes	2–6"	4–8	X	Spring, white		Succulent with rosettes of small, round, light green leaves; creeper.
Silene acaulis (Moss campion)	X	1, high mountains in other areas	Sun	Tundra location or scree conditions	1"	3–5		Summer, red-purple	X	Bright green, mosslike foliage, grows compactly, spreads to 6", mat-forming.

PLANT NAME	N	REGIONS	LIGHT REQ.	SOIL	HEIGHT	ZONE	E	BLOOM TIME & COLOR	B	COMMENT	W
Sisyrinchium bellum (Blue-eyed grass)	X	6,9,10	Sun to part shade	Dry, poor; can take heat	3–8"	8–10	X	March to May, blue flowers		Clump-forming with grasslike foliage that will stay evergreen with adequate moisture. Best for naturalizing with other low grasses.	
Stachys olympica (Lamb's-ears; 'Silver Carpet' is a nonflowering form)		2,3,5,9	Sun	Well-drained, to dry	8"	4–8	X	Late spring, purple, in whorls on 18" stem, not very attractive, can just prune off		Herb that forms a mat of large, woolly, soft whitish green leaves. Cut back any foliage with winter damage in spring.	
Teucrium chamaedrys 'Prostratum' (Wall germander)		2,3,5,6,7, 8,9,10	Sun or shade but prefers sun	Average to poor, well-drained; drought tolerant once established	6" (*T. majoricum* 'Cossonni' 2–3")	5–9	X	May, purple to pink		Prostrate subshrub with small, dark green, fine-textured, glossy leaves; spreads to 2'. Cut back winter damage in spring. Aromatic.	X
Thymus pseudolanuginosus (Woolly thyme)		2,3,5,6,9	Sun	Well-drained	1"	4–8	X	Summer, pink	X	Creeping perennial herb with tiny, hairy, gray leaves; forms a dense mat. Can take light foot traffic.	Bees
T. serpyllum (Creeping thyme; similar species often sold under this name is *T. praecox arcticus*, called Mother-of-thyme)		2,3,5,6, 9	Sun	Well-drained, tolerates dry soil for short time	3–4"	4–8	X	Summer, pinkish purple		Creeping, perennial herb with tiny medium green foliage; forms a mat.	Bees

Plant		Region	Light	Soil	Height	Zone		Bloom		Remarks
Vaccinum vitis-idaea minus (Mountain cranberry)	X	1,2	Sun	Rocky, peaty, acid, moist	6"	3–6	X	Spring, pink; then bright red fruit	X	Prostrate shrub that forms a dense mat with small, oval, shiny green leaves; spreads by rhizomes.
Verbena bipinnatifida (Dakota verbena, Vervain)	X	5,7,8,10	Sun	Well-drained; extra water in driest part of summer promotes continued bloom	8–12"	7–10		June until frost, lavender	X	Prostrate perennial with gray-green foliage that spreads to 2'; above zone 7 may die back in winter but self-sows readily. May need to blend with another evergreen ground cover or short grass.
V. canadensis (Clump verbena)	X	3, 7, 8, parts of 2,5	Sun	Must be well-drained, tolerates dry conditions	8"	6–10		Throughout the summer, red or pink	X	Low, spreading perennial with clumping habit. Stems root where they lie along the ground. Cut back in fall if stems lose leaves or get too long.
V. peruviana	X	lower part of 3,5, 6; also 7,8,10	Sun	Well-drained to dry; drought tolerant once established	3–4"	7–10		Spring through summer, bright scarlet	X	Low perennial related to the native *V. canadensis* that hugs the ground; stems root as they creep; dark-green foliage; prune back in fall to encourage dense growth.

PLANT NAME	N	REGIONS	LIGHT REQ.	SOIL	HEIGHT	ZONE	E	BLOOM TIME & COLOR	B	COMMENT	W
Verbena tenuisecta (Moss verbena)		3,7,8,10 naturalized in the South	Full sun to part shade	Well-drained soil, can tolerate sandy conditions	6–8"	8–10	X	Spring through fall, purple	X	Low perennial with divided, ferny foliage that spreads by stems rooting along the ground. Cut back in winter to renew. Can shear with lawn mower set at 3".	X
Viola labradorica (Labrador violet)	X	1,2,3 if given sufficient moisture, 5,6	Shade	Well-drained needs moisture if in sun	1–4"	3–8		Early spring, mauve	X	Ovate dark green foliage; spreads rapidly by creeping rhizomes, and seeds create carpet.	X
V. pedata (Bird's-foot violet)	X	2,3,5	Sun to part shade	Well-drained soil, will tolerate dry, poor soil	2–6"	4–9		Spring for 3 weeks, blue and violet with yellow stamens	X	Tufted perennial with green palmately lobed leaves; spreads by rhizomes; does well naturalized in short grass meadows.	X
V. pubescens (Downy yellow violet)	X	2,5	Shade	Fertile, moist (not wet) soil	6–8"	3–7		Early spring, yellow	X	Tufted perennial with green, kidney-shaped leaves that have soft hairs; spreads by rhizomes.	X
V. sororia (Blue woods violet, Confederate violet)	X	2,3,5	Shade	Fertile, moist, in a site protected from wind	6–8"	3–8	X	Spring, pale to deep blue, sometimes white	X	Tufted perennial with dark green, heart-shaped leaves; self-sows readily, forming colonies; can take light foot traffic.	X

Name	Native	Zones/Region	Light	Soil	Spacing	Hardiness		Bloom		Notes
Waldsteinia ternata (Barren strawberry)		2,3,5,6 9	Sun or shade	Dry or cool, moist	6"	4–8	X	Spring, yellow		Perennial with glossy green leaves; spreads by rhizomes to form a carpet.
Wedelia trilobata		Florida portion of 3,4	Sun to part shade	Sandy, well-drained, needs some moisture; salt tolerant	6–8"	9–10	X	Summer, daisylike, yellow		Stems creeping and rooting, can be invasive. Plant where you don't mind it spreading rapidly. Not native, but naturalized. Can mow it to renew.
Zauschneria californica (California fuchsia)	X	10	Full sun to light shade	Dry, likes stone crevices	10–15"	8–10		Aug.–Oct. scarlet-orange	X	Soft, downy gray leaves; spreads underground to form a loose, low, broad mound. Hummingbirds love it. Cut to ground after bloom, will regrow.
Zinnia grandiflora (Prairie zinnia)	X	5,7,8,10	Sun	Dry, tolerates poor soil and heat, a tough plant	6"	5–10		All summer, dark yellow	X	Perennial that spreads by underground rhizomes to form a cover; wiry, grass-like leaves turn tan in winter and disappear. Flowers dry to a straw color. Shear back to 4" in spring.

Transforming all or part of your turfgrass lawn into a "wild lawn" of mostly native, low-growing plants is an exciting educational process. You will learn more about the site on which you live and the plants that once grew there. You will find yourself studying the plants along back roads to try and spot particular species that you have read about and are considering for your site. As the process continues, so does the learning. Native plant communities are dynamic and ever-changing. People who have been involved in restoration or natural landscaping for years still are surprised at how plants behave and what techniques work one year but not the next. Every site and natural landscape is unique and is a cooperative process between you and nature.

While Lorrie and I stood quietly in Milt Ettenheim's yard, surrounded by the prairie flowers, a red admiral butterfly landed nearby. And while we were visiting the prairie planting in Rae Sweet's front yard, two cedar waxwings suddenly appeared on the serviceberry tree and began feasting on the ripe berries.

One day in late September I was standing at the kitchen sink, looking out the window across my own meadow, when two male wild turkeys stepped out of the grasses and goldenrod and strolled across the yard—not more than ten feet from me. These birds have declined to such an extent that they are being reintroduced in some parts of the state and hunting laws are more restrictive. I wondered if they had shown up because we stopped mowing an eight-acre meadow that had been kept as lawn for ten years. Had they found two of their favorite foods—deertongue (*Panicum clandestinum*) and switchgrass (*Panicum virgatum*)—which were now allowed to make seed? On the trails that we've cut through the meadow we've seen fox, box turtles, and pheasant. Kestrels, red-tailed hawks, and merlins soar overhead when the house is quiet, and deer eating fallen fruit from our apple trees are so close that we can hear them snort when they are startled and leap away.

By changing the plants in our yards, Rae, Milt, and I have created the possibility for these events, which are routine for the butterfly, the birds, and the other animals, but become special when we recognize that their occurrence depends on the existence of particular species of plants in certain parts of the country.

This book is my report to you about how Rae, Milt, and other homeowners have created "wild lawns" all across the United States that are distinctive to the regions in which they live. It is also filled with details about the plants and techniques that you need to transform your lawn into a more natural landscape that does not require chemicals, synthetic fertilizers, or supplemental watering. The photographs (see color insert) show you how some of these "wild lawns" look.

Installing and Maintaining a Wild Lawn

Whatever plants you choose to replace your lawn, some ground preparation will be needed. Once you have developed an overall plan for the changes, including a rough sketch to scale, you can begin the transformation in small stages, doing a bed each year, or all at once. Either way, follow the guidelines below to prepare the soil. Most meadow and prairie species are adaptable to sand, silt, or clay soils and you can select the ones that favor dry, moist, and wet conditions to match your site. Other alternative plant choices, such as heathers, moss, or sedums, are less adaptable. Unless your site fits their requirements, it would be best to consider a suitable ground cover, a native and ornamental grass planting, or a blend of native grass and wildflowers.

The first and most important step is site preparation. Since your goal, whether you plant seed or plants, is to give them the very best chance to get established so that weeds will not invade and compete, clearing the existing vegetation is key. If you are starting with a bare site (say you have moved into a recently constructed home), and the ground is dry, run a sprinkler for thirty minutes three days in a row and wait a week. This will cause whatever seeds are present in the soil to germinate. Presuming that what germinates is weeds, destroy them by whatever means you choose. Repeat the procedure twice; be ready to plant after the second time.

I have asked many people about whether a meadow can be started by just cutting the existing grass very low and using a grain drill or a slit seeder to plant right into it. The majority said they would not recommend it because it is unlikely that the warm-season native bunch grasses could compete successfully in the first two years against the exotic, sod-forming turfgrasses and any rhizomatous weeds that might exist. So, the two choices are: 1) clear the ground of all vegetation and sow seed; or 2) let the lawn grow and remove unwanted plants. The latter method is how I began. I spent many hours during the first year of "no mowing" identifying the grasses and wildflowers. This process is essential so that you can manage the area to favor the native and noninvasive exotics and remove noxious weeds. It is also very exciting, especially when you discover a plant that you never expected to find—for me it was blue-eyed grass (*Sisyrinchium angustifolium*). I have identified six native grasses, three nonnative grasses (which so far seem compatible), and thirty-six wildflowers. The plants I had to remove include thistle, multiflora rose, and honeysuckle.

If you choose the "stop mowing" technique, you may want to start with a small area first. Continue to cut along your property borders and near your house. If the unmown area is larger than 500 square feet, you may want to cut pathways through it as well. Identify your plants, keep a journal (including name and location), remove noxious weeds, and manage it by cutting or burning (with a permit) once a year as described later in this chapter. There are two excellent sources—and as far as I know, the only ones—to guide you: the pamphlet "Energy Conservation on the Home Grounds: The Role of Naturalistic Landscaping" and *The Wild Gardener in the Wild Landscape*—both listed in Appendix IV.

If you choose to clear the ground either for a meadow or for other alternatives and have a weed-free turf, rent a sod-cutter and remove the sod. It will come off in long strips about eighteen inches wide and three inches thick. You can pile it upside down in a place where you would like to have a small berm, cover it with topsoil to shape it, and then put a thick layer (six inches or more) of mulch over the top until you are ready to plant. If you do not want to create a raised area, just pile the sod strips upside down in an out-of-the-way place and cover them with black plastic. Eventually they will decompose and you will have a pile of compost.

After the sod is removed, loosen the soil with a shallow tilling (no deeper than one to two inches) or, if it is a small area, just rake or hoe to loosen the top layer. Wait one week to see if any weeds germinate. If not, you are ready to plant. If they do, dig them out before planting the seeds.

If your lawn is a mix of turfgrasses and weeds and you want to take it all out and replant the entire area at once, you will need to use one of the methods below to kill the vegetation.

How to Get Rid of Lawn

1. **Smother it.** For a small area (a few thousand square feet or less), you can cover the ground in the fall, or at least three months before you plant, with six inches of wood chips, heavy duty black plastic, a layer of newspapers twenty sheets thick and overlapped with wood chips on top, or four-by-eight-foot pieces of plywood. Some of the prairie gardeners I visited in Wisconsin who have heavy clay soil laid down a thick layer of newspaper, covered it with a foot of sand, and then plugged in plants.

2. **Remove it mechanically.** A sod-cutter is the quickest way to remove the lawn and be ready to plant. Available at most rental centers, this machine slices horizontally just below the surface, taking off about a three-inch layer of turf and soil in strips. This leaves a bare surface ready for planting. Have all your seeds, plants, mulch, and watering equipment ready before you rent the machine. Since the soil surface will be bare, you need to plan this to correspond with the correct time for planting in order to avoid erosion and the germination of seeds brought in by the wind or birds.

    To remove lawn grass and weeds by cultivation, rotary till the area two or three times about a week apart. Timing is important. If you wait longer between tilling, the plants that you are trying to kill may reroot.

If you know that you have tough weeds like quack grass or Johnson grass which have rhizomatous root systems, you may need to cultivate at intervals throughout the growing season to get rid of them.

3. **Remove it chemically.** Many people involved in natural landscaping feel that this option defeats the whole purpose of gardening in a more natural way. They do not recommend it and neither do I. But, if the other methods do not work for you, or if you decide to go with this technique, use only one of the glyphosate-based herbicides (Roundup, Kleenup, or Ranger), reported to be of lower toxicity and nonpersistent; or the salt-based Sharpshooter by Safer. Read the label, wear protection, and follow the directions precisely. After everything turns brown (usually ten days to two weeks), cultivate, and plant.

These three techniques are used to get rid of perennial plants. Since annual weed seeds may still be present in the prepared bed, you can water, wait a week, and cultivate shallowly to kill any that have germinated. Or, if you live where you can expect a regular rain every few days, wait seven days after it occurs and then cultivate. Be ready to plant right after the cultivation.

Choosing Species to Suit Your Site

Since this book is focused on alternatives to front lawns, most of my suggestions are for open, sunny areas—meadow and prairie plants, sedums, heathers, and many of the ground covers. The only exceptions are moss and shade-loving wildflowers and ground covers. If you have a shady front yard with numerous tall trees, see Chapter 5 and Table 2 (pages 47–63) for possibilities. Whether you have a sunny or shady site, your selections still need to be made with consideration for the type of soil you have, its pH (most woodland soil is acid), and its moisture level.

There are three main types of soil—sandy, clay, and loam. Sandy soil has large particles, and water drains very rapidly from it. It feels gritty to the touch and will not hold together well if you squeeze a handful. Sandy soils are low in nutrients compared to clay and loam and tend to be dry.

Clay soil, on the other hand, is composed of tiny particles that are compressed together and it drains very slowly; on heavy clay, water stands in puddles for a long time after a rain, and plant roots can literally be drowned. Clay is nutrient rich but can be very compacted, lacking organic matter—the decaying remains of plant or animal waste (manure)—which keep the soil loose and provide energy for soil microorganisms whose activity helps release nutrients from the soil so that plants can take them up. Soil with a high clay content feels slick and smooth and will hold together in a clump if you squeeze it.

Loam is categorized between clay and sandy soil. It is the ideal medium, being a mixture of different-sized particles, possessing a good level of fertility, and holding moisture well while at the same time draining readily. It will hold together when squeezed but not as stiffly as clay. It feels somewhat gritty and, when dry, you can feel another substance that is flourlike in texture. That substance, called silt, is a soil particle somewhere between the size of the large sand particle and the tiny clay particle.

Soil pH is a measure of its level of acidity or alkalinity. The scale runs from 0 to 14, with 7 in the middle as neutral. Zero indicates the highest degree of acidity and 14, the highest degree of alkalinity. Most soils fall between 5.0 and 7.5; those to the east of the Mississippi River tend to be acid, those to the west tend to be alkaline, particularly in the Southwest. Most of the plants discussed in this book are adaptable to varying soil pH. Tables 1 and 2 indicate the few that require more acid or more alkaline conditions. Although you can amend your soil with lime to raise the pH, or with sulfur to lower the pH, it is best to select plants that are suited to the existing soil.

The moisture level of soil has three categories: dry (xeric), medium (mesic), and moist (hydric). Dry soil is usually sandy and poor in nutrients. Turf grasses do not grow well on it, nor do many other cultivated garden species. But there are whole groups of native and well-adapted plants that like dry, sandy soil—some of the prairie and meadow species, sedums and sempervivums, and desert and drought-tolerant ground covers. Medium soils include well-drained loams and clay loams, and the widest range of plants prefers this type of soil moisture. The last category, moist, includes soils that have moisture in the subsoil year-round and may have water standing on them in spring and fall. They occur in lowland areas, along pond edges and streambanks, and in rich garden soil that receives regular, abundant water.

Since most readers of this book will be converting an area of turfgrass or a mixture of turf and a few weeds, extensive soil improvement should not be necessary for planting a meadow, prairie, or native grasses. However, if you will be planting ground covers, sedums, or heathers, you will need to dig the soil a spade's depth (about twelve inches), loosen the subsoil beneath it, and add organic matter (a three- to four-inch layer mixed in). For most of the ground covers, you will also need to work in a long-lasting organic fertilizer (available commercially or blend your own, see box). For more on planting these other types of plants, see the separate sections below.

Organic Fertilizer Blends

2 parts bloodmeal (or cottonseed meal or soybean meal)
1 part bonemeal or rock phosphate
1 part greensand or granite dust (or 3 parts wood ashes)

Use 4 to 5 pounds per 100 square feet.

The addition of organic matter for a prairie/meadow will be helpful but is only absolutely necessary for compacted clay or very poor soil. To improve these poor soils, work in compost, rotted leaves, or well-composted aged manure. This will break up heavy soil, add nutrients, and improve air circulation. For light, sandy soils it will improve water-holding capacity. Another way to add organic matter is to plant a cover crop, also called "green manure." Some suggestions are buckwheat, winter wheat, annual rye, hairy vetch, and annual alfalfa. Plant them in the spring and let them grow all season, then till or turn them under in the fall. Some can be planted a few weeks before the first fall frost, left in all winter, and turned under in late spring or early summer after they have put on some new growth. Talk with your local extension agent to determine the best ones for your site.

Planting a Prairie or Meadow

When to sow seed and whether to sow grasses and wildflowers at the same time are both subjects on which you will find conflicting information. Part of this is because different methods work better under different conditions, part of it is because the techniques for sowing and managing these plantings are still being developed. Keep the following two facts in mind when making your decision about whether to plant in spring, early summer, or fall. One, most prairie and meadow plants, especially the grasses, are warm-season plants, which means they germinate best when the soil is warm and grow most vigorously during warm weather. Two, since the seed or transplants are usually put out in a large area that is not easily watered, it is best to plant them when you can count on nature's assistance, that is, regular rainfall.

Planting can be done in late spring or fall, although most sources say that best results are usually obtained with late spring or early summer sowings. In Georgia and the Southeast, Will Corley, University of Georgia extension horticulturalist, recommends fall seeding since the soil has cooled off and the area will have the advantage of fall, winter, and early spring rain. He says spring plantings can be made from March through May but irrigation needs may be higher since rainfall is less at that time. In Maryland, wildflower specialists recommend sowing from mid-September to late October or early March to late April. In Pennsylvania, roadside plantings of wildflower-only mixes were done in November, January, February, March, and April. The wildflowers planted in April resulted in the best establishment. Early to mid-May is the recommended planting time for central Missouri, early summer for Wisconsin. In the Southwest, if you are using a mix that has warm-season grasses and wildflowers, sow when the soil warms up in the cold-winter parts of the region and sow anytime in the mild-winter parts to take advantage of the natural rainy season. In Colorado, individuals and sources recommend May to early June before hot weather begins. In California, plant very early in spring before the hot dry summer begins, or wait until fall when the rains return.

For small areas (anything less than two acres), the seed can be broadcast by hand. Mechanical seed drills pulled by small tractors will be needed for larger sites. Mix the seed with sand, calcined clay (for example, untreated kitty litter), vermiculite, sawdust, or peat moss so that you will be able to

Some Helpful Measures

Length

Field guides to wildflowers, native grasses, and weeds often give the length of leaf blades and flower stems in centimeters. I have written in the back of my guides the following helpful conversions:

1 inch = 2.5 cm
1 foot = 30.5 cm
1 yard = 92 cm = .9 m

Area

9 square feet = 1 square yard
43,560 square feet = 1 acre
1,000 square feet = an area about 32 by 32 feet or 50 by 20 feet

Seeding Rates

Native grass alone or blended with wildflowers:

10 pounds per acre
1 pound per 4,000 square feet

Use approximately 50 percent each of grass and wildflowers. If your budget is limited, increase the amount of grass, which costs less than the wildflower seed.

spread it more evenly. If you use one of the last three, it will need to be moistened slightly so that the seed will adhere to it. For the other materials, use about a bushel basket per half-pound of seed. Use about four pounds of clay or sand to one pound of seed.

Take half of the mixture and broadcast it over the area, then broadcast the rest in a pattern that is perpendicular to your first broadcasting. Rake the area to cover the seed one-quarter to one-half inch deep. For large areas, this can be done by dragging a piece of chain-link fence attached to a tractor over the site. To improve seed-to-soil contact, enhancing germination and preventing moisture loss, lightly compact the site with a walk-behind lawn roller (fill with water to the amount of weight that you can push without struggling). Lawn rollers are available at most rental centers and the usual width of the roller is thirty-six inches. For large areas, use a tractor with a roller attachment having at least 200 pounds of weight. Apply a light covering of wheat or oat straw as a mulch and water the area thoroughly. Do not use hay—even old hay bales—because it contains seeds of Eurasian grasses and weeds. Water every other day for four weeks, skipping days when it rains.

If you are sowing a very small area, you may want to try this tip from Judi Davenport, a member of the Wild Ones, from Downers Grove, Illinois. She suggests sowing your wildflower seed mixture a few seeds at a time in soilless media in small peat pots. After they germinate, plant the pots in the garden and mark them with wooden plant labels or sticks. Anything that grows that is not marked, you can pull out. She says that this way you will be watering and tending the wildflowers and not the weeds. Another benefit is that it will also help you identify wildflower seedlings.

If you use transplants, start them a year ahead and either grow the wildflowers in deep pots so that the roots have plenty of room to grow down, or start them in small pots and transplant them into a protected garden bed to grow for one season before they are moved to the prairie or meadow area. Grasses have fibrous roots and the deep pots are not crucial for them. Space plants on eight- to twelve-inch centers and alternate grasses with wildflowers. Within two years, the spaces will fill in but you may want to apply mulch between the plants in the meantime if the area is not too large for that to be impractical. Some gardeners I talked to started their stand with grass seed first and put in wildflower seed and transplants the second year in the bare spots where the grass did not germinate well or where weeds had been pulled out. Still others started the area first with wildflower seed and later plugged in grass transplants.

The First Three Years

The early years of a meadow or prairie planting require the most expense and labor. But patience and diligence during that time will pay off because once the plants are established, the site takes care of itself. You will only need to inspect once or twice a year to remove any undesirable plants that show up and either mow or burn to prevent woody species from developing in the Eastern states and to remove the buildup of plant debris elsewhere. The first year, the grass and wildflowers will be tiny, ground-hugging plants, most likely in a sea of weeds. They are directing most of their energy downward, developing root systems.

Mow several times the first season to control annual weeds. The first mowing should be before the weeds reach eight inches high. Set the mower to a height of about four inches (just above the developing plants) and use a rotary or flail type that chops the clippings into small pieces. Remove any large clumps that might remain which will smother the young prairie or meadow plants. It is best not to try and pull out the weeds because you may pull the desirable plants along with them and disturb the soil, which will cause other weed seeds to germinate. If you prefer not to mow, you can cut weeds off at or just below ground level with clippers.

Mow often enough to prevent the weeds from getting taller than eight inches or developing flower and seed heads. If you miss a seed head, cut if off and remove it completely from the planted area so that it does not drop seed. Do not do a final low mowing of the entire area until late winter or early spring of the next year. If it is possible, rake off the mowed clippings to expose the ground to sun and air. During the second season, you will again have to be vigilant about weed control. Remove undesirable plants by cutting them off at ground level or pulling carefully.

Prescribed Burning

In mid-spring of the third season, you can begin to use an annual burning instead of mowing as the method of management if you live in an area where you can obtain a permit and you educate yourself about the necessary techniques and equipment needed to do a prescribed burn safely. If your meadow or prairie area is larger than 2,000 square feet or you have several patches throughout your yard, you may want to alternate burning and mowing. The two techniques favor different species and will prevent one or two from becoming more dominant than the others.

The best day for a prescribed grassland fire is one with temperatures from 40° to 60° F and moderate humidity between 45 and 60 percent. A slight steady breeze (about two to three miles per hour) is helpful because it will cause the fire to burn in one direction. Firebreaks—either paved driveways or sidewalks and mowed lawngrass pathways—need to be thoroughly soaked and cleared of all debris. Assemble a team of people who have been instructed and educated about grassland fires and make sure you have a hose, backup sprayer, fire flapper (a 12-by-18-inch piece of reinforced rubber attached to a 5-foot handle), and fire rakes (an iron garden rake with a 12-inch metal extension between the wooden handle and the rake head that is used to spread the fire). The flapper is used to smother flames at their base. Because it is rubber, you have to pause periodically to let it cool off or have someone spray it with water. Inform your neighbors and the local fire department of the day of the burn. Once set, the fire will burn about thirty feet in ten minutes (this is the spread of a backing fire which burns into the wind). A head fire (a stronger, faster fire that is carried with the wind) will burn as fast as 200 feet in ten minutes. The fire will stop and go out when it reaches firebreaks. Make sure to obtain the booklet by Wayne R. Pauly from the Dane County Park Commission, Madison, Wisconsin, (see Appendix IV) or other similar information from your forest service or extension agent in order to teach yourself the proper method for burning a grassland.

During the first three years or at any time you want to add a species to your prairie or meadow, you can start plants yourself or buy them from a nursery and clear a small area (at least 12 inches in diameter for each plant) so that you can plant them. Keep in mind that disturbing the soil causes any remaining dormant weed seeds to germinate. You may want to try cutting the existing plants to 1 or 2 inches high and digging a narrow, deep hole, just wide enough to be able to insert the new plant.

Rick Brune, a prairie gardener in Lakewood, Colorado, offers this tip when planting out a new wildflower transplant: After planting, mulching, and watering the new plant, place next to it a one-gallon plastic bottle filled with water with a pinhole pricked in one bottom corner. This provides slow, deep watering for plants that are becoming established.

Ground Covers

Most ground covers will be installed as plants. Those that can be started by seed should be broadcast in the same manner as seed for a prairie, meadow, or native grass planting. The ground should be cleared of competing vegetation as for a prairie or meadow planting, and if the soil is not easily dug and well-drained, till or dig the area to a depth of 12 inches and work in some organic matter.

In general, rooted cuttings of ground covers should be spaced on 6- to 10-inch centers in staggered rows. A quicker and more uniform cover will be achieved by pulling good-sized plants (in a 2- or 4-inch pot) apart and planting the pieces closely than planting large plants and waiting for them to spread. To calculate how many plants you will need, multiply the number of square feet of the area to be covered by the number of plants you plan to use per square foot below:

Spaced on Center	Plants per Square Foot
6 inches	4
8 inches	2.25
10 inches	1.44
12 inches	1
18 inches	.44

For instance, if you want to cover 200 square feet and plan to space the plants on 6-inch centers, multiply 200 by 4. You will need 800 plants. Or, if you plan to cover an area only 25 square feet and want to space the plants 12 inches apart, multiply 25 by 1. You will need 25 plants. Depending on the price of the plants and your budget, you can purchase them all at once and plant the entire area or do small patches at a time. Another possibility is planting just a few of the species that you select into a nursery bed. You can take cuttings or divide them, gradually increasing the number of plants until you have a sufficient quantity to complete the area, or at least plant another portion of it.

Since most ground covers will take two years to fill in, it is important to apply mulch at planting time and replenish it as needed to keep out unwanted plants. A general rule-of-thumb is that one cubic yard of mulch will cover about 100 square feet to a depth of four inches. Check the area at least once a week and remove weeds while they are still young and easy to pull.

On slopes where rain might wash away young plants, cover the area with a several-inch-thick layer of straw and top it with a net of strings fastened to stakes on all sides. Pull back enough straw to create an opening to put in plants. If the area is steep and rocky and would erode if all vegetation were removed, clear small areas here and there and prepare a planting hole three to four times as wide as the plant. Mulch around it. Keep the remaining unwanted vegetation cut back with a string trimmer or clippers. As the ground cover fills in, that remaining vegetation can be pulled out in stages.

Herbs, sedums, sempervivums, heaths, and heathers are particular types of ground cover plants. For details about their installation and care, see Chapter 6.

Woodland Areas

Deciding what species to plant in a wooded front yard depends on the spacing and type of trees. If the trees are very close, then very little light will be able to reach the forest floor. The soil in woods dominated by oaks or conifers will be more acid than a forest of mostly maples. The level of moisture in the soil also varies from the dry, sandy floor of pine/oak woods in the Southeast to the moist, humus-rich soil of New England birch/maple/hemlock forests.

A good place to start would be deciding where pathways will be and laying down a thick layer of wood chips, sawdust, or finely crushed stone to

Fire-Resistant Landscaping

Periodic burning of the natural vegetation occurred for thousands of years in most of the western United States, except for the coastal areas of Oregon, Washington, and part of northern California. These fires occurred as a result of the semi-arid environment and the buildup of dead shrubs, branches, and leaf litter and were usually started by lightning. During the last century, these fires have been suppressed as a forest management technique. But the Yellowstone fires of 1988 and 1989 and other smaller wildland fires have demonstrated the faultiness of the prevention policy.

As the population of the interior West has increased, so have the occurrences of wildland fires destroying homes. In 1985 research foresters began to organize conferences and workshops to discuss the problem and devise policies and techniques to teach homeowners methods of landscaping that would minimize the damage from a fire.

"Often when people move into a wildland area, they do so because they want privacy and to be closer to wilderness," says Steve Arno, research forester, Missoula, Montana. "They don't understand that building a house in a thick stand of trees and then not managing the landscape makes them vulnerable to the wildland fires that are inevitable." Wildland vegetation accumulates and requires cropping to prevent it from fueling a wildfire. Homeowners can prune, compost, and thin stands of trees to greatly reduce the risk of severe fire damage.

define them. This will help you see where you want to plant some understory shrubs and where sufficient light filters through to establish massed plantings of spring ephemerals. If your area has long periods without rain and your water source is far from where you will be planting young woodland plants, run a water line of some kind into the area so that you will not have to carry buckets of water over a long distance.

To help you determine your home's risk, you can order a "Wild-land Home Fire Risk Meter," which also has suggestions for reducing the risk (see Appendix IV). Other sources listed in the bibliography give more detailed information. Some general rules include:

1. Grassy areas should be kept mowed up to thirty feet around the home. Riding trails, pathways, and circle drives around the home create fire barriers. Use gravel or concrete walkways right next to the structure to prevent direct flame contact.

2. Shrubs and dwarf conifers 30 to 100 feet from your home should be thinned so that the distance between them is five times the plant height. Prune off dead branches and rake up plant debris. These materials can be shredded and composted.

3. Thin dense stands of mature trees so that the crowns do not touch. If the trees are growing very close together, this should be done in two stages to prevent other trees from falling due to wind damage. Take out about one-half of what is required and wait five to ten years, then take out the rest.

4. Prune up the live and dead branches from trees a minimum of ten feet above the ground.

5. Prescribed burns can be used to reduce litter and the buildup of nonmown grasses, but they should only be done with the supervision of a fire expert from your area.

6. Use only low-growing species near the house and irrigate them. Trees should be no closer than thirty feet to the house, and it is best not to put small shrubs beneath them.

If any grass remains in the forested area, remove it. If moss exists in patches, encourage it. If you have not been letting the leaves fall and remain, then you will need to add a five- to six-inch-deep mulch of wood or bark chips to redevelop the humusy soil that woodland shrubs and wildflowers require. Add shredded leaves as well. Avoid planting wildflowers in rings around shrubs or trees; instead, plant them in groups alongside the trail or just put in one or two and let them spread where they want to go. Leave old logs and stumps to rot in place. Because of shrub and tree roots, you cannot use a tiller to prepare a wide area for planting. Dig individual holes for each plant. If you hit a large root, just move over to an open space. If the soil seems dry and hard, add compost or leaf mold to the soil before pushing it back in the hole around the plant.

Plant in spring or fall and avoid planting during the hot part of summer. Always water plants regularly until well-established, which may be up to six weeks, especially if there is little rain. Some of the ground-cover plants listed in Table 2 are suitable for shady forested sites. Consult field guides and local sources to determine other native wildflower species to include in your woodland habitat.

Noxious and Invasive Plants

The plants listed here have characteristics that make them capable of destroying existing native plant cover or displacing entire native plant communities, particularly in the habitats that are indicated. Most municipalities and states have official "noxious weed lists," which enumerate specific plants that cannot be planted purposely and must be controlled wherever they show up. Most of these lists were designed for agricultural communities and may be inappropriate now, especially if the area has become urbanized. Form a citizens' group in cooperation with your local officials to review the lists. Make sure to include a botanist in the group. In some cases weed commissioners are appointed to enforce the weed ordinances; make sure yours is at least an amateur botanist or is trained to identify noxious plants.

Some groups have already started this process, taking native flowers or grasses that are not troublesome off the list and adding alien plants that are known to be invasive and overwhelming to native plant communities in particular habitats. A good example is purple loosestrife (*Lythrum salicaria*), an escaped garden perennial with beautiful striking deep-pink blooms from July to September. An old-world plant, it was introduced to the United States years ago and has naturalized here, but it is not indigenous. A tall, bushy plant, it has choked out the native plants in countless freshwater wetlands, particularly in New England and the northern states, now spreading west.

Illinois, Minnesota, Missouri, Ohio, and Wisconsin have banned *L. salicaria* and *L. virgatum* from sale in their states. Several mail-order nurseries used to offer what is known as a sterile hybrid, a cross between *L. alatum* and *L. virgatum,* but if the flower spikes were not removed as the blooms faded, it would interbreed with local populations. Because of the controversy around the problems that *Lythrum* has caused, these nurseries have discontinued selling it.

Determining what plants are noxious or invasive is sometimes a complicated issue. One plant, which although native to river marsh habitats around the world (including the United States), has overtaken those habitats where the natural water level has been artificially altered. Giant reed (*Phragmites communis* or *P. australis*) can often be seen in ditches along roads and other places where water stands. A member of the grass family, it grows twelve to thirteen feet tall and has striking purplish silky flowers in late summer that turn grayish-tan and persist through the winter. A rhizomatous plant, it spreads to form impenetrable strands and excludes other native plants. Human alteration of water levels and pollution have caused it to proliferate more than usual. This reed requires a wet soil with a neutral pH. Where it has spread quickly is an indication that sewage runoff has altered the natural acidity of the water. Mowing and burning only encourage it, but botanists know that it cannot survive changing water levels. It is not listed in the following table because this book focuses on front lawn settings, few of which would have marsh conditions. However, if you have a wet area on your property, you would want to avoid this plant.

Most of the species on the list are annuals that can usually be controlled by mowing and/or handpulling the first few years. Others will require more persistent efforts. Spending the time on soil preparation at the beginning to ensure that roots of perennial problem plants are removed will prevent the difficulty of battling these plants if they show up after you have planted a meadow, prairie, ground-cover area, or woodland floor.

You may see plants on this list that have not been a problem for you. Gardeners in some parts of the country told me that lily-of-the-valley, knap-weed, and Queen Anne's lace had not become unmanageable in their locations. Still, they are listed because of their aggressive habit. Check with local experts such as extension agents, native plant society groups, Audubon Society or Nature Conservancy chapters to verify the species that are particular problems in your state.

GRASSES

Name	Habitat Invaded
Agropyron repens (Quack grass)	Prairie
A. smithii (Western wheatgrass)	Although a native throughout the West, in some prairie plantings it has taken over the wildflowers.
Bromus inermis (Smooth brome)	Prairie
B. japonicus (Japanese brome)	Prairie
B. tectorum (Downy chess)	Prairie, meadows
Cortaderia jubata (Andean grass)	California grassland
Cynodon dactylon (Bermuda grass)	Meadows
Digitaria spp. (Crabgrass)	Meadows
Imperata cylindrica (Japanese blood grass)	Has escaped to thousands of acres in Alabama, Florida, Louisiana, and Mississippi spreading by runners and seed. Not to be confused with *I. cylindrica* 'Red Baron' (Japanese blood grass) — a popular ornamental grass—which spreads slowly by short rhizomes and does not produce viable seed, according to horticulturist Barry R. Yinger.
Pennisetum clandestinum (Kikyku grass)	California grassland
Phalaris arundinacea (Reed canary grass)	Wetland, prairie
Sorghum halepense (Johnson grass)	Fallow fields, woodland, riverbanks

PERENNIALS, BIENNIALS, ANNUALS

Name	Habitat Invaded
Alliari officinalis (Garlic mustard)	Woodland
Amaranthus palmeri (Palmer amaranth)	Prairie
A. retroflexus (Redroot pigweed)	Prairie
Ambrosia artemisifolia (Ragweed)	Prairie
A. psilostachya (Ragweed)	Prairie
Arctium minus (Burdock)	Woodland
Brassica nigra (Mustard)	Disturbed sites, fields
B. sativus (Wild radish)	Disturbed sites, fields
Campanula rapunculoides (Creeping campanula)	
Carduus acanthoides (Bristly thistle)	Prairie
C. nutans (Nodding thistle)	Prairie
Centaurea maculosa (Knapweed)	Prairie
Chenopodium album (Lamb's-quarter)	
Cirsium arvense (Canada thistle)	Prairie
C. vulgare (Bull thistle)	Meadows, prairie
Convallaria majalis (Lily-of-the-valley)	Woodland
Convolvulus arvenis (Field bindweed)	Prairie
Conyza canadensis (Horseweed)	Meadows
Coronilla arvensis (Emerald crown vetch)	Prairie
Cyperus spp. (Nutsedge)	Meadows
Daucus carota (Queen Anne's lace)	Meadows
Datura stramonium (Jimsonweed)	Meadows, prairie
Euphorbia cyparissias (Cypress spurge)	Prairie
E. esula (Leafy spurge)	Prairie
Lythrum salicaria (Purple loosestrife)	Wetland
Malva neglecta (Mallow)	Prairie
Melilotus alba (White sweet clover)	Prairie
M. officinalis (Yellow sweet clover)	Prairie
Pastinaca sativa (Wild parsnip)	Prairie
Polygonum cuspidatum (Japanese knotweed)	Woodland

PERENNIALS, BIENNIALS, ANNUALS (CONTINUED)

Name	Habitat Invaded
Ranunculus ficaria (Lesser celandine)	Woodland
Silybum marianum (Milk thistle)	Meadows, prairie
Sonchus asper (Sow thistle)	Prairie
Trifolium repens (Dutch white clover)	Prairie, meadows

SHRUBS/VINES

Name	Habitat Invaded
Ampelopsis brevipedunculata (Porcelain-berry vine)	Hedgerows, fields, woodland
Campsis radicans (Poison ivy)	Meadow, woodland
Celastrus orbiculatus (Oriental bittersweet)	Fields, woodland
Euonymus fortunei (Climbing wintercreeper euonymus)	Woodland
Ligustrum sinense (Chinese privet)	Fields and hedgerows in southeast
L. vulgare (Common privet)	Fields and hedgerows in northeast
Lonicera japonica (Japanese honeysuckle)	Prairie, woodland, meadows
L. maackii (Bush honeysuckle)	Wetland, prairie, woodland
L. morrowii (Bush honeysuckle)	Wetland, prairie, woodland
L. tatarica (Bush honeysuckle)	Wetland, prairie, woodland
Pueraria lobata (Kudzu)	Meadows, woodland in the south but has crept as far north as Massachusetts
Rosa multiflora (Multiflora rose)	Meadow, prairie, woodland

TREES

Name	Habitat Invaded
Acer platanoides (Norway maple)	Woodland
A. pseudoplatanus (Sycamore maple)	Woodland
Elaeagnus angustifolia (Russian olive)	Prairie
E. umbellata (Autumn olive)	Fields, prairie
Melaleuca quinquenervia (Punk tree)	Threatens entire Everglades ecosystem in Florida
Populus alba (White poplar)	Prairie
Rhamnus catharticus (Buckthorn)	Woodland
R. frangula (Glossy buckthorn)	Wetland
Robinia pseudoacacia (Black locust)	Native from Pennsylvania to southern Indiana, west to Oklahoma but an escapee from cultivation in Wisconsin where it has become a problem in prairies
Schinus terebinthifolis (Brazilian pepper)	Disturbed sites in Florida

Prairies and Native Grasses

A prairie is a unique ecosystem—a mix of native perennials including grasses and flowering plants of the legume and composite families—that may contain as many as 300 species. In addition, these plants are part of a distinct interrelated community of soil organisms, insects, birds, and other animals. When vast ranges of prairie still existed, a combination of high summer temperatures, strong winds, late summer drought, and accumulations of dead vegetation set the stage for naturally occurring fires, which prevented trees and other woody plants from becoming a part of the system. The perennial plants of the prairie develop deep roots enabling them to withstand drought, wind, and fire; the fire actually stimulates them to grow better and promotes the germination of seeds.

Prior to the arrival of European settlers, all of the land from Illinois west to the Rocky Mountains and from Texas north to the Dakotas was prairie. Of the original 400,000 square miles, only about 6,200 remain in scattered protected remnants throughout the area. Although you may not be able to achieve the incredible diversity of the original prairie in your yard, with the right preparation and attention you can turn your lawn into a small prairie planting. Thousands of residents, particularly in Illinois and Wisconsin, have proved it. Every year as they pass along what they have learned, more prairie plants appear in front yards throughout the area, even in downtown Milwaukee.

Based on soil and climate, three general communities are discernible — the shortgrass prairie, the desertlike western edge (twelve inches or less of rain annually); midgrass or mixed grass prairie (a transition zone between the moister conditions of the eastern side and the drier conditions of the west, with fifteen to twenty inches of rain annually); and tallgrass, the area adjacent to the forested eastern edge (about thirty-five inches of rain annually). Some grass and wildflower species are common to all three communities; others occur in only one of them. Tallgrass prairie is the furthest eastward strip, running as far south as Oklahoma. As you move west, the midgrass prairie comes next—an area about 200 miles wide again reaching from the top of the country down into Texas, and finally, the shortgrass prairie, which is the furthest west and also extends into Texas. Spots of short- and midgrass prairie occur in a few of the Southwestern states and in the middle part of Washington and the upper middle part of Oregon.

The major grasses in tallgrass prairie are big bluestem (*Andropogon gerardii*), little bluestem (*Schizachyrium scoparium*), Indian grass (*Sorghastrum* spp.), switchgrass (*Panicum virgatum*), prairie dropseed (*Sporobolus heterolepis*), and prairie cordgrass (*Spartina pectinata*); in midgrass, little bluestem, porcupine grass (*Stipa spartea*), needle-and-thread (*S. comata*), Western wheat grass (*Agropyron smithii*), prairie dropseed, sand dropseed (*Sporobolus cryptandrus*), and sideoats grama (*Bouteloua curtipendula*); in shortgrass, buffalo grass (*Buchloë dactyloides*), blue grama (*Bouteloua gracilis*), and sideoats grama.

There are hundreds of flowering prairie plants, and some are best suited for dry soil (called xeric), some for well-drained (mesic), and some for moist areas (hydric). They bloom at different times during the season and they range in size from the well-known five- to eight-foot-tall specimens such as compassplant (*Silphium laciniatum*), cupplant (*S. perfoliatum*), and yellow prairie coneflower (*Ratibida pinnata*) to midsized two- to four-foot types such as black-eyed Susan (*Rudbeckia hirta*), purple coneflower (*Echinacea purpurea*), prairie blazing star (*Liatris pycnostachya*), and bergamot (*Monarda fistulosa*) to the small, low-growing pasque flower (*Anemone patens*), Canada anemone

(*A. canadensis*), prairie smoke (*Geum triflorum*), and wild petunia (*Ruella humilis*). Obtain catalogs from prairie nurseries and books about prairie plants and learn about the different species so that you can make selections that will fit the conditions of your site. Most catalogs offer mixes for dry, medium, and moist soils. If you prefer to blend a custom selection, experts at quality prairie nurseries (see Appendix I) can help.

Some of the most popular flowering prairie plants—because they are available and are easy to get started on a prepared site—are butterfly weed (*Asclepias tuberosa*), leadplant (*Amorpha canescens*), lanceleaf coreopsis (*Coreopsis lanceolata*), prairie larkspur (*Delphinium virescens*), purple coneflower (*Echinacea purpurea*), prairie smoke (*Geum triflorum*), asters (*Aster* spp.), sunflowers (*Helianthus* spp.), hairy puccoon (*Lithospermum caroliniense*), lupine (*Lupinus perennis*), bergamot (*Monarda fistulosa*), prairie clover (*Petalostemum candidum* spp.), yellow prairie coneflower (*Ratibida pinnata*), black-eyed Susan (*Rudbeckia hirta*), stiff goldenrod (*Solidago rigida*), prairie dock (*Silphium terebinthinaceum*), compassplant (*S. laciniatum*), cupplant (*Silphium perfoliatum*), Culver's root (*Veronicastrum virginicum*), rattlesnake master (*Eryngium yuccifolium*), blue false indigo (*Baptisia australis*), nodding pink onion (*Allium cernuum*), shootingstar (*Dodecatheon meadia*), oxeye sunflower (*Heliopsis helianthoides*), Queen of the prairie (*Filipendula rubra*), boneset (*Eupatorium perfoliatum*), Joe-Pye weed (*E. maculatum*), Turk's cap lily (*Lilium superbum*), rosinweed (*Silphium integrifolium*), and ironweed (*Veronia fasciculata*).

Choosing Species

Most prairie plants prefer well-drained soil and, in the case of shortgrass types, dry soil. A few species can tolerate somewhat wetter soil and clay (see Table 1, pages 35–45). For best results, plant prairie species in full sun and select ones that suit the soil on your site.

Determine the size of the area that you plan to plant so you will know how much seed or how many plants you will need. Order early in the season (December to February) since the supply of some species is limited. Try to buy seed that was harvested within 300 miles of your location since it will be better adapted to your situation and will help preserve the gene pools for plants in your area. The supplier will give you recommendations for how much to plant per 1,000 square feet or per acre. The general recommendation is one-quarter to one-half pound per 1,000 square feet and ten pounds per acre. Many experienced people that I talked to suggested doubling that amount if you can afford it because a thicker stand means less space for unwanted plants to invade the planting.

For a showy display of flowers, use a mixture that is about 50 percent grass and 50 percent wildflowers. In a natural prairie, the ratio is weighted more toward the grass, at about 60 percent to 40 percent. Andy Larsen, chief naturalist for Riveredge Nature Center near Newburg, Wisconsin, says that when they sowed grasses and flowers together, the grasses came on so strong that the perennial flowers were not able to become well established. They switched to seeding only the flowers and plugging in grass plants after the flowers were established.

John Diekelman, a landscape architect who specializes in using native plants, recommends sowing a 50/50 mixture of nonspreading forbs (wildflowers) and nonspreading grasses. He says to leave out, initially, such aggressive species as switchgrass (*Panicum virgatum*), prairie coreopsis (*Coreopsis palmata*), wild strawberry (*Fragaria virginiana*), flowering spurge (*Euphorbia corollata*), whorled milkweed (*Asclepias verticillata*), and sunflowers (*Helianthus* spp.). The goal is to have a plant every square foot—if possible—alternating grasses and forbs.

The prairie will look odd in the first year—the plants will be very small and you will need to pull out weeds as they appear. The plants are small because they spend the first two years growing *down*, putting their roots deep into the soil. This characteristic is what has enabled them to withstand drought, wind, grazing, and so forth for centuries. More upward growth will be visible the second year and by the third year the prairie will be established and only need your vigilance to remove the occasional weeds that might show up and to provide an annual mowing or burning.

Another way to obtain plant material and to share information is to join one of the various organizations throughout the Midwest that is actively involved in prairie restoration (see Appendix II).

How Others Did It

About nine years ago, John Clegg of Arlington, Texas, decided that he wanted to try and create a small prairie plot in his yard. He knew that just letting the area grow wild would not work because the practice of cotton farming had eliminated all native seed sources for hundreds of miles around his home. He used a combination of techniques including putting plants and seed into an area that he prepared by tilling, planting into existing sod, and using a chemical to kill vegetation before planting.

The major plot, a sloping nine-foot-square area in the front yard, was mostly Bermuda grass that was difficult to keep watered and as a result was always brown. In the fall of 1985, he dug out portions of the dormant and dying Bermuda and put in clumps of little bluestem dug from a nearby field. He cleared some spots and sowed wildflower seed. The following summer he heard about a native hay meadow that was going to be bulldozed for development. He tilled another area of his front yard, about six-by-nine, and applied Vapam. (Vapam is a trade name for sodium methyldithiocarbamate, a chemical that is registered as a soil sterilant, fungicide, and herbicide. It kills all life in the soil and is not recommended by prairie experts.) He transplanted clumps of big bluestem and Indian grass from the meadow into one half of the prepared site, with their centers about two feet apart. After tamping the soil down in between the clumps, he planted wildflower seed. On the other half of the area, he sowed seed of little bluestem and sideoats grama.

"Grasses are the framework of the prairie," says Clegg, "and even though wildflowers were only about five percent of the native prairie, over a large area they made quite an impact." The grasses in Clegg's prairie planting include little bluestem, big bluestem, Indian grass, and sideoats grama. Although switchgrass and eastern grama were found in low areas of the prairie, Clegg says "they are too aggressive and I do not recommend them for small plots." Over the years he has come to revere big bluestem: "Despite some scholarly studies to the contrary, I believe big bluestem was the primary component of tallgrass prairie," says Clegg. "It is the 'Cadillac' of grasses and you should include as much of it as you can find." In general, the native grasses are slow to establish from seed (sideoats is the exception), and he did water them some to help them become established. He had the best results when planting clumps in January because there was less need for supplemental water.

Clegg grew some of his grass plants in containers — from two-inch pots to five-gallon pails. "My very best prairie," he says, "was established by using the rescued clumps of native grass." After three years the area where he planted clumps right into Bermuda sod looked better than the area where he sowed seed. The Bermuda has completely disappeared from his plot except for a strip along the driveway which he presumes is persistent because it gets extra water in that location.

Although in a natural prairie flowers are a small part of the grass: flower ratio, Clegg says, "I have aimed at making wildflowers fifty percent, and that requires consistent human intervention." Clegg starts perennial wildflowers from seed to have ready to plug into holes where he removes undesirables such as Dallis grass (*Paspalum dilatatum*) or Johnsongrass (*Sorghum halepense*). He has found that a one-gallon container allows the plant to develop enough of a root system so that it does not have to be watered after a few weeks. Clegg sows the seed of prairie forbs in his garden as row crops, then transplants the mature plants into containers or right into the prairie.

Annuals such as Texas bluebonnet (*Lupinus texensis*) and Indian blanket (*Gaillardia pulchella*) disappeared after a few years because "they could not compete with the grasses," says Clegg, and certain perennial wildflowers have become prominent — cutleaf (or Engelmann) daisy (*Engelmannia pinnatifida*), mealy sage (*Salvia farinacea*), wine cup (*Callirhoe involucrata*), prairie phlox (*Phlox pilosa*), spiderwort (*Tradescantia ohiensis*), purple coneflower (*Echinacea purpurea*), and gayfeather (*Liatris punctata*). "I recently added skullcap (*Scutellaria integrifolia*) and prairie larkspur (*Delphinium virescens*)," he says. "I've had trouble with purple paintbrush (*Castilleja purpurea*) and have decided that it needs the drainage of a rocky mound and is not suitable for my deep clay soil." Wild foxglove (*Digitalis purpurea*) has proven to be short-lived, so he keeps a supply that he starts in pots to plug in occasionally. (Wild foxglove is not native; it was introduced from Europe and has naturalized in various parts of the United States.) Wildflowers that have been too aggressive for his small plot are goldenrod (*Solidago* spp.) and Maximilian sunflower (*Helianthus maximiliani*). He completely removed the sunflower and pulls out some goldenrod plants to keep them from dominating. Evening primrose and Mexican hat were not able to compete and disappeared.

"I have had very little weeding to do in my prairie," says Clegg, "much less than my lawn. In the spring I might find a few dandelions or thistles."

He cuts the prairie once a year in mid-December to six inches and then rakes it in early spring. This simulates the effect of burning by allowing light to penetrate to the ground. The debris is composted. "The best way to maintain a native prairie is by periodic burning," says Clegg, "but because I don't want to hassle with the fire department, I cut mine."

On a prairie restoration project near Austin, Texas, the amount of native grass sown per acre was fifteen pounds of little bluestem, fifteen pounds Indiangrass, seven pounds switchgrass, and seven pounds Haskell sideoats. Lee Stone, editor of the Native Prairies Association of Texas newsletter and botanist with the Austin Parks and Recreation Department, directed the project. After several years of managing the site, she said that doubling the amount of sideoats would have been helpful because it came up, matured, and produced seeds the first season. Now little bluestem is dominating and the Indiangrass gets stronger every year. She also regrets not adding some buffalo grass, as she feels it would have helped in the early years to cover ground and keep out weeds.

Mickey and Bob Burleson of Temple, Texas, restored 250 acres of prairie. They advise planting only perennials to begin with and after these are well-established—in two to three years—to overseed or plug in annuals. They also recommend planting seeds no more than one-quarter inch deep and rolling or somehow packing down the soil after they are covered.

Pat Armstrong, a biologist and prairie design consultant in Woodstock, Illinois, planted her third-of-an-acre yard with prairie and native woodland plants in 1983. Over the years, she has seeded others and added some as transplants so that the small plot now contains 300 species—200 prairie and 100 woodland. The day that I visited in August, forty-eight different types of plants were in bloom around her solar-heated home. When her home was built, the entire area around it was covered with Hungarian brome grass (*Bromus inermis*) and quackgrass. To begin, she tilled the entire area in the fall and planted. Pat broadcast seed by hand, seeding more densely than would be the case with a mechanical seeder.

The original planting consisted of thirty-five to forty pounds of native prairie grasses. She added many pounds of native forb seed at the same time and continued to do so through the years. In the spring of the first year, she had a crop of mostly Queen Anne's lace and red clover. She mowed it off at six inches several times the first season and handweeded around the baby prairie plants.

Pat sowed the shortest grasses around the house for a "lawn" area (fifteen pounds buffalo grass, three sideoats grama, and three blue grama), then the midgrass area which also included sideoats (six pounds), little bluestem (six pounds), and some prairie dropseed, then the tall grasses along the back and side borders of the yard (three pounds Indian grass, three big bluestem, one wild rye [*Elymus canadensis*], and one switchgrass). "The blue grama declined and disappeared," says Pat, "which I think is because there is too much moisture here for it."

The front of the house is shaded by a huge burr oak; there she put down six inches of wood chips and gradually planted native trees, shrubs, and shade-loving wildflowers. The first two years she weeded and cut the shortgrass area several times. Now she cuts the shortgrass area once a year and burns the entire prairie in March. She applies for a permit each time, prepares a firebreak around the house by laying down soaked newspapers, and invites friends over to help and to celebrate. The fire lasts about fifteen minutes. Then the prairie is black until early May.

There are small stone pathways winding through the prairie. Pat says, "I take the loose-prairie approach; the plants move around—seeding themselves here and there. You can leave some or dig them out and move them. If you want things to stay put—for instance, the tall plants at the back and the short ones in the front—then you need to pull out the volunteers or dig them up and move them back where you want them."

Besides the plants already mentioned, Armstrong's prairie includes white and purple prairie clover (*Petalostemum candidum* and *P. purpureum*), compassplant (*Silphium laciniatum*), mountain mint (*Pycnanthemum verticillatum*), partridge pea (*Cassia fasciculata*), prairie dock (*Silphium terebinthinaceum*), flowering spurge (*Euphorbia corollata*), Culver's root (*Veronicastrum virginicum*), rattlesnake master (*Eryngium yuccifolium*), prairie rose (*Rosa setigera*), cupplant (*Silphium perfoliatum*), wild bergamot (*Monarda fistulosa*), oxeye (or false) sunflower (*Heliopsis helianthoides*), dogbane (*Apocynum cannabinum*), butterfly weed (*Asclepias tuberosa*), prairie coreopsis (*Coreopsis palmata*), asters (*Aster* spp.), Queen of the prairie (*Filipendula rubra*), sunflowers (*Helianthus* spp.), black-eyed Susan (*Rudbeckia hirta*), goldenrod (*Solidago* spp.), nodding onion (*Allium cernuum*), and coneflower (*Echinacea* spp.).

Even after eleven years, some invaders still come in by seed carried on the wind or in bird droppings. Pat handweeds or digs out the unwanted plants, mainly in the spring after the burn when things first start to come up. She does not water or fertilize.

Armstrong has helped hundreds of other people install small prairie plantings in the area west of Chicago. Her advice in getting started is to think about what you want, how much money you can invest, how much lawn you want to get rid of at once, and how long you are willing to wait for things to look mature. She usually recommends that you start with a small area first and if you want faster results, to plant "plugs" (small plants that have been started from seed in pots). Seeding costs less but the overall planting will take longer to become established.

Julie Marks, with the help of her friends in the Wild Ones (an organization whose members are committed to native prairie plantings in their yards), installed numerous plants on two clay soil berms in front of her house in Milwaukee, Wisconsin, in 1988. When the earth-moving equipment was there, Julie had them shape the mounds to give the impression of two sleeping animals in winter. The berms, ten feet high, twenty feet wide, and each about fifty feet long, provide privacy from the street and block some of the noise and pollution.

Although mulch was placed around the plants, the first year the area was invaded by quackgrass (*Agropyron repens*) and Queen Anne's lace (*Daucus carota*). Because of the shape of the berms, they would have been difficult to mow and Julie did not want to risk losing any of the prairie plants. So, the unwanted plants were removed by hours of tedious handweeding.

Additional plants were plugged into bare spots that year and in the next few years. Gradually, the prairie plants dominated, and only an occasional weed needs to be pulled out in the spring. The eight-year-old planting includes a wide variety of prairie grasses and flowers. On the tops of the berms where the soil is dry the grasses are prairie dropseed (*Sporobolus heterolepis*), sideoats grama (*Bouteloua curtipendula*), and little bluestem (*Schizachyrium scoparius*) and the featured flowers (which need a dry soil) are prairie smoke (*Geum triflorum*), nodding onion (*Allium cernuum*), shooting star (*Dodecatheon meadia*), columbine (*Aquilegia canadensis*), compassplant (*Silphium laciniatum*), and butterfly weed (*Asclepias tuberosa*). The grasses used at the base of the berms where the soil is moist are Indian grass and big bluestem. Flowers needing a moist soil are featured there; they include five different types of perennial sunflowers (*Helianthus* spp.), blue iris (*Iris shrevei*), golden alexanders (*Zizia aurea*), Queen of the prairie (*Filipendula rubra*), prairie dock

(*Silphium terebinthinaceum*), bottle gentian (*Gentiana andrewsii*), Turk's-cap lily (*Lilium superbum*), and pale Indian plantain (*Cacalia atriplicifolia*).

Other plants, which can adapt to a range of soil conditions, grow on the slopes and are spotted here and there on the top and at the base. They include yellow prairie coneflower (*Ratibida pinnata*), cupplant (*Silphium perfoliatum*), purple coneflower (*Echinacea purpurea*), pale purple coneflower (*E. pallida*), various asters (*Aster* spp.), bergamot (*Monarda fistulosa*), prairie blazing star (*Liatris pycnostachya*), and stiff goldenrod (*Solidago rigida*). A small area of lawn between the berms and the house is kept mowed.

I saw a number of front lawns in the Milwaukee area for which the transformation to prairie gardens had been started. Some residents had marked off an area in an interesting kidney or oval shape—about sixty or seventy square feet—and stopped mowing. The gradually declining grass was barely visible in the plantings which included the lower-growing prairie flowers such as blazing star (*Liatris spicata*), rattlesnake master (*Eryngium yuccifolium*), bergamot (*Monarda fistulosa*), purple coneflower (*Echinacea purpurea*), black-eyed Susan (*Rudbeckia hirta*), nodding onion (*Allium cernuum*), and the native grass, little bluestem (*Schizachyrium scoparium*). Other residents had put up a split-rail fence near the front edge of their yard and planted along both sides, keeping the space from the road edge to the fence (about eight feet) mowed.

Lorrie Otto, of Bayside, Wisconsin, is a heroine in her state for two main reasons—she was instrumental in the banning of DDT there in 1969, and she has become known as the "prairie lady" for her personal and public efforts to replace lawns with the original plants of the Wisconsin prairies, woodlands, wetlands, and oak openings. She has not only convinced many of her neighbors to plant prairies, but her reputation has spread across the country, with photographs of her standing among the dramatic prairie plants in her "wild" yard appearing in several national books and magazines. She began converting her two-acre yard to native plants in 1955 and put in what she calls her "sand laboratory" in 1988 with tallgrass prairie. Her site was so shaded by sixty existing Norway spruce when she arrived in 1952 that all had to be cut down to create openings for the sun. "Besides," Lorrie says, "they are nonnative trees and are overplanted in our community."

The "sand laboratory" was an experimental method that Lorrie used to create a suitable site for prairie plants. She needed to kill the existing nonnative grass and, because her soil was mostly clay, had to find a way to alter it in order to provide the well-drained conditions that prairie plants require. So she put down a thick layer of newspaper, then leaves, then six to eight inches of sand, more leaves, and more sand. Into this "sand sandwich," she planted bare-root plants of pale purple coneflower (*Echinacea pallida*), downy sunflower (*Helianthus mollis*), white false indigo (*Baptisia leucantha*), nodding onion (*Allium cernuum*), bergamot (*Monarda fistulosa*), yellow prairie cone-flower (*Ratibida pinnata*), blazing star (*Liatris spicata*), spiderwort (*Tradescantia ohiensis*), plantain (*Cacalia atriplicifolia*), prairie coreopsis (*Coreopsis palmata*), New Jersey tea (*Ceanothus americanus*), Joe-Pye weed (*Eupatorium maculatum*), and others. Right after she planted, the drought came. The plants survived that, but in the summer of 1993 the deer ate the prairie dock (*Silphium terebinthinaceum*), columbine (*Aquilegia canadensis*), prairie smoke (*Geum triflorum*), baptisia (*Baptisia leucantha*), and others. Otto regretfully put up an eight-foot fence to protect the planting. She is now adding the native grasses—little bluestem (*Schizachyrium scoparium*), prairie dropseed (*Sporobolus heterolepis*), and sideoats grama (*Bouteloua curtipendula*).

Otto says she started planting native plants for aesthetic reasons, but soon it was also to attract and feed wildlife and restore their native habitat. She sees numerous species of birds, insects, and butterflies, five types of bats, two types of squirrels, deer mice, meadow voles, shrews, chipmunks, and the deer, which have reached abnormal population levels without the presence of their natural predators and are a serious threat to native plants in many parts of our country.

Small pathways of mulch or stepping-stones wind through the yard— sunny in front, shaded on the sides and in back. She removed the blacktop from the driveway and replaced it with turf stones—patterned cement blocks that allow the rain to pass through and into the soil. In this way, all of the rain that falls on her property stays there, she explains, and does not run off into an urban drainage system which eventually dumps into streams, caus-ing them to rise quickly and erode banks or giving them a concentrated dose of the pollutants carried in the water.

Otto describes her yard as low-maintenance, not no-maintenance—a misconception that many have about natural landscaping. Her main job is keeping things cut back so that the paths stay open and pulling out weeds and small seedlings of exotic or unwanted species. Major culprits are white clover (*Melilotus alba*), garlic mustard (*Alliaria petiolata*, formerly *A. officinalis*), honeysuckle (*Lonicera × bella*), Norway maple (*Acer platanoides*), and buckthorn (*Rhamnus cathartica* and *R. frangula*).

Otto continues to give lectures on natural landscaping, writes the lead article for the newsletter of the Wild Ones, and does two cable television shows year. The Garden Club of America awarded her the Margaret Douglas Medal for conservation education in 1991.

Milton and Toni Ettenheim, Lorrie's neighbors, were inspired by her and installed a prairie planting in their yard when they built their house eighteen years ago. In August, I wandered along the narrow path through the chest-high plants blooming in shades of yellow, gold, lavender, and white. Butterflies and birds were all around us. "When I began," says Milton, "it was difficult to find native plants or seeds. Lorrie and I used to go together to places where we had permission to collect and brought back plants to plug into spots."

The worst problem that Milton faced in the beginning was the persistence of Canada thistle and reed canary grass. "My wife and I actually handpulled and dug out the thistle and grass," he said, because they did not want to use an herbicide and, besides, the unwanted plants were so intertwined with the prairie plants that it would have been very difficult to kill one without killing the other. "In the first year the plants were so small and we were still battling the weeds," says Milton, "that it looked unattractive. I didn't want the neighbors to be distressed about it so I planted larger-sized plants with blooms along the borders that were visible from the street and along the driveway."

His planting includes prairie dock (*Silphium terebinthinaceum*), cupplant (*S. perfoliatum*), compassplant (*S. laciniatum*), yellow prairie coneflower (*Ratibida pinnata*), Culver's root (*Veronicastrum virginicum*), black-eyed Susan (*Rudbeckia hirta*), purple prairie clover (*Petalostemum purpureum*), bergamot (*Monarda fistulosa*), downy sunflower (*Helianthus mollis*), western sunflower (*H. occidentalis*), Joe-Pye weed (*Eupatorium maculatum*), purple coneflower (*Echinacea purpurea*), sky-blue aster (*Aster azureus*), and stiff goldenrod (*Solidago rigida*). He put up a fence several years ago to protect the area from deer.

Gradually over the years he has removed all the weeds and continues to add prairie plants, although some have spread by themselves. He starts seeds of prairie wildflowers in pots in the spring. When they are a good size, he plants them out into a screened, protected area to let them grow undisturbed through the summer. In the fall, he gives them away to friends who are starting prairie gardens and puts some into his own planting.

In a subdivision in Mequon near Milwaukee, the common land at the entrance and along the main road leading into the homesites is maintained as a natural landscape—some native shrubs and trees were installed and the banks were sown with native wildflowers and grasses. One couple, Marsha and Richard Krueger, has turned most of their front and back yard into a prairie planting. Only a small area right in front of the entrance and to the side is still kept cut as a lawn.

About ten years ago, the front yard—much of it bare from being re-graded—was tilled several times and seeded with a mixture of prairie grasses and forbs by Bob Ahrenhoerster, prairie garden designer and owner of Prairie Seed Source in North Lake, Wisconsin. The mix included bee balm (*Monarda fistulosa*), purple coneflower (*Echinacea purpurea*), yellow prairie coneflower (*Ratibida pinnata*), big bluestem (*Andropogon geradii*), little bluestem (*Schizachyrium scoparium*), goldenrod (*Solidago* spp.), aster (*Aster laevis* and *A. ptarmicoides*), compassplant (*Silphium laciniatum*), blue false indigo (*Baptisia australis*), and black-eyed Susan (*Rudbeckia hirta*). A few nonnative species can be spotted here and there—Queen Anne's lace, chicory, white clover, and what is left of the Kentucky bluegrass—but these could be weeded out at any time. Narrow pathways wind through the plants in front and back. They mow the planting each spring and rake afterwards to stimulate the effect of burning. They also pull out invasive species that show up during the growing season.

The front area was expanded in the spring of 1993 by laying down newspapers, covering them with a deep layer of sand, and sowing seeds of perennial plants over it. When I visited in the summer, the area had the typical look of a new prairie or meadow planting, the tiny green rosette plants covering the ground with spaces between them and a few grass seedlings here and there. This is the key time to identify plants and pull out or clip off ones that you know are unwanted weeds.

In the back yard, they stopped mowing the bluegrass lawn and plugged in prairie plants here and there. Over the years, as they have continued to mow once in spring and plug in plants that they wanted, the prairie species have come to dominate the bluegrass which is gradually declining. The prairie plants sow themselves and they help the process along by gathering seeds and scratching them into bare spots throughout the front and back areas.

Prairies and Children

One question that skeptics usually bring up when they hear about a prairie or meadow planting is, Where will the children play? Two homes that I visited — both with young children — showed this was not a problem. Quite the contrary, as both parents told me, as soon as the plants grew tall and the paths became hidden passageways through the mass of five- to six-feet-tall plants, the children were drawn like magnets. Debbie Harwell, past president of the Wild Ones, was so inspired by the prairie in her own yard that her enthusiasm and ability to influence others spread to the school officials at the nearby Indian Hills Elementary School.

The prairie and other native plantings at the school are now in their third year. The entire front schoolyard, about three-fourths of an acre, features small displays of Wisconsin's native habitats — a native woodland, a tallgrass prairie planting, and a wetland. The children went on digs to bring plants back and some were purchased from a native plant nursery. They helped put down the newspapers and sand, and they help weed when unwanted species show up. They know the names of the plants and can recognize nonprairie species. When they look out the windows of their school, they see the plants that are their native heritage as well as the numerous butterflies, birds, and insects that are attracted.

In the spring of 1992, David Cavagnaro of Decorah, Iowa, took advantage of the fact that the ground had been disturbed all around his new home during its construction. When the house was completed, he broke up the rough area (about three acres) with a disc harrow and pulverized it thoroughly with a toothed drag. He planted the large seeds first and pulled a smooth board drag over them. "I broadcast the fine seeds over the smooth area by hand and with a hand-cranked seeder," says David, "and then just waited for the hard summer rains to work them in."

To control annual grasses and weeds, David mowed the area several times through that first summer. "As ridiculous as it sounds, I used a hand-pushed lawn mower set at the highest height," says David, "because we had not gotten a brush hog for the tractor yet." David said he would have preferred cutting at the higher height that a brush hog would have provided but "I was glad not to be chewing up the seedlings with tractor tires, too."

As is typical in that part of the country, by midsummer everything was very dry. This resulted in poor germination in some spots. He collected seed that fall and sowed it in those areas to overwinter. "The following spring," David says, "I noticed a much more vigorous germination, and by midsummer the area was a thick stand of blooming wildflowers."

Since his area is so large and prairie wildflower seed is expensive, he collected seed himself. Several species that he wanted and could not find locally, he ordered from a seed company, started them in his garden, and then saved seed from the plants. Grasses were a minority in his mix but he did collect and sow big bluestem, Indian grass, and sideoats grama. Altogether he had about three grocery bags full of seed for the three acres. That's roughly seven to eight pounds per bag, or twenty-one pounds. Even though he did not record the rate of application per acre, he was close to the usually recommended rate of ten pounds to the acre of a wildflower/grass mix on a well-prepared site.

David reports that so far none of the native grasses are obvious. "Several species of nonnative perennial grasses were present in the area when we started," says David, "and the plowing and discing only set them back a bit. Until I have established clumps of blooming native bunch grasses, they will be hard to detect." Even with the nonnative grasses present, "the wildflowers are holding their own."

Since the first season, David has not burned or mowed again and has no plans to as of now—"I like the look of the dry stalks in the winter snow." If he did decide to burn, a car-width "lawned" road and a wide perennial border separate the meadow from the house. And, a wide firebreak would be cut on the "other perimeters of the meadow to keep fire from spreading into the surrounding woods."

Ken and Barbara Root, also of Decorah, turned two large sections of their yard into native prairie gardens more than ten years ago. They had just completed their passive solar home which they had designed to blend into the natural landscape and to be energy efficient. The house was set far back from the street and the north side was in full sun and mostly bare as a result of the construction. Barbara did not want a lawn because she thinks it is boring and did not want to spend weekends on a riding mower polluting the atmosphere with fumes and noise. From talking to a biologist friend who had a written a booklet on prairie plantings, she realized that she could use prairie plants instead.

Her goal was to sow a blend of grass and wildflower seed of plants that would have been on the site before it was disturbed. Since few people were involved in prairie restoration at the time, she sought advice from as far away as Wisconsin and Minnesota. "I knew that it was important to collect or purchase seed from sources no farther than 200 miles from my location," says Barbara, "but to obtain seed for some of the species that are important prairie components, I had no choice."

She and her husband rotary tilled the clay soil in two areas, about 1,000 square feet each, two or three times, then hand-picked the plant roots and debris until the area was bare. Because soil needs to be warm for prairie seed to germinate, they did not plant until June 10. "We mixed the seed with sand and spread it with rakes," says Barbara, "then watered once to settle everything and waited." The seed mix — about two pounds — contained about half native bunch grasses and half wildflowers, with about a half-pound of annual rye as a nurse crop. Nurse crops germinate and grow rapidly without competing with the native grasses and wildflowers; thus they occupy space that might otherwise be invaded by annual weeds and help reduce the weed problems in the first year.

"We had been warned not to expect much in the first three years," she says. "We were told that patience was needed because the prairie plants would spend the first three years sending down roots and there would not be much growth above ground." A lot of the plant material that was visible above ground the first year was weeds. "Some people mow the first two years with the blade set at its highest point to control annual weeds," says Barbara, "but I did not want to risk damaging the plants that I wanted to nurture." So she spent hours kneeling over the ground, clearly identifying the plants, and then handclipped the weeds.

Some of the plants began to bloom in the second year and by the third year the grasses were apparent as well. Now the site is a mixture of blue grama (*Bouteloua gracilis*), little bluestem (*Schizachyrium scoparium*), and sideoats grama (*Bouteloua curtipendula*) with white and purple prairie clover (*Petalostemum candidum* and *P. purpureum*), butterfly weed (*Asclepias tuberosa*), leadplant (*Amorpha canescens*), false indigo (*Baptisia leucantha*), compassplant (*Silphium laciniatum*), partridge pea (*Cassia fasciculata*), black-eyed Susan

(*Rudbeckia hirta*), various sunflowers (*Helianthus* spp.), purple coneflower (*Echinacea purpurea*), bergamot (*Monarda fistulosa*), and yellow prairie coneflower (*Ratibida pinnata*). Two more areas were planted in the next few years so that now the majority of the ground in the landscaped area is prairie—about 4,000 square feet.

From the beginning, Barbara was sensitive to her neighbors. She invited them all to a picnic around the time that they planted the first beds. "I showed them the landscape plan and explained all about the prairie plants," she said, "I told them why I was including them in the yard." Everyone responded favorably and even though they have consistently told her through the years how much they enjoy the "prairie," none of them have been inspired to change their lawns. There is even one neighbor who sprays with pesticides and uses chemical fertilizer.

To maintain a neat appearance, the Roots mow a strip around the house and around each of the prairie patches. It varies in width from eighteen inches to about three feet. It also serves as a firebreak. They obtain a permit each spring and burn the patches. Barbara says the fire zips through the prairie area and stops dead at the mowed strip. The only other maintenance is going out in early June when the weeds come up quicker than the prairie plants and pulling them out. "I don't mind pulling out those weeds," Barbara says, "I consider it part of the joy of having the prairie plants. They attract birds and butterflies and are not harmed at all by the droughts that occur almost every year."

Barbara says the patience that is required in the first three years pays off because you end up with a beautiful field of grasses and wildflowers that provides an everchanging palette of color and interest. You do not have to fertilize or water or worry about the plants dying from harsh weather. "Some people call the initial purchase of seed expensive," says Barbara, "but looked at over the long term, it really isn't."

Shortgrass Prairie

Rick Brune of Lakewood, Colorado, has been planting prairie gardens since 1980 in various locations, including his own yard, the Denver Botanic Garden, and Chatfield Arboretum. He is the author of *The Prairie Garden: A*

Step-by-Step Guide to Creating a Shortgrass Prairie Garden, a pamphlet available from the Colorado Native Plant Society (see Appendix II).

Since Rick's front yard has two very large elm trees and is too shaded to grow his favorite native plants—prairie species—he established a 4,000-square-foot shortgrass prairie planting in his backyard. He used a combination of rotary tilling and herbicides to remove the existing vegetation, then planted a blend of warm-season native grasses in late May.

He recommends using treated buffalo grass seed which will germinate in seven to ten days; untreated seed germinates over a period of three years. He made one-inch-deep furrows about six to twelve inches apart, broadcast the seed, and raked to cover the furrows. He broadcast blue grama over the same site and raked it lightly. The entire area was rolled with a lawn roller to ensure good seed-to-soil contact. He also sowed some sideoats grama and little bluestem in patches.

He began adding wildflowers to the site a year later. During the winter, he starts wildflower seed in pots and plants them into the site in early spring after the last killing frost—from late April onward. The young seedlings can stand a slight frost and will do fine as long as they are provided with regular moisture. Since many prairie plants have deep taproots, Rick plants out seedlings when they are very small—often with just one or two pairs of true leaves—to avoid the problem of the taproot becoming coiled up in the bottom of the pot. "I also insert a one-inch wide by twelve-inch long piece of cedar shingle next to each plant," says Rick, "to provide a bit of sun and hail protection. I think it is a waste of wildflower seed to broadcast it along with the grasses, because you don't know what type of weed control will be needed. That is why I start seed in pots where I can control water and temperature, and there are no weeds."

Because of his years of experience, Rick now gives advice to many people. He says that he regrets not following his own advice in terms of controlling all of the weeds on the site first before planting anything. The ones that are most important to remove in his area are ones that he still does battle with—bindweed (*Convolvulus arvensis*), thistle (*Cirsium arvense*), and perennial grasses such as bluegrass (*Poa pratensis*) and quackgrass (*Agropyron repens*). When he digs out unwanted plants, he uses the bare area to put in a wildflower seedling.

Although Rick disagrees with broadcasting wildflower seed in a mix because of possible weed problems, he says many species can be direct seeded successfully when sown in bare patches. Using this method, the species that work well for him include groundplum (*Astragalus crassicarpus*), fringed puccoon (*Lithospermum incisum*), silky sophora (*Sophora sericea*), and slim-flowered scurfpea (*Psoralea tenuiflora*). Those that he plants as seedlings include gayfeather (*Liatris punctata*), white-flowered penstemon (*Penstemon albidus*), narrow-leaved penstemon (*P. angustifolius*), prairie coneflower (*Ratibida columnifera*), evening primrose (*Oenothera caespitosa*), Easter daisy (*Townsendia exscapa* and *T. grandiflora*), spreading wild buckwheat (*Eriogonum effusum*), copper mallow (*Sphaeralcea coccinea*), sand sage (*Artemisia filifolia*), larkspur (*Delphinium geyeri*), *Senecio tridenticulatus*, Nuttall's violet (*Viola nuttallii*), and scarlet gaura (*Gaura coccinea*).

Unlike many other prairie gardeners, Rick does not have established pathways through his prairie garden. "I just walk right into it," says Rick. "It doesn't hurt the plants. After all, these plants evolved along with grazing animals such as the bison that ranged over them." He mows the area once a year in November to a height of three inches with a lawn mower. He mows around the wildflowers and shrubs to provide a variety of heights during the winter and to leave seeds to drop into the prairie area. He gathers seed from any wildflowers that would be cut down and sows it after the mowing. "I collect the clippings to prevent litter from accumulating," says Rick. "That accumulation would cause the grasses to thin out, slow the warming of the soil in the spring, and prevent the seeds from reaching the soil to germinate."

Florida Prairie

Although few people realize it, most of Florida was a prairie grassland covered with native grasses and wildflowers—from coast to coast—before wet areas were drained, before Bahia grass and Brahman cattle, before canals and orange groves. The population explosion, which began about 1960, only made things worse since everyone brought along the "lawn" mentality as housing developments went in, instead of keeping what native species might have remained. Exotic warm-season grasses such as Bahia, Bermuda, and St. Augustine were used for lawns.

One of the few vast acreages of Florida prairie left is the 8,000-acre National Audubon Society Kissimmee Prairie Sanctuary near Okeechobee.

The major grasses are wiregrass or pineland three-awn (*Aristida stricta*), bluestems (*Andropogon virginicus*, *A. tenarius*), muhly grass (*Muhlenbergia capillaris*), dropseed (*Sporobolus junceus*), Florida gama grass (*Tripsacum floridanum*), and lopsided Indian grass (*Sorghastrum secundum*). Wildflowers include hatpins (*Eriocaulon compressum*), bog buttons (*Lachnocaulon anceps*), coreopsis (*Coreopsis* spp.), black-eyed Susan (*Rudbeckia hirta*), bladderworts (*Utricularia* spp.), butterworts (*Pinguicula* spp.), narrowleaf sunflower (*Helianthus angustifolius*), horsemint (*Monarda punctata*), rosinweed (*Silphium* spp.), and rayless goldenrod (*Bigelowia nudata*). Other plants include saw palmetto (*Serenoa repens*), wax myrtle (*Myrica cerifera*), and creeping runner oak (*Quercus minima*).

The prairie is a fire-maintained community, explains Scott Hedges, manager of the Kissimmee sanctuary. In earlier times when it stretched for miles and miles, lightning would strike at the height of the hot, dry summer and the fire would spread, traveling about two miles per hour, until the prairie was all burned. But because the area is much smaller and the fire cannot be allowed to burn out of control, he burns plots from 50 to 300 acres in size one at a time. This is done on a hot day, with moderate humidity, sometime between May and July.

Scott says homeowners could successfully replace their lawn with a Florida prairie planting using a blend of the grasses and wildflowers that are available from nurseries. He recommends that it be mowed or burned every two or three years once it is established. The mature height of the prairie is three feet but plants could be selected to maintain a lower height if that is preferable.

Landscape architect Bill Bissett, who has been in the business for twenty years, says the trend is starting to move back toward natives, but it is slow. There is a rising demand and the supply is slowly increasing to meet it. There are about forty-five small nurseries in Florida that specialize in native plants but it is still difficult to find sufficient quantities of plants when they are needed. According to the Association of Florida Native Nurseries plant and service directory, homeowners can find plants of many native cultivars, but rarely seed.

Homeowners in Florida who want to develop a meadow of Florida native grasses and wildflowers will have to begin with plants available from nurseries in the state and obtain the seed of appropriate species (some are the same as those found in coastal plain meadows and even the prairies in the Great Plains) from out of state. Bill says advice is available from any of the many local chapters of the Florida Native Plant Society, which was formed twelve years ago.

Native grasses for use in mass plantings to replace lawns in Florida are listed in Table 1 (pages 35–45). Other possibilities include woods grass (*Oplismenus setarius*), two to eight inches tall with small light green foliage that needs shade and can be mowed like other grasses; wiregrass (*Aristida stricta*), eight to fifteen inches tall with fine-textured foliage and awns along the flowering stem, often occurs with saw palmetto (*Serenoa repens*) in palmetto prairies; *Eragrostis elliotii*, a lovegrass species about eighteen inches tall with billowy reddish purple flower heads from late June through August about one foot above the foliage that prefers a sunny, well-drained site; key grass (*Monanthochloe littoralis*), six to eight inches tall with tufts along the upright stems, spreading and rooting as it goes along in muddy seashores and tidal flats; marsh hay or saltmeadow cordgrass (*Spartina patens*), six to twelve inches tall, spreads by slender rhizomes, in salt marshes and sandy meadows along the coast; and pineland dropseed (*Sporobolus junceus*), ten to fifteen inches tall, growing in dense bunches with airy panicles in pine barrens throughout the coastal plain area. I will mention one more that may be too tall for a mass planting to replace a lawn but perhaps has possibilities: Florida gama grass (*Tripsacum floridanum*), a warm-season grass that likes moist areas and ditches, forms a two- to three-foot arching clump, and is evergreen in warm climates. Choose species based on the soil and moisture conditions of your location and consult with local gardeners or the extension office in your county.

Buffalo Grass and Other Native Grasses

Buffalo grass is a low-growing, warm-season native grass that occurs throughout the prairie, but tends to be dominant in areas that are very dry or grazed. It spreads along the surface of the ground by stolons that root as they go.

The seed heads appear all summer and look like tiny combs on stems reaching above the foliage. If left unmowed, it will never grow higher than six inches, and some new varieties have been developed that grow only four inches. In the last few years, its use as a lawn grass has spread extensively throughout the Midwest and Southwest.

Several years ago, horticulturists at the University of Nebraska in Lincoln began observing samples of buffalo grass that had been gathered from all over the Midwest, and selected strains for breeding. Funded by the United States Golf Association, the purpose was to find a grass to use on course roughs to reduce the use of water. However, the grass has so many advantages, particularly drought tolerance, that it is now being widely used as an alternative to conventional lawn grasses such as Kentucky bluegrass, Bermuda, and St. Augustine.

Buffalo grass resists disease and insects, needs little or no mowing, and uses 50 percent less water than Kentucky bluegrass. The variety '609' was released as a result of the research. Two other varieties, '315' and '378', which are more adapted to northern, colder parts of the country, are currently available only in Nebraska, but Terrance P. Riordan, head of the research program, expects them to be more widely available in a year.

All three of these varieties, as well as 'Prairie', which was developed by the program at Texas A & M, are called vegetative types. They are available only as sod or plugs. Named, improved varieties that are available as seed include: 'Texoka', 'Comanche', 'Sharp's Improved', 'Bison', 'Topgun', and 'Plains'.

Crenshaw Doguet Turfgrass Inc. of Austin, Texas, produces 'Prairie' and '609' sod. The plants in the sod of these two species are all female so they do not produce pollen or visible seed heads, which some people, oddly enough, find objectionable. They are selling sod to homeowners, commercial property owners, and highway departments. More than 500 homes in the Austin area have switched to buffalo grass sod, says Barbara Bauer, sales manager.

I visited an exclusive subdivision northwest of Austin where property owners were given a choice of St. Augustine or buffalo grass sod when their homes were built. Bauer says the benefits of the buffalo grass were explained to them, and about half chose it. As I walked through the area in late April, the healthy buffalo grass lawns stood out. They were bluish green with a fine texture in contrast to the coarse St. Augustine lawns which had dead patches and looked dried out.

Buffalo grass is also showing promise in the eastern part of the country. Although native only to the area of the central plains from the Rocky Mountains to the Mississippi River and from Canada to southern Mexico, its tough character, ability to thrive without fertilizer or mowing, and its drought tolerance have led researchers and highway roadside managers to test it in places east of the Mississippi. In Florida, the department of transportation has been experimenting with buffalo grass sod and seed in various locations to determine if it can be used for roadsides, especially where irrigation is impossible. Ralph Carter, who oversees a sixteen-county area in the panhandle, says the sodded areas have been doing well for three years but his observations are not complete enough to say it is a definite for Florida.

Buffalo grass sod was installed on the grounds of Ki Hill Energy Efficiency Services north of Tampa, Florida, in July 1993 and a year later it was thriving. Ken Olson, partner in the company, said they installed sod and plugs in a patchwork pattern over prepared bare ground. They watered a lot—apparently too much—in the beginning to make sure that it would become established, and the grass turned brown. They stopped the water and it became green again. Now they apply only one-eighth inch of water with sprinklers if the grass shows stress, which only happens when it receives no rain or irrigation for two weeks during the hottest months. In its native environment, buffalo grass goes dormant—turns brown—when there is no water but does not die. It revives as soon as it receives moisture again.

Olson says the grass has a soft texture and they receive a lot of questions about it from people passing by. He says even though buffalo grass is low-growing and does not need to be mowed, they prefer keeping it at a height of about two to three inches, so they mow about once a month. The grass spreads very slowly. Since it did not seem to be growing at all, they decided to fertilize and water regularly to stimulate growth. Although in its native environment, buffalo grass would not respond well to this treatment, it may be that the sandy soil and hot, humid conditions in Florida cause it to behave differently.

Whether buffalo grass can be used successfully as an alternative lawn grass or as a component in a low-growing meadow blend east of the Mississippi River is still under study. Two research stations in the mid-Atlantic states—Cornell University and Rutgers University—have been observing trial plots of buffalo grass for more than five years.

Interestingly, historical evidence shows that buffalo grass was once used as a "lawn" in the Eastern states. Dr. David Huff of Rutgers in New Brunswick, New Jersey, has a photograph from the late 1800s showing a healthy buffalo grass lawn in Washington, D.C. He has also found written reports that it was doing well as a lawn in Yonkers, New York. "There is a site here on the campus where buffalo grass naturalized in compacted soil," he said, "it has been thriving for fifteen years and we don't mow it or fertilize it."

Two problems that Huff sees with buffalo grass for the East is susceptibility to disease (due to combined high humidity and heat in the summer) and invasion by other species, mainly cool-season European grasses, in higher moisture soils. Buffalo grass does best in heavier soils and with lower precipitation because it can thrive when many other plants cannot. But he says he thinks this grass still has potential for the East because some of the strains that he is observing show better disease resistance.

Buffalo grass sod provides the look of a conventional lawn without the high amounts of water and fertilizer that nonnative species require. But, planted from seed, it can also be blended with other native grasses and low-growing wildflowers for a more diverse and interesting cover that is truly an alternative to the conventional lawn. Fine fescues, which Huff recommends for low-maintenance turf, grow in a bunching-type pattern and thus can also be blended successfully with wildflowers. They are low-growing; you can get by with cutting them only twice during the season—once to knock down the seed heads and later to reduce the height before winter. The fine fescue group (*Festuca rubra* subspecies) includes creeping red, chewings, and hard fescue. A similar grass, although a different species, is fine-leaved sheep's fescue (*F. tenuifolia*). Red fescue (*F. rubra*) is a native grass and many cultivars have been developed from it. All fescues are cool-season grasses; red fescue spreads by short rhizomes, whereas chewings, hard, and fine-leaved are bunch grasses.

This ability to blend with other plants and to grow slowly made fine fescue one of the choices for the ecology lawn mixes developed by Nichols Garden Nursery of Albany, Oregon, in association with Oregon State University. Rose Marie Nichols McGee, co-owner of Nichols, and Tom Cook, associate professor of horticulture and head of the turf program at Oregon State, were looking at the closely cropped lawn at the botanic garden in

1. Ken and Barbara Root of Decorah, Iowa, replaced most of their lawn with this native prairie planting ten years ago. In late summer the plants in bloom include yellow prairie coneflower (*Ratibida pinnata*), bergamot (*Monarda fistulosa*), purple prairie clover (*Petalostemum purpureum*), and various sunflowers (*Helianthus* spp.). The native grasses, which support and provide a contrast for the flowers, are just beginning to send up seed heads—little bluestem (*Schizachyrium scoparium*) and sideoats grama (*Bouteloua curtipendula*). *Photo by David Cavagnaro*

2. In this fall scene at my home near Hellertown, Pennsylvania, the lower meadow displays the orangish golden seed stems of broomsedge (*Andropogon virginicus*) and little bluestem (*Schizachyrium scoparium*), beige billowy heads of purpletop (*Tridens flavus*), faded brown heads of goldenrod (*Solidago* spp.) and New York ironweed (*Vernonia noveboracensis*), tiny white blooms of calico aster (*Aster lateriflorus*) and small-flowered white aster (*A. vimineus*), and the bleached white, coarse stems of orchard grass (*Dactylis glomerata*). Unwanted species are removed and replaced with native plants, and large 100- to 200-square-foot patches have been cleared completely and reseeded with native grasses and wildflowers. *Photo by Stevie Daniels*

3. Water is a scarce resource in the Southwest, and many homeowners are turning to landscapes of low-growing native grasses and forbs that do well with the natural rainfall such as this example near Albuquerque, New Mexico. Russ and Irene Howard asked garden designer and nursery owner Judith Phillips to reseed an area (left bare by excavation) to match the mostly native vegetation surrounding their home. The grasses include blue grama (*Bouteloua gracilis*), purple three-awn (*Aristida purpurea*), little bluestem (*Schizachyrium scoparium*), and sideoats grama (*Bouteloua curtipendula*). The cactuslike plant (far left) is cholla (*Opuntia cylindropuntia*). *Photo by Charles Mann*

4. A weed-free, evergreen lawn that never has to be cut—planted with penny grass (*Dichondra micrantha*)—is featured at the home of Charles Stein near Pasadena, California. Ground covers used in the rest of the landscape include trailing pink verbena (*Verbena peruviana*), blue fescue (*Festuca ovina* 'Blue Finch'), sageleaf rock-rose (*Cistus salviifolius*), rosemary (*Rosmarinus officinalis*), and caraway thyme (*Thymus herba-barona*). *Photo by Jerry Pavia*

5. In spring, the pink and white blooms of heath intermingled with prostrate junipers and the flat gray surfaces of granite boulders create a dramatic front garden at the home of Eloise Lesan in southern Connecticut. The plants include *Erica carnea, E. c.* 'Springwood White', *E. darleyensis*, and *Bruckenthalia spiculifolium. Photo by Karen Bussolini*

6. A canopy of mature tulip poplars, oaks, beech, and birch creates so much shade that trying to grow lawn grass would be folly. Dave Benner of New Hope, Pennsylvania, simply encouraged the moss and began planting ground covers and shade-loving wildflowers more than twenty-five years ago. This garden of intriguing foliage colors and textures is at its peak for four to five weeks in spring. The reddish blooms (far left) are columbine (*Aquilegia canadensis*), the blue is creeping phlox (*Phlox stolonifera*), and the white blooms are foamflower (*Tiarella cordifolia*). *Photo by Stevie Daniels*

7. Several years ago, Randy Davis planted a mixture of annual wildflowers from Plants of the Southwest and western wheatgrass (*Agropyron smithii*), a native cool-season grass, for his front lawn in Santa Fe, New Mexico. The site was mostly bare as the nonnative lawn died without regular irrigation. He raked the surface and planted in early spring. In this late summer view, the golden beige dormant color of the wheatgrass complements the bright yellows of the cape marigolds (*Osteospermum auriantacum*), Plains coreopsis (*Coreopsis tinctoria*), and the deep crimson of scarlet flax (*Linum rubrum*). *Photo by Charles Mann*

8. This view—in August—of the heather "lawn" created by Jim Thompson of northern California is a breathtaking blend of colored foliage and blooms. Because he has included more than 100 different varieties of these evergreen, low-growing plants in a 100-by-100-foot area, the beauty continues through every season. Flowering time varies with the species, beginning with heaths in the spring (*Erica carnea*), then *E. cinerea* and *Daboecia* spp., followed by *Erica tetralix* and others in midsummer, then the true heather (*Calluna vulgaris*) in fall. Foliage includes all shades of green as well as copper, pink, gold, and silver-gray. *Photo by Jim Thompson*

9. Oak and pine trees with cedars and dogwoods scattered beneath them create filtered shade down one side of Eloise Lesan's yard in southern Connecticut. Even though some sun comes through, moss thrives on the steps that lead up the slope. Other plants include Christmas fern (*Polystichum acrostichoides*), prostrate juniper, *Sedum ewersii*, and fire pink (*Silene virginica*). *Photo by Karen Bussolini*

10. The garden of Ernie and Marietta O'Bryne in Eugene, Oregon, covers about one acre and includes more than 4,000 types of plants. Only a rough lawn and a few trees existed when they arrived over twenty years ago. The prominent low-growing plants in this entry area (shown in April) include pearlwort (*Sagina subulata* 'Aurea'), the light green, ground-hugging plant in foreground; buttercup (*Ranunculus montanus* 'Molten Gold'), yellow blooms in center; *Hacquetia epipactis*, to the right of the buttercup; saxifrage (*Saxifraga moschata*), pink and red blooms; spirea (*Spiraea bullata*), right edge of the boardwalk; and dwarf false cypress (*Chamaecyparis pisifera* 'Minima Aurea'), just behind the spirea. *Photo by Michael S. Thompson*

11. In this Baltimore suburban garden, ornamental grasses are the major feature, accented with blooming perennials and ground covers. Concrete and slate pathways lead through the garden of astilbe (*Astilbe* x *arendsii*) (right); fountain grass (*Pennisetum alopecuroides*) lining the walkways; yellow black-eyed Susan (*Rudbeckia fulgida* 'Goldsturm') with *Miscanthus sinensis* 'Morning Light'; feather reed grass (*Calamagrostis acutiflora stricta*); amber flowers; and tufted hair grass (*Deschampsia caespitosa*). The garden, shown in midsummer, is the creation of Oehme, van Sweden & Associates, Inc. of Washington, D.C. *Photo by Derek Fell*

12. The owners of this home near San Diego, California, seeded treasure flower (*Gazania rigens*) into their front yard. With the intense heat and lack of rain in summer, the grass goes dormant but the flowers, which begin to open in spring, will continue into early winter. A perennial in warm climates (zone 9), the plants spread by rhizomes. New hybrids have been developed that are lower growing and have a wider range of color. *Photo by Derek Fell*

13. When Jack Biesencamp bought his house in Haddonfield, New Jersey, the ground beneath the mature tulip poplars and oak trees had patches of dying lawn grass and areas of thriving moss. He helped the moss spread and pulled out any weeds that showed up when they were young. By the fifth year, he had an evergreen lush moss lawn. *Photo by Walter Chandoha*

14. Trying to grow a lawn in the Southwest, which receives seven inches or less of rain each year, is environmentally unsound and, as this intriguing landscape of Cliff and Marilyn Douglas near Phoenix, Arizona, shows, the desert plants that thrive on their own are a more interesting alternative. In the foreground are flat-padded prickly pear (*Opuntia* spp.), barrel cactus (*Ferocactus* and *Echinocactus* spp.), agave, chuparosa (*Justicia californica*), and Arizona yellowbells (*Tecoma stans*).

The towering cacti are saguaro (*Carnegiea gigantea*) and the trees closer to the house include shoestring acacia (*Acacia stenophylla*), desert willow (*Chilopsis linearis*), and blue palo verde (*Cercidium floridum*). The branch on the ground is the skeleton of a dead saguaro and the plant with tall, thin stems behind it is ocotillo (*Fouquieria spendens*). *Photo by Christine Keith*

15. The front yard of Noreen Went's home in Pennsylvania has perennial borders close to the house, a strip of lawn, and a wildflower area beyond. This show of color occurs only in the first year of a wildflower mix planting on cleared ground. Shown in early summer after having been planted in March, the blooms include corn poppies (*Papaver rhoeas*), cornflower (*Centaurea cyanus*), and a few wallflowers (*Cheiranthus allionii*). In following years, weeds had to be removed and more seeds added. A long-term planting was started in a new area in 1994 with warm-season grasses and native perennials. *Photo by Grant Heilman, courtesy of Lefever/Grushow*

16. Two attractive, spreading ground covers were used to replace most of the lawn of this sloping front yard in Martinsburg, West Virginia. Moss phlox (*Phlox subulata*) is covered with pink blooms in spring that blend well with the white candytuft (*Iberis sempervirens*) which is also evergreen in winter. Pink dogwoods (*Cornus florida* 'Rubra') and a rock outcrop planted with bulbs and sedum complete the scene. *Photo by Grant Heilman/Grant Heilman Photography*

Oregon. They noticed that it also included yarrow, clover, and other plants and decided it would be possible to develop mixtures of turf grass, clovers, wildflowers, and herbs suitable to the different geographic regions of the country that would not require mowing, spraying, fertilizing, and irrigation schedules.

They began developing the mixes in 1983 and the growth of sales has been steady since they were introduced through the catalog eight years ago. Their goal was to create an ecologically stable blend of grasses that would not grow too fast or come back quickly when mowed, and broadleaf plants that were tough, drought resistant, and could be cut or left to grow. Grasses make up 80 to 90 percent of the mix by weight but the appearance of the lawn changes as the various flowering plants that are included come into bloom. Fine fescue, along with perennial rye, is used in the dryland mix; colonial bentgrass in the northern mix; and improved turf-type tall fescue (a cool-season, bunch-type grass) in the southland mix. Strawberry and Dutch white clover, yarrow, and baby blue-eyes are common to all. Other herbs and low-growing wildflowers appropriate to the climate for which the various mixes were developed are included as well. For instance, wild English daisies, used in the northern and dryland mixes, bloom in the spring and fall.

Rose Marie says the mix is one answer to the dilemma that many homeowners face who want a soft green patch for themselves and their children to sit and play on, but do not want to use pesticides and fertilizers and mow the lawn every weekend. The clovers in the mix provide nitrogen for the grasses. In trial plots that Tom has observed for seven years, the mix has been balanced and long-lived; the grass stays green in winter, the clover and yarrow are green in summer when the grass is mostly dormant, and the daisies bloom from March to about June. The baby blue-eyes disappeared after the first year but the Roman chamomile, which they thought was gone, has made a strong appearance the last few years.

In the trials, they mow once every three weeks at about two inches and irrigate once a month in the summer. It is not necessary to mow that often but "the planting loses its integrity as a turf environment when it is let go," says Tom. Although individual weeds come in here and there, they are not a problem in this plant community. Tom is interested in trying some other low-growing flowers in the mix, but has had trouble finding seed for them.

In the Southwest, many homeowners are replacing their nonnative turf lawns with a blend of two low-growing, drought-tolerant native species — buffalo grass and blue grama (*Bouteloua gracilis*). Left unmowed, the lawn will have a soft, wavy look. Buffalo grass will reach about six inches in height and blue grama about twelve. For a tidy lawn appearance, you only need to mow twice a year. These grasses are tough; once established they can be played on and walked on just like any other turfgrass. In addition, these two species can be blended with a small amount of wildflowers for an effect that is similar to the ecology lawn mixes. Plants of the Southwest, of Santa Fe, New Mexico, offers a blend for the southwest region called "Tame Wild Lawn Collection," which, by weight, is sixteen ounces of the two native grasses with one ounce of wildflowers chosen according to the elevation of the customer's site. The silver-gray fine-textured foliage of fringed sage (*Artemisia frigida*) is a wonderful contrast placed here and there among the unmown grass.

Grasses native to the Southwest can also be planted in drifts. Garden designer Judith Phillips used this technique at the home of Bob Levin in Albuquerque, New Mexico. Most of the lot was in the back of the house and was long and narrow. "My idea was to plant drifts of grasses, low to high to low again, with a path winding through to make the space seem more open," says Judith. Blue grama and buffalo grass were mixed together and used closest to the house with flagstones placed in it here and there. Bob mows this area occasionally as a spot for his grandchildren to play. To either side is sand lovegrass (*Eragrostis trichodes*) and in the middle area is a blend of little bluestem and sideoats grama. Judith sows native grasses from seed using a rate of 5 to 6 pounds per 1,000 square feet, where weed competition is intense (urban areas), and a lower rate in the foothills, where a lot of native vegetation remains.

In Colorado, the highway department has begun to use native grasses along roadways in unirrigated areas. Janet Hughes, a transportation specialist in the environmental division of the Department of Transportion, says Kentucky bluegrass is still used for most home lawns in the Denver area and even along the roadsides despite the fact that it requires irrigation wherever it is planted in the West. The department planted '609' buffalo grass sod in one area and they received numerous calls from residents who wanted to know what type of grass it was and where they could obtain it for their yards.

A new planting of little and big bluestem went in a year ago, and Hughes is anxious to see how the public responds. She planned to sow a 40-acre site in the spring of 1994 with a trial blend of sideoats grama, buffalo grass, blue grama, and little bluestem.

The predominant native grass in the West is western wheatgrass (*Agropyron smithii*). A cool-season grass that spreads by rhizomes to form a sod, it has rich blue-green foliage and a mature height of about two feet. Extremely drought tolerant, it will turn beige during dry spells and green up again when it rains. Some Southwest gardeners have had success mixing it with wildflowers. Gary Feinsted, of the Soil Conservation Service in Lakewood, Colorado, says a beautiful fall combination is the blue blades of western wheatgrass with the purplish seed heads of blue grama mixed in it.

Meadows

The word "meadow" creates a vision in our minds. Each person's may be slightly different, but what seems to be common to all is an image of an open, sunny area filled with grasses and wildflowers about knee-high, with low shrubs and trees at the margins. The possibility of having these visions manifest in their own yards caused the attention of homeowners to be captured by the "meadow in a can" promotions of the 1980s. But meadows are not climax communities (the last stage in an evolutionary succession of native plants), as prairies are. They have to be maintained to keep them from gradually developing back into a forest—the natural climax community of most of the eastern United States.

The popularity of wildflower meadows, which began in the mid-1980s, has continued to rise along with the desire to use suburban ground to preserve native species. Even though many homeowners were disillusioned with their first efforts, interest has not diminished; instead, the lessons learned have resulted in better techniques. In too many cases, even though the ground may have been cleared of existing vegetation and the seeds sown properly, by the second year the desired plants had been crowded out by invaders and, by the third year, many called it a "weedy mess" and mowed it down.

Wildflower Bed Problems

The reason for these failures? First, nearly all of the mixes available in the major retail outlets and through catalogs contained *only* wildflower seed. Many contained exotic (not indigenous to the United States but naturalized here) wildflower seed such as Queen Anne's lace (*Daucus carota*), cornflower (*Centaurea cyanus*), or chicory (*Cichorium intybus*). In some cases, the percentage of annual species in the mix was too high. While that provided a dazzling show of color the first year, it meant that the small perennial seedlings trying to get established got too much shade and could not make a good stand. So, the second year, when the annuals did not self-sow because they were not native to the region in which they were planted, the bare spots that were left between the perennials were quickly invaded by exotic rhizomatous grasses and weeds. Homeowners who were able to identify seedlings of unwanted plants pulled them out and sowed more seed or plugged in transplants.

Another outcome was that one perennial wildflower would become dominant by the end of a three-year period. Oxeye daisy (*Chrysanthemum leucanthemum*), which is not native to the United States, becomes dominant in the mid-Atlantic area; in the south, lance-leaved coreopsis (*Coreopsis lanceolata*), although it is native, does the same. Two other species can be used in this manner: blanketflower (*Gaillardia aristata*) and black-eyed Susan (*Rudbeckia hirta*).

In every area that I visited, these problems had occurred. The situation was handled in different ways, depending on the site and on the gardener's taste. Some homeowners were perfectly happy to have one dominant species. In that case, maintenance included removing woody or weedy species that showed up and cutting the area to a height of six inches in late fall or early winter. Those who wanted more diversity and the showy flash of colorful annuals in spring and early summer had to reseed and plug in good-sized plants of different varieties. In only a few cases was the area completely done over—tilled repeatedly to kill everything and replanted.

Another alternative to the "meadow in a can" is to plant a few native trees and shrubs, especially if your lot has none or very few, and to stop mowing an area that you would like to develop into a natural meadow with wildflowers and native grasses. Kentucky bluegrass (*Poa pratensis*)—the dominant lawn grass in the eastern part or country—is not indigenous to the

United States. Where taller native grasses are encouraged and left undisturbed for two to three years, it will be shaded out, according to a classic book by J. E. Weaver, who was a grassland specialist at the University of Nebraska. I asked Dr. Terrance Riordan, a turf specialist at the university today, if this would be true throughout the United States. He says that the bluegrass would decline in the Midwest due to lack of adequate, consistent rainfall and in any other area where that was true, but in the East, because of regular rainfall, it most likely would not decline. However, William A. Niering, botanist at Connecticut College and research director of the arboretum, reports that the Kentucky bluegrass in the lawn that he stopped mowing in 1970 did decline while the red fescue (*Festuca rubra*) did not. Little bluestem (*Schizachyrium scoparium*), which was already present, increased over the years but the fescue has been pushing it out in some spots. The possible persistence of rhizomatous turfgrasses is the reason they need to be removed from a site where you want to establish native grasses and wildflowers.

Leaving an area unmown does not mean simply neglecting it. You will need to identify which species are growing on the site so that you can distinquish between natives and nonnatives. Some of the nonnatives will be species that have naturalized and do not pose a threat to the balance of the meadow. You can leave those unless you want a completely pure stand of natives. Remove all plants on your local and state "noxious weed" list, and any woody plants that show up. Some native species are very aggressive and may dominate unless you place other similarly aggressive species adjacent to them, which will keep both in check. If you are in a conventional suburb, explain to your neighbors what you are doing and keep the boundary around the meadow-in-progress mown and neat.

Using Grasses with Wildflowers

If you start from bare ground, use a seed mixture that contains native grasses and wildflowers. Some gardeners have been successful sowing the grasses alone at first and waiting a year or two to plug in plants of selected native wildflowers. If your goal is to have a low-maintenance, nearly self-sustaining meadow, then you will need to use a higher percentage of grasses than flowers. Having a field of only wildflowers in bloom throughout the growing season that comes back on its own every year is a fantasy. If that is what you desire, then it is important to understand that you will need to use mostly annuals and replant every year.

John Thomas of Wildseed Farms in Eagle Lake, Texas, says they used to carry native grass seed but customers who used it thought it should not be in the planting and often killed it. "Our customers want a solid carpet of wildflowers and instant color," says Thomas, "so our mixes have a dominance of annuals." By late summer, the plantings usually have a lot of brown stalks with drying seed heads and many people do not like how it looks, so they cut it at that time. "If they had a native grass in the planting," says Thomas, "they would lose the benefit of its late summer and fall beauty anyway because that is when the flowering stems emerge."

Thomas says they have decided to concentrate on providing wildflower mixes that are low growing and give the customer the instant, thick burst of color they want. They urge anyone new to this idea to start with a small area and see how they like it before doing more. Perennials take three to four years to really get established, and he says many people are too impatient to wait or do not understand the process. Customers who are successful and take care of the planting until the perennials become established are very pleased. They often oversow with some of the annuals they like the best.

In naturally occurring meadows, the grasses are dominant with various wildflowers blended in that bloom in succession through the season. Some will bloom and the foliage will disappear, others will grow slowly through the summer and bloom in the fall.

The grasses serve as a background and support to the flowers through the summer and then send up attractive seed heads in the fall which continue to provide beauty and interest through the winter. They also fill in the ground between wildflowers, preventing unwanted nonnative grasses or weeds from taking hold. Also, the foliage of the grasses turns appealing shades of rust, orange, and beige in the late fall.

Neil Diboll of Prairie Nursery, who consults with homeowners who are installing meadow plantings in the East, generally recommends sowing forty to sixty seeds per square foot, grasses not exceeding twenty seeds per square foot or they will dominate. The number of seeds per ounce for wildflowers is much higher than for grasses. For example, bergamot (*Monarda fistulosa*) has

78,000 seeds per ounce; yellow prairie coneflower (*Ratibida pinnata*) has 27,000 per ounce; and columbine (*Aquilegia canadensis*) has 25,000. Compare these amounts to those for grass: little bluestem (*Schizachyrium scoparium*), 8,800 per ounce; sideoats grama (*Bouteloua curtipendula*), 8,000; and prairie dropseed (*Sporobolus heterolepis*), 14,000. So, if you use a mixture that is half grass and half wildflowers, you will actually be broadcasting more flower seed per square foot. This also explains why you can increase the ratio (by weight) of grasses and still obtain the end result of a showy display of flowers dispersed throughout the planting.

Diboll further explains that it is the teamwork of the grasses and wildflowers together to occupy the soil environment so completely that prevents weeds from getting a foothold. He also warns that the taller grasses, such as switchgrass (*Panicum virgatum*) (three to six feet) and big bluestem (*Andropogon gerardi*) (five to eight feet), tend to form a sod which will discourage all but the most vigorous wildflowers. The lower-growing bunch grasses leave spaces between their clumps, a characteristic that favors the spread of wildflowers and makes for such a successful coexistence of the two types of plants. Sherri Evans of Shooting Star Nursery, Frankfort, Kentucky recommends a ratio of 60 percent grass to 40 percent forbs by weight for prairie/meadow plantings and a higher ratio of wildflowers (75:25) for naturalizing smaller areas where an intensive flower display is desired (4,000 square feet or less). The nursery's mixes contain such native grasses as little bluestem (*Schizachyrium scoparium*), broomsedge (*Andropogon virginicus*), sideoats grama (*Bouteloua curtipendula*), Indian grass (*Sorghastrum nutans*), prairie dropseed (*Sporobolus heterolepis*), big bluestem (*Andropogon gerardii*), and prairie switchgrass (*Panicum virgatum*).

Keep in mind that using blends of native grasses or blends of grasses with other wildflowers and perennials is a completely new field of landscape practice in many parts of the country. If you are trying a combination that you invented, take an experimental approach. Try it in a small area first to make observations and to develop effective methods of maintenance before tilling under the entire front lawn. Make selections based on what is indigenous to your area and on your knowledge of the plant's preferred growing conditions. The suggestions in Table 1 (pages 35–45) and the combinations used by homeowners reported in the previous chapter and here will give you a starting point. You may develop successful plantings that have not been used before and will be helpful to other homeowners in your region.

Native grasses take longer to get established—up to three years. But once they are, you will have a self-sustaining stand that requires your participation only to keep out the few weeds that may crop up as a result of seeds being brought in by the wind or by birds, and to cut (or burn) once a year to prevent woody species that sow themselves from getting a start. Warren Kenfield, author of *The Wild Gardener in the Wild Landscape*, which is the story of the knowledge he gained during the twenty-one years that he spent developing an Eastern meadow, says there are very few woody shrubs that will invade a well-established stand of native grass.

Choosing Species

When planning your meadow, select the grass species first as they are the dominant feature in a meadow, and then choose a compatible mix of native or naturalized (noninvasive) wildflowers. The nurseries that carry native grass as well as wildflower seed (see Appendix I) have good guidelines for developing a custom mix, or you can begin with one of the blends that they have developed for specific soils and locations. Grasses recommended for most of the eastern United States include little bluestem (*Schizachyrium scoparium*), sideoats grama (*Bouteloua curtipendula*), Junegrass (*Koeleria cristata*), switchgrass (*Panicum virgatum*), broomsedge (*Andropogon virginicus*), silver beardgrass (*A. ternarius*), Indian grass (*Sorghastrum nutans*), Prairie dropseed (*Sporobolus heterolepis*), big bluestem (*Andropogon gerardii*), and Canada wild rye (*Elymus canadensis*).

Rick Darke, Curator of Plants for Longwood Gardens, Kennett Square, Pennsylvania, and a specialist in native and ornamental grasses, says there are two different ways to go about creating a meadow: 1) discontinuing to mow; and 2) disking, spraying to kill the vegetation, and resowing with the desired meadow species. When you stop mowing, the idea is to let the plants grow in order to determine what natives and desirable naturalized plants are present. How well it will work depends on the soil, the site (whether you live close to agricultural fields, which might contain undesirable plants like thistle that could seed into your meadow or close to a natural area that has native plants that would be welcomed if they seeded in), what plants are there now, and how much moisture the area receives.

With sufficient existing natives, you can gradually remove the unwanted plants and replace them with clumps of native wildflowers and grasses. Being able to identify the plants is essential to knowing which ones to encourage and which to eradicate. You can get help from professionals who give workshops or symposiums in your area or through the use of field guides. If the site you want to try this on has numerous woody shrubs, weeds, and rhizomatous grasses, the competition will be too fierce to just cut it and hope for native species to return.

Darke himself chose the first method because less labor is involved. He was banking on the fact that a lot of natives were already there and others would seed in, and they did. He stopped mowing a third of an acre on his home grounds to develop a meadow. Over the last six years he has watched the area, attempting to remove and control invasive, weedy plants. At this point, the meadow includes at least five native grasses, various species of native goldenrod and asters, and two nonnative, naturalized aliens—Queen Anne's lace and chicory—among other plants. He put in one plant of Indian grass and now has fifteen. He mows the area once a year in spring using a commercial mower with blades set at three-and-a-half inches.

Plants that have continued to be a problem are honeysuckle, Canada thistle (*Cirsium arvense*), wild grape (*Vitex riparia*), poison ivy (*Campsis radicans*), Russian olive (*Elaeagnus angustifolia*), and multiflora rose (*Rosa multiflora*). Darke says the latter two plants can be dug or removed mechanically and managed, but the vining plants are an incredible problem. He has come to the conclusion that regular applications of a broadleaf herbicide may be the only solution. He is not recommending that but says it is important for homeowners to realize that meadows still require maintenance and may, if persistent invasive plants are present, call upon them to constantly weed or use an herbicide.

The reason nonnative seeds are included in the wildflower mixtures, according to various seed companies, is that they are naturalized in the areas that the seed is intended for and that their customers want a mix that will give them blooms for as long as possible through the season. Neil Diboll of Prairie Nursery says the nonnative species are often included because "natural" Eastern meadows are almost always the result of recolonization of old fields by both native species and naturalized exotic species.

Perennial wildflowers that have been used successfully in meadows in Pennsylvania and could be used throughout the northeast and as far south as Virginia include white yarrow (*Achillea millefolium*), Siberian wallflower (*Cheiranthus allionii*), oxeye daisy (*Chrysanthemum leucanthemum*), lance-leaved coreopsis (*Coreopsis lanceolata*), purple coneflower (*Echinacea purpurea*), black-eyed Susan (*Rudbeckia hirta*), prairie coneflower (*Ratibida columnifera*), blue flax (*Linum perenne lewisii*), and New England aster (*Aster novae-angliae*).

Two grasses used in some plantings, which, even though they grow in a bunching pattern suitable for blending with wildflowers, did not become established consistently throughout the plantings—sheep's fescue (*Festuca ovina*) and hard fescue (*F. longifolia*)—are both nonnative, cool-season types. They were sowed at eight pounds to the acre. However, once they have taken hold, they will eventually dominate when sown in a stand with wildflowers, according to studies in Pennsylvania and Maryland. Trials are underway in both states using native grasses.

How Others Did It

A one-quarter-acre meadow at Garden in the Woods, the grounds of the New England Wild Flower Society, was installed ten years ago. Woody plants were removed and an herbicide was used to kill persistent perennial weeds. The soil was rotary tilled several times during the summer. In midsummer, nearly 3,000 wildflower transplants were planted into the area, spaced about one plant per every three or four square feet. They were kept watered during the first year. Thirty species were selected well in advance so that they could be started from seeds and cuttings. The goal was to have a grass-to-flower ratio of three or four to one. Four native grasses—little bluestem (*Schizachyrium scoparium*), sideoats grama (*Bouteloua curtipendula*), Junegrass (*Koeleria cristata*), and Northern (or prairie) dropseed (*Sporobolus heterolepis*)— were sown at twice the recommended rate in the fall. The entire area was covered with a half-inch layer of salt marsh hay.

Based on their experience, the staff now recommends sowing the grass as seed or as plugs in early May. Compatible wildflower seed can be sown at the same time and an annual companion crop, which will help keep out weeds, can also be planted. Oats is a good choice. After the grasses have established themselves (two to three years), transplants of wildflowers can be installed in large drifts. In the first year the site should be kept mowed at a height of six to eight inches and any weeds that show up should be pulled or dug out. Some undesirable species that have shown up in the meadow are purple loosestrife (*Lythrum salicaria*), Canada goldenrod (*Solidago canadensis*), and hog peanut (*Amphicarpa bracteata*).

The society's list of recommended native grass species for northeastern meadows includes those listed above as well as switchgrass (*Panicum virgatum*). Some of the wildflowers that they recommend are Canada anemone (*Anemone canadensis*), butterfly weed (*Asclepias tuberosa*), New England aster (*Aster novae-angliae*), blue false indigo (*Baptisia australis*), lance-leaved coreopsis (*Coreopsis lanceolata*), purple coneflower (*Echinacea purpurea*), Queen of the prairie (*Filipendula rubra*), wild geranium (*Geranium maculatum*), sneezeweed (*Helenium autumnale*), blazing star (*Liatris spicata*), wild lupine (*Lupinus perennis*), monarda (*Monarda fistulosa*), obedient plant (*Physostegia virginiana*), black-eyed Susan (*Rudbeckia hirta*), sweet black-eyed Susan (*R. subtomentosa*), rosinweed (*Silphium dentatum*), gray goldenrod (*Solidago nemoralis*), seaside goldenrod (*S. sempervirens*), stiff goldenrod (*S. rigida*), New York ironweed (*Vernonia noveboracensis*), Culver's root (*Veronicastrum virginicum*), and bird's-foot violet (*Viola pedata*).

One of the longest-term naturalistic landscapes in the East is a half-acre site at the Connecticut Arboretum in New London. More than forty years ago, an abandoned orchard that was reverting to forest was cleared of trees, leaving desirable shrubs and small trees such as highbush blueberry (*Vaccinium corymbosum*), virburnums (*Virburnum* spp.), huckleberry (*Gaylussacia baccata*), sweet fern (*Comptonia peregina*), gray birch (*Betula populifolia*), red cedar (*Juniperus virginiana*), and flowering dogwood (*Cornus florida*). Grasses and wildflowers intermingle with the shrubs, and the native Virginia creeper (*Parthenocissus quinquefolia*) climbs some of the trees. The main grass is little bluestem (*Schizachyrium scoparium*); others include Pennsylvania sedge (*Carex pensylvanica*), hair grass (*Deschampsia flexuosa*), and two nonnatives: red top (*Agrostis alba*) and sweet vernal grass (*Anthoxanthum odoratum*). Wildflowers include butterfly weed (*Asclepias tuberosa*), black-eyed Susan (*Rudbeckia hirta*), New England aster (*Aster novae-angliae*), goldenrod (*Solidago* spp.), sunflowers (*Helianthus tuberosus, H. occidentalis*), and two naturalized nonnatives: oxeye daisy (*Chrysanthemum leucanthemum*) and hay-scented fern (*Dennstaedtia punctilobula*). Niering points out that there are many other suitable species—some native and some nonnative—that can be added to increase the beauty of the meadow. Some are orange daylily (*Hemerocallis fulva*), yellow daylily (*H. flava*), Japanese iris (*Iris kaempferi*), Siberian iris (*I. siberica*), bouncing bet (*Saponaria officinalis*), blazing star (*Liatris spicata*), moss pink (*Phlox subulata*), May apple (*Podophyllum peltatum*), and loosestrife (*Lysimachia ciliatum*). For more wildflowers as well as shrubs that suit a naturalistic landscape, see the pamphlet available from the arboretum (see Appendix II).

In the early years at the arboretum natural landscape, undesirable plants were dug out, girdled and left to die, or were killed by cutting and applying herbicide to the stump. Girdling can be done by removing a complete section of bark around the tree with an axe in any season, or pulling off sizeable sections of bark in the early spring when the tree is actively growing. These trees can be left to die in place. In the last ten years, very little maintenance beyond the annual burning (done with permits) is required. Studies have shown that the burning actually increases the amount and vigor of the dominant grass, little bluestem.

Meadows are suitable for open sunny areas throughout the eastern United States, parts of the Southwest, and even along the West Coast. Most of the area in the middle of the country is more suited to a prairie planting. Some grass and wildflower species may be found in all of these regions but most are different, particularly where temperature, soil, and rainfall patterns are not the same. One of the most valuable membership services of the National Wildflower Research Center in Austin, Texas, is its clearinghouse. Members can request an extensive list of recommended wildflowers and grasses for their state as well as shrubs, trees, and vines. They also offer brochures on native plant nurseries and how to create a wildflower meadow or a prairie garden.

The southern states—because of the heat and high humidity in summer—are a good example of how the species vary by location. In Georgia, Will Corley, a University of Georgia Extension Service horticulturalist located at the Agricultural Experiment Station in Griffin, has been researching wildflowers and grasses (both native and ornamental) for more than twenty years. He screened and evaluated about 400 forage grasses for possible use as ornamental plants. Out of those, he kept fifteen. Five years ago a wildflower project was established at the Griffin station. It evolved from a statewide beautification program sponsored by the Garden Clubs of

Georgia, county Clean and Beautiful Commissions, Georgia State Parks, and the Adopt-a-Highway program. Corley had already begun evaluating more than eighty wildflower species to select perennials that had heat tolerance and lower height. He also evaluated southeastern wildflower mixes that were available from wholesale catalogs.

He selected thirteen species for the UGA basic mix including yarrow (*Achillea millefolium*), black-eyed Susan (*Rudbeckia hirta*), goldenrod (*Solidago* spp.), crimson clover (*Trifolium incarnatum*), pink primrose (*Oenothera speciosa*), and partridge pea (*Cassia fasciculata*). He later developed a UGA color mix to provide more variety and longer-lasting color—seventeen species ranging from baby blue-eyes (*Nemophila menziesii*), cornflower (*Centaurea cyanus*), corn poppies (*Papaver rhoeas*), and crimson clover (*Trifolium incarnatum*), to rocket larkspur (*Delphinium ajacis*), lemon mint (*Monarda citriodora*), lance-leaved coreopsis (*Coreopsis lanceolata*), plains coreopsis (*Coreopsis tinctoria*), partridge pea (*Cassia fasciculata*), blanketflower (*Gaillardia aristata*), blue sage (*Salvia farinacea*), black-eyed Susan (*Rudbeckia hirta*), and goldenrod (*Solidago* spp.) to provide blooms from March to early November. He is currently researching some new mixes to find a blend for partial shade performance and one that is all native species (both grass and wildflowers) for restoration of plant communities.

The roadside planting sites in the Athens area did not include any native grasses. On one site, which was on a slope, a grass was included for erosion control only—tall fescue (*Festuca arundianacea*). This cool-season, bunching grass would eventually compete with, rather than complement, the wildflowers. Once the wildflowers were established, a grass herbicide was applied to kill it. This, of course, left open spots for weeds to come in. Corley says he is looking for one or more native grasses to use instead that would not have to be killed. He has been collecting native grass seed to use in trial plantings of grass and wildflowers together.

You do not have to wait for the results of these trials to select native grasses for your meadow in the southeast. Corley recommends broomsedge (*Andropogon virginicus*), bushy bluestem (*A. gomeratus*), silver broomsedge (*A. ternarius*), hairy-awn or purple muhly (*Muhlenbergia capillaris*), Indian grass (*Sorghastrum nutans*), purple top (*Tridens flavus*), plume grass (*Erianthus* spp.), and switchgrass (*Panicum virgatum*). Another species suited for meadows is purple lovegrass (*Eragrostis spectabilis*).

The major management problems for wildflower areas in the Southeast are that they can brown out by midsummer due to heat and that they can be invaded by unwanted species such as white clover (*Trifolium repens*), plantain (*Plantago major* and *P. lanceolata*), cheat grass (*Bromus secalinus*), and Queen Anne's lace (*Daucus carota*). Corley usually advises three properly timed cuttings no lower than four inches—late June after spring species' bloom ends, late August when things look somewhat brown and bedraggled, and December to clean up the area. Because the mixture and the site can be so variable, Corley advises homeowners who are interested in the idea to select a good mix for their particular area, prepare a small site well, and try it. He feels that is the best way for someone to determine the species that will work best for their site and what management techniques will be needed.

Darrel G. Morrison, professor at the University of Georgia School of Environmental Design, is known for his prairie restoration work in Wisconsin. Since his move to Georgia ten years ago, he has used southeastern native plant communities in various projects and in some field trials. Based on what he has seen so far, the grasses and wildflowers that he would recommend for a native meadow in the Southeast are broomsedge (*Andropogon virginicus*), split-beard bluestem (*A. ternarius*), purple lovegrass (*Muhlenbergia capillaris*), Indian grass (*Sorghastrum nutans*), lance-leaved coreopsis (*Coreopsis lanceolata*), black-eyed Susan (*Rudbeckia hirta*), butterfly weed (*Asclepias tuberosa*), rough blazing star (*Liatris aspera*), partridge pea (*Cassia fasciculata*), and wild bergamot (*Monarda fistulosa*). The grasses should be the major part of the blend, with wildflowers no more than 20 percent of the mix.

He tried buffalo grass (*Buchloë dactyloides*), blue grama (*Bouteloua gracilis*), and sideoats grama (*B. curtipendula*) in some areas but they did not do well. He thinks they may need drier sites and less competition and is still experimenting with ways to use them in southeastern landscapes—pathways that are occasionally mowed is one possibility. He advises that in order to have the best success with a meadow, use only native species.

He says if you currently have a lawn of mostly bluegrass, Bahia, St. Augustine, or other imported, rhizomatous species, the best method is to till it repeatedly to remove it all before sowing a native seed mix. If your lawn is an old field that is mowed or your home is in a new subdivision that used to be an undeveloped area, you might want to wait a year and see what plants are there. A colleague of his moved into a new subdivision in August in the

Athens area and did not mow. By December it was clear that his front yard was a beautiful, pure stand of broomsedge.

In 1987, Ruth and Dennis Mitchell of Griffin began planting a cottage-style garden around the house of her family's 200-year-old farm. In the large grassy area—about an acre—beneath the pecan grove in the front, they planted one patch of oxeye daisies (*Chrysanthemum leucanthemum*). They usually mowed the area about once every two weeks but, as the daisies spread, they began leaving those areas uncut. When I visited in May last year, the area was nearly filled with daisies, and some other wildflowers have shown up on their own as well. Now they cut only around the edges and over the few areas without flowers about once a month.

The areas in front, on the left side, and around the back of the house are planted more intensively with all types of small shrubs, herbaceous perennials, wildflowers, and ground covers. "Five years ago when I started planting here," says Ruth, as we stood in the front of the house, "this was hard bare soil that had been swept clean for more than 100 years—an old custom in the South." The area is now a blend of herbs and perennials including verbena (*Verbena canadensis*), Siberian wallflower (*Cheiranthus allionii*), yarrow (*Achillea* spp.), various artemisia species including *Artemisia Stellerana*, crambe (*Crambe cordifolia*), bronze fennel (*Foeniculum vulgare*), and garlic chives (*Allium tuberosum*). "I plant in the fall or spring when the ground is moist and rainfall is consistent," says Ruth, "so I don't have to do any watering myself. The plants that are able to establish themselves and start growing get to grow."

What is now a meadow area with small pathways through it was originally covered with privet, honeysuckle, and small pines. They had someone pull out the woody plants with a tractor and chains. It was plowed, tilled, and after a two-week waiting period, a glyphosate herbicide was used to kill the remaining weeds. They planted 125 hybrid tea roses and some other perennials. A southeastern wildflower meadow mix was sown in 1987 and the area has just developed on its own since.

The combination of Ruth's gardening philosophy and the fussiness of most hybrid teas resulted in the demise of nearly all the roses. The ones that remain are now part of the rambling diverse mixture of self-sowing annuals, perennials, and creeping ground covers such as wild strawberry (*Fragaria virginiana*) and yarrow (*Achillea* spp.). The garden provides a tapestry of blooms that is constantly changing from spring through fall. Species include Siberian wallflowers (*Cheiranthus allionii*), native verbena (*Verbena canadensis*), garlic chives (*Allium tuberosum*), larkspur (*Delphinium ajacis*), gaura (*Gaura biennis*), cockscomb (*Celosia cristata*), globe amaranth (*Gomphrena* spp.), spider flowers (*Cleome spinosa*), ageratum (*Ageratum* spp.), California poppies (*Eschscholzia californica*), iris (*Iris germanica*), cornflower (*Centaurea cyanus*), sedum (*Sedum spectabile* 'Brilliant'), Shirley poppies (*Papaver rhoeas*), opium poppies (*P. somniferum*), wild geranium (*Geranium maculatum*), Mexican hat (*Ratibida columnaris*), phlox (*Phlox paniculata*), bergamot (*Monarda fistulosa*), and violets (*Viola odorata*).

Grasses are mixed into the flowers but not enough to outcompete them. Ruth, in her later years, says she just cannot pull it all out even though she thinks the overall look is a bit unkempt.

"People come from all types of garden clubs and organizations to see my garden," says Ruth. "They say they love the wild look and want to go home and create a garden just like it, but they rarely do." Will believes people are hesitant because the approach is unconventional and they are not confident that it will work for them. "I always suggest that people start with a small plot in the backyard," he says, "to try it and see how it works, then make it larger and if they like it, eventually expand it to the front yard as well."

Fox McCarthy of Conyers, Georgia, former president of the Georgia WaterWise Council and current water conservation coordinator for the Cobb/Marietta Water Authority in Cobb County, sowed a one-and-a-quarter-acre wildflower meadow four years ago using a southeastern wildflower mix from Pennington Seed. He deep-tilled (to seven inches) in August and sprayed glyphosate two times before broadcasting the seed at a rate of ten pounds to the acre (he used twelve pounds in all) in November. He dragged a chain harrow over the area and then the rains came. The mix included yarrow (*Achillea millefolium*), cornflower (*Centaurea cyanus*), partridge pea (*Cassia fasciculata*), lance-leaved coreopsis (*Coreopsis lanceolata*), plains coreopsis (*C. tinctoria*), rocket larkspur (*Delphinium ajacis*), California poppy (*Eschscholzia californica*), annual and perennial gaillardia (*Gaillardia pulchella* and *G. aristata*), baby blue-eyes (*Nemophila menziesii*), Shirley poppy (*Papaver rhoeas*), black-eyed Susan (*Rudbeckia hirta*), blue salvia (*Salvia farinacea*), and crimson clover (*Trifolium incarnatum*).

"The poppies reseeded for the first three years but none showed up the fourth," says Fox. "I planted only one oxeye daisy plant and it has spread throughout the meadow." Sheep sorrel (*Rumex acetosella*), wild strawberry (*Fragaria virginiana*), spiderwort (*Tradescantia virginiana*), and sneezeweed (*Helenium autumnale*) showed up on their own and blend well. The only one that could prove troublesome is the sorrel since it is of European origin and has naturalized throughout the Southeast. It spreads by rhizomes but does so slowly, and since it is shallowly rooted an overabundance could be pulled up. Unfortunately ragweed (*Ambrosia artemisiifolia*), lespedeza (*Lespedeza virginica*), greenbrier (*Smilax rotundifolia*), and an unidentified vine showed up as well, which he does not want.

"I usually cut the area once in the fall," says Fox, "but last year I cut it in August hoping to kill or discourage the invaders." The fescue that was in the mix is still around and is becoming dominant. Since he does not want a lot of grass, he is planning to renovate the entire area next year using a method he tried on a small plot near his office. He prepared the ground as above except tilled it to a depth of only two inches and used the same wildflower mix but without any grass species in it.

Derickson W. and Barbara Bennett of Fair Haven, New Jersey, stopped mowing their front lawn and began planting wildflowers and well-adapted perennial flowers in 1983. The mixture includes viper's bugloss (*Echium vulgare*), chicory (*Cichorium intybus*), butterfly weed (*Asclepias tuberosa*), Deptford pink (*Dianthus armeria*), wild columbine (*Aquilegia canadensis*), milkweed (*Asclepias syriaca*), daylilies (*Hemerocallis fulva*), evening primrose (*Oenothera biennis*), and carpet bugleweed (*Ajuga reptans*). Even though it created a controversy which has continued through the years, they are not in violation of the local ordinance which says only that "grass should be maintained in a proper fashion." The Bennetts say that their "lawn" requires less water, avoids chemical fertilizer, and eliminates the noise pollution created by lawn mowers.

In California, much of the open ground used to be a native grassland, filled with more than 300 species. Then came development and overgrazing. Many of the native species have been displaced by imported forage grasses or weeds. Three years ago the California Native Grass Association was formed for the purpose of reestablishing the native grasses along roadsides and in parks and helping individuals who want to do the same on their land.

They have installed demonstration sites to evaluate species and to show residents what their state's native grasses look like.

Although the grassland was predominantly grasses, colorful wildflowers were also part of the habitat. Some of the species they have been working with include the state grass—purple needlegrass (*Stipa pulchra*), Idaho fescue (*Festuca idahoensis*), onion grass (*Melica californica*), wild rye (*Elymus glaucus*), meadow barley (*Hordeum brachyantherum*), California poppy (*Eschscholzia californica*), a native lupine (*Lupinus benthamii*), and blazing star (*Mentzelia lindleyi*).

The combination of prescribed fire during the dry season and short-term grazing (by sheep, in this case) in the wet season (early spring) enhances the growth of purple needlegrass and suppresses exotic annual grasses. That was the conclusion of Andrew R. Dyer, Department of Agronomy and Range Science, University of California, Davis. He observed trial plots sown with purple needlegrass seed in 1988. Summer grazing combined with burning increased the presence of native wildflowers as well. Although you may not be able to have sheep grazing in your yard, you can simulate the effect by using a lawn mower.

Other important native grasses which would work successfully in a blend with wildflowers in California include California fescue (*Festuca californica*), deergrass (*Muhlenbergia rigens*), and California oat grass (*Danthonia californica*).

Some additional native wildflowers to consider, besides those mentioned above, are blue-eyed grass (*Sisyrinchium bellum*), a clump-forming perennial with grasslike foliage that is evergreen in mild climates and has small blue flowers from March to May; *Allium unifoloium*, a perennial reaching eighteen inches in height with long, thin, flat leaves and rose flowers in a ball-shaped cluster in spring; *A. dichlamydeum*, similar to the plant above but reaching only one foot in height with thinner leaves and deep purple flowers; sulfur buckwheat (*Eriogonum umbellatum* var. *polyanthum*), an eighteen- to twenty-inch perennial with olive leaves that blooms in May with its yellow flowers held about three inches above the foliage; Pacific coast iris (*Iris munzii*, *I. fernaldii*, *I. purdyi*, *I. innominata*, and others), displaying a wide variety of foliage and flower color, most of them evergreen, ranging in size from eight to eighteen inches high and self-sowing; California fuchsia (*Zauschneria californica*), a creeping perennial with soft gray-green leaves and brilliant, scarlet-orange flowers from July through mid-October; tidytips (*Layia platyglossa*), an annual with fuzzy, light green leaves and two-inch yellow flowers from March to June that grows about a foot tall and spreads about two feet, will self-sow; and penstemons.

A number of small California native shrubs will work in a mass planting of grasses, wildflowers, and perennials. A selection of these include monkeyflower (*Mimulus bifidus*, *M. clevelandii*, *M. aridus*, and others), a short-lived (four to five years) two-foot subshrub that blooms in June in colors including white, apricot, yellow, orange, rose, and red, and will readily reseed; sandhill sage (*Artemisia pycnocephala*), an eighteen-inch mounding subshrub with fine-textured silver-blue-green foliage that sends up tall flower spikes; woolly blue curls (*Trichostema lanatum*), a shrub reaching three to four feet with twisted trunk and branches covered with peeling tan bark and fragrant medium green leaves, displays twelve- to eighteen-inch flower spikes for eight months if the spent blooms are removed and it receives moderate water (it is short-lived, eight to ten years, but will reseed); and Cleveland sage (*Salvia clevelandii*), a two- to three-foot shrub with blue flowers.

Moss Lawns and Woodlands

In many ways, homeowners who live on wooded sites have an easier job of converting what lawn there is into an alternative planting of moss, understory small shrubs, and low-growing, shade-loving wildflowers. Turfgrass does not like shade or acid soil. If there are turfgrass species in a yard with large trees that is shaded most of the day, it is a real struggle to keep it going. The first step, then, is simply to stop struggling. Most likely, moss has been growing in the grass for years, and ironically, many lawn care books and experts describe moss as a "pest" and "invader" and recommend ways to kill it. You can have an evergreen ground cover that does not require mowing, watering, or fertilizing simply by letting the moss take over. And walking on moss does not hurt it and actually encourages its growth as long as you have on flat-soled shoes and do not drag your feet as you go.

Encouraging Moss

To speed up the process, kill the grass. That's what Dave Benner, of New Hope, Pennsylvania, did. When he moved to his two-acre property more than twenty-five years ago, there was a small area of lawn in the front. His plan was to create a garden requiring very little maintenance and no mowing. "I knew grass could not survive on very acid soil," he says, "so I applied sulfur to the entire area. In six weeks, the grass was dead." After four to five months of pulling weeds that showed up, he said, "I noticed a light green film completely covering the bare areas...it turned out to be moss." In the following years, he encouraged it by simply pulling out invading weeds and removing leaves in the fall. In two years the moss was well-established and, after two more years, only occasional weeds needed to be pulled.

Mosses are nonflowering, nonvascular, rootless plants that reproduce by spores. Instead of the vascular tissue which most plants have to allow fluids to flow through them, mosses have "ducts" which open when moistened and close to retain the moisture. Moss plants go completely dormant without moisture and become active as soon as they receive moisture again. When the spores land in a suitable environment—possessing shade, moisture, and good drainage—they branch out into miniscule filaments. This network of filaments on bare ground creates the green tint. As the moss continues to mature, it develops both male and female parts and eventually sheds more spores. Mature moss plants can also reproduce themselves from a single cell. The plants can be sheared off and the pieces scattered over a favorable environment. Soon each piece will begin to grow into a plant.

Benner's property is gently sloped from back to front and the house sits about halfway. The acre at the highest point in the back was left natural—the ground layer of leaves prevents weeds. Deer, whose population levels have created a real problem in his area, roam through the back, but a twenty-foot-high green mesh fence keeps them out of the rest of the property. The trees include tulip poplars (*Liriodendron tulipifera*), oaks (*Quercus* spp.), beech (*Fagus grandifolia*), and birch (*Betula* spp.). The understory includes Japanese maple (*Acer japonicum*), redbud (*Cercis canadensis*), fetterbush (*Leucothoë* spp.), lilac (*Syringa vulgaris*), Japanese skimmia (*Skimmia japonica*), azaleas, rhododendrons, pieris (*Pieris japonica* and *P. floribunda*), flowering raspberry (*Rubus odoratus*), and dwarf evergreens and boxwoods.

The rest of the ground is completely covered with perennial plants, including forty species of evergreen ground covers and numerous wildflowers. For the last ten years, he has had no weeds. "I do not water, fertilize, or prune," says Benner. "I avoided the need to prune by choosing plants for the right location and placing them so they could grow to their mature size with plenty of space." One native shrub that was present, mapleleaf viburnum (*Viburnum acerifolium*), he describes as "weedy" and has gradually removed and replaced it with other shrubs, leaving only one small patch.

The ground covers include climbing hydrangea (*Hydrangea anomala* subsp. *petiolaris*), two types of colchis ivy (*Hedera colchica*), English ivy (*H. helix*), club moss (*Lycopodium clavatum*), partridgeberry (*Mitchella repens*), barrenwort (*Epimedium* spp.), and Christmas fern (*Polystichum aerostichoides*). Wildflowers include bluets (*Hedyotis caerulea*), toad trillium (*Trillium cuneatum*), wild columbine (*Aquilegia canadensis*), creeping phlox (*Phlox stolonifera*), foamflower (*Tiarella cordifolia*), lady's slipper (*Cypripedium calceolus* var. *pubescens*), variegated fairy bells (*Disporum sessile* 'Variegatum'), shooting star (*Dodecatheon meadia*), fire pink (*Melandrium virginicum*), sweet woodruff (*Galium odoratum*), bloodroot (*Sanguinaria canadensis*), goldenstar (*Chrysogonum virginianum*), and Solomon's seal (*Polygonatum biflorum*). Two other perennials that are not American wildflowers but suit the setting and blend harmoniously are fumewort (*Corydalis lutea*) and many species of hosta.

Small, rust-colored gravel is used for the driveway that curves in front of the house and for the narrow footpaths that wind throughout the property. Some of the paths are laid with flagstone and others are moss-covered. Low stone walls hold the soil in various places, creating terraced levels from the back of the property to the small patio behind the house.

Mosses are indigenous to every part of the United States wherever the conditions include shade, moisture, and acid soil. If your yard is shade to part shade or has patches with those conditions, you can create a moss lawn.

I visited the home of Beverly Bremer in Atlanta, Georgia, where she and her landscape architect, Rick Anderson, have just begun their efforts to finish off what lawn grass remains and encourage the moss to take over. A grove of mature beech trees (*Fagus grandifolia*) covers a large mound in the front of the house that is built into a slope which drops off into a deeply wooded area below. "For years, the lawn maintenance crew has been trying to kill the moss," says Anderson, "and work feverishly to get the grass to grow." He finally realized that it made no sense and told them to stop. The moss is thriving but still has small blades of grass throughout.

"I prefer not to use herbicides," says Anderson, "but because we might have to resort to it in the parts where the grass is thickest, I have done a small test patch with glyphosate to see if it will totally kill the grass without harming the moss." Their plan is to hand pull as much as possible and only use the glyphosate in small targeted areas where the grass is thickest.

Mondo grass (*Ophiopogon japonicus*) and English ivy (*Hedera helix*) are used for ground cover close to the house. Ground-cover plants around the pool area, which is mostly sunny, include prostrate juniper (*Juniperus horizontalis*), Southern shield fern (*Dryopteris austriaca*), hay-scented fern (*Dennstaedtia punctilobula*), and plum yew (*Cephalotaxus drupacea*). Azaleas and rhododendrons are the understory for large pines in the front.

Another example of a moss lawn is part of the woodland garden of Barbara and Harold Herr of Wilmington, Delaware. When they moved to the site they preserved the native woodland flowers, shrubs, and trees that were already present and added the native mountain laurel (*Kalmia latifolia*), barrenwort (*Epimedium* spp.), which is not native but does not outcompete the natives, and lungwort (*Pulmonaria* spp.), which is also not native but not invasive. "Moss was already growing in a small area," says Barbara, "and there were bare spots where the lawn grass had died. We watered the bare areas and added patches of moss rescued from neighbors and friends who wanted to get rid of it." They brought back small patches from trips to New England and Mt. Rainier and added them to the area.

Diminutive bluets (*Hedyotis caerulea*) and taller spring beauties (*Claytonia virginica*) grow at the edges of the moss with a few springing up in it. Other ground covers include wild ginger (*Asarum virginianum*), woodland phlox (*Phlox divaricata*), creeping phlox (*P. stolonifera*), and Allegheny spurge (*Pachysandra procumbens*). They also removed a Japanese holly hedge near the front porch and replaced it with a bed of native wildflowers and ferns including Jacob's ladder (*Polemonium reptans*), bleeding heart (*Dicentra eximia*), and foamflower (*Tiarella cordifolia*).

Two weeds that have invaded the area at the back of the property near a creek are lesser celandine (*Ranunculus ficaria*) and garlic mustard (*Alliaria officinalis*). Both are European plants that infiltrate native woodlands and displace indigenous species. Celandine spreads by way of fleshy tuberous roots. "Celandine is a terrible pest," says Barbara. "We dig it out in the areas close to the house but cannot keep up with it in the low-maintenance area in the back." The battle against it is made even more difficult because the bordering neighbors do nothing to control it on their properties despite explanations about its destructive nature.

In the 1970s, Dr. Jack Biesencamp began encouraging his moss lawn in Hadenfield, New Jersey, which covered almost two acres. He sold the house recently and does not know what plans the new owners have for the landscape. Nevertheless, his expertise and experience in creating a moss lawn are of great benefit to those who are just beginning.

When he bought the house, the property had a thick stand of mature tulip poplars and oak trees. The soil was sandy and very acid. The moss was already present in patches and what little grass was there was dying. "I wanted to create a low-maintenance landscape," says Jack, "but I had no intention of cutting down the trees." He knew that the environment was exactly what moss wants so he just helped it thrive. By the fifth year the moss had filled in completely and was lush and thick.

The first few years, he would run the lawn mower over the areas of well-established moss to shave them and catch the clippings. He spread those pieces over an area where he wanted the moss to spread. Spores also spread themselves in the spring and he brought some mosses back from his trips. "Some weeds invaded the moss the first two to three years," he says, "but I just walked around and checked regularly, especially in the spring, and pulled them when they were very young and easy to remove."

Because that part of New Jersey has been settled for hundreds of years, many of the home landscapes and sides of the streets have beautiful, large, mature trees. Moss thrives nearly everywhere and, he says, "unfortunately, the city crews and homeowners keep trying to kill it." In the mid-1980s when news articles brought his moss lawn notoriety, thousands of people came on tours to see it. Some told him that they had trouble getting moss to work for them. "They were usually trying to keep it confined in small patches," says Jack, "but it really needs an expanse to become lush and healthy." He also says that even though moss loves snow cover, it does not like being covered with leaves since it requires good air circulation. He used a blower to remove the leaves each fall.

Other shrubs and trees on the property include paper birch (*Betula papyrifera*), hemlock (*Tsuga canadensis*), mountain laurel (*Kalmia latifolia*), and rhododendrons. He brought in boulders and good soil to create planters for perennials that he wanted to grow but knew would not make it in the barren New Jersey sand. Jack is currently creating a native plant landscape at his home in Boca Raton, Florida.

After four years, Jerry and Roberta Silbert of Guilford, Connecticut, successfully established a complete moss lawn on their one-and-a-half-acre property. Deeply shaded by hemlock, pine, and sugar maple, facing a lake which caused almost constant dampness, and having acid soil, the site was anathema for turfgrass. "I noticed that moss was growing on its own beneath the sparse grass," says Jerry, "so I began to wonder if I could create a moss lawn. I pulled out patches of grass and moss grew in to cover the bare area."

As he worked to spread the moss, he noticed that urine from the neighbor's dog killed it. He built a barrier of brush to keep him out. The hemlock needles also interfered with the growth of the moss, he says, "so periodically I lightly sweep them away with a broom." When he moved patches from other parts of the yard or from places where he gathered it, he noticed that they took hold and began to thrive better if he moistened the ground first.

Maintenance includes removing all the leaves in fall and pulling out the few birch tree seedlings that take root in the moss-covered ground. The Silberts are enchanted with their moss lawn and its quiet, evergreen beauty. Even though moss species are some of the most difficult plants to identify, Jerry has pinpointed at least twenty-five different types in his lawn.

Shady Front Yards

Another possibility for wooded, shady sites is to establish shrubs and woodland wildflowers beneath the trees, with pathways winding through. Moss may occur naturally in patches here and there but in less expansive areas than the moss lawns discussed above.

Mills Tandy of Austin, Texas, took this approach. When he moved to his house about seventeen years ago, the 100-by-150-foot lot contained an old hackberry tree (*Celtis laevigata*), a few pecan trees (*Carya illinoinensis*), some oaks (*Quercus virginiana* and *Q. macrocarpa*), and a lawn of St. Augustine grass. A botanist and professional nature photographer, he decided to create a landscape that would be low maintenance and would represent small versions of the native plant communities of Texas, mostly those that occur in shady conditions.

The front of the house is a woodland with a slope at the wood's edge next to the street and a moist forest close to the house. In the center where the tree canopy is open enough for the sun to come through is a prairie glade. In the moist forest area, Tandy uses drip irrigation to replicate the moist woodland environment that would occur along streams. He turns it on for an hour twice a week during the hottest part of the summer; no other part of the yard is irrigated. He doesn't have to replenish mulch because the leaves that fall from the trees do it for him.

As the trees have grown larger, causing a decrease in the amount of sun, the prairie area has grown smaller. It includes big bluestem (*Andropogon gerardii*), bushy bluestem (*A. glomeratus*), silver bluestem (*Bothriochloa saccharoides*), sideoats grama (*Bouteloua curtipendula*), Texas grama (*B. rigidiseta*), seep muhly (*Muhlenbergia reverchoni*), little bluestem (*Schizachyrium scoparium*), spiderwort (*Tradescantia* spp.), western ironweed (*Vernonia baldwini*), gray goldenrod (*Solidago nemoralis*), frostweed (*Verbesina virginica*), black-eyed Susan (*Rudbeckia hirta*), slenderleaf hymenoxys (*Hymenoxys linearifolia*), Maximilian sunflower (*Helianthus maximilani*), blue mist flower (*Eupatorium coelestinum*), Indian blanket (*Gaillardia pulchella*), purple coneflower (*Echinacea purpurea*), Texas aster (*Aster texanus*), heath aster (*A. ericoides*), straggler daisy (*Calliptocarpus vialis*), Indian paintbrush (*Castilleja indivisa*), prairie paintbrush (*Castilleja purpurea*), obedient plant (*Physostegia virginiana*), white heliotrope (*Heliotropium tenellum*), puccoon (*Lithospermum incisum*), butterfly weed (*Asclepias tuberosa*), green milkweed (*A. viridis*), evening primrose (*Oenothera speciosa*), gaura (*Gaura lindheimeri*), western primrose (*Calylophus hartweggi*), wine cup (*Callirhoe digitata*), and Turk's-cap lily (*Malvaviscus drummondii*).

Through the years the collection of species has grown to 300; he has added numerous shade-loving perennials, vines, ferns, shrubs, and small understory trees. Because of the leaf layer, the soil is fairly loose and moist so he does not have to amend the soil when he plants. He waters the new addition regularly until it is well-established. Some native plants, such as box elder (*Acer negundo*) and baby blue-eyes (*Nemophila phacelioides*) have shown up on their own. Some of the smaller trees and shrubs include redbud (*Cercis canadensis*), Wright acacia (*Acacia wrightii*), mock orange (*Philadelphus argenteus*), Texas hawthorn (*Crataegus texana*), apache plume (*Fallugia paradoxa*), Texas persimmon (*Diospyros texana*), Texas silverbell (*Styrax texana*), eastern red cedar (*Juniperus virginiana*), mountain cedar (*J. ashei*), spice bush (*Lindera benzoin*), agarita (*Berberis trifoliolata*), wax myrtle (*Myrica cerifera*), Texas buckeye (*Aesculus arguta*), and American beautyberry (*Callicarpa americana*).

"Many of the plants self-sow themselves around the property," says Mills, "but I don't have invasive plants showing up except for Japanese honeysuckle which I had to kill to get rid of." Fallen branches and prunings are piled in a large area to compost slowly. When thoroughly rotted, it is added as mulch around plants or used for a new planting.

Another example of adding native plants beneath a canopy of existing trees is the landscape of Rich and Marion Patterson, of Cedar Rapids, Iowa. They began transforming their one-acre suburban lot in 1979 after hearing Lorrie Otto of Milwaukee, Wisconsin, who has been called the "high priestess of natural landscaping," make one of the statements that she is famous for: "Anyone who mows their yard ought to be put in jail."

The Pattersons found some fescue grasses beneath the existing six white oaks (*Quercus alba*) and a few hickories (*Carya ovata*) that were there. "We just stopped mowing to see what other plants might appear," says Rich, director of the local nature center. "The ground on which our home is located used to be oak savannah," he says, "and given a chance, native plants will often revive, since their seeds are in the soil 'bank.'" Unlike some newer housing developments where the topsoil is scraped off and taken away, the Pattersons live in an older neighborhood where this was not done. Oak savannah, also called oak barrens, is the name for an ecological region with vegetation that is a transition between deep forest and prairie. Scattered groups of oak and hickory trees occur here and there through the same grasses and wildflowers that dominate the tallgrass prairie. The appearance is park-like, with large open areas between the groups of trees. Today, little savannah remains because it was all destroyed for agricultural purposes.

The Pattersons, knowing what vegetation used to be there, could make selections appropriate to the site. They added native shrubs and wildflowers—the understory layer that was missing due to continuous mowing. They planted highbush cranberry (*Viburnum trilobum*) and shade-tolerant trees such as basswood (*Tilia americana*) and sugar maple (*Acer saccharum*), which will eventually be as high as the oaks, and smaller ones like pagoda dogwood (*Cornus alternifolia*). Since they did not start from bare ground, and the falling leaves through the years had served as a natural mulch, they were able to plant without extensive soil preparation. "We do not have to water except to help new plants get established when we first plant them," says Rich, "and our landscape thrives without the use of pesticides or fertilizers."

Three years after they stopped mowing, colonies of Solomon's seal (*Polygonatum canaliculatum*), wild strawberries (*Fragaria virginiana*), lady fern (*Athyrium filix-femina*), wild ginger (*Asarum canadense*), and wood violets (*Viola blanda* and *V. sororia*) appeared. The area being too shady for most of the native grasses of the savannah, the only one that has shown up is Pennsylvania sedge (*Carex pensylvanica*). They added wild sweet William (*Phlox maculata*) and bergamot (*Monarda fistulosa*). Two invasive exotic plants that have shown up and are weeded out are gill-over-the-ground (*Glecoma hederacea*) and garlic mustard (*Alliaria officinalis*).

The Pattersons have kept a lawn area in back for their son to practice baseball on and there is a small front area, but overall the lawn has been reduced by half. "We don't fuss with the lawn area," Marion explains, "we just cut whatever is there—some of it is turfgrass but there is also clover and probably some lawn weeds." When they mow, they use the highest setting for the blade. The leaves are left where they fall in the restored woodland areas and the ones raked from the lawn go to the garden for mulch.

With the restoration of this small woodland, the Pattersons have watched the return of rose-breasted grosbeaks, warblers, waxwings, wood ducks, barred owls, hawks, pileated woodpeckers, wild turkeys, tree frogs, toads, and red foxes. They see which plants thrive and which decline during a drought and vice versa in a wet year. They have not only the satisfaction and joy of restoring a native woodland but also privacy. A neighbor's home only a few dozen feet away cannot be seen from their porch or backyard. However, they say, "there's a fine line between privacy and claustrophobia, so we maintain our landscape to keep a blend of shrubs and open vistas."

Ground Covers and Front-Yard Gardens

"Ground cover" is a term that describes plants which can be planted together in large masses to create a uniform layer. Although some plants that can be used successfully in this manner are three to five feet high, in selecting plants for lawn alternatives the focus is on low-growing species. These particular plants stay low, spread by creeping over the ground, and, once well-established, provide the same landscape benefit as a lawn, that is, a low expanse of vegetation serving as a foreground and balancing tall elements such as trees and structures and medium ones such as shrub groupings or perennial borders.

Some of these special plants are evergreen, while others go dormant in the cold season. Many will be covered with blooms at certain times, whereas others, which are used because of their interesting foliage or grasslike appearance, will have inconspicuous flowers or none at all. In general, stands of ground covers are established by spacing individual plants four to twelve inches apart (depending on the size and rate of growth of the species used) and watering regularly until they are established. A light mulch is placed between the plants to prevent weeds from sprouting, and annuals may be planted as filler the first season if desired.

Plants that can be used as ground covers may come from any of the following groups—shrubs, perennials, herbs, and ornamental grasses. This chapter includes wide-ranging examples from the yards of homeowners who have used ground covers as an alternative to the front lawn. The selection begins with examples that feature one particular kind of plant, such as herbs or heathers, and concludes with front-yard gardens that combine all types of low-growing plants. All of these lawn alternatives are for full sun with perhaps some filtered shade. If your front yard is heavily shaded, see Chapter 5 for suggestions. As with other alternatives to the lawn, the key ingredients for success and low maintenance are selecting species that are suited to the amount of rainfall and type of soil at your location and preparing the site thoroughly before you plant.

Important questions to ask yourself when you review the ground-cover plants listed in Table 2 (pages 47–63) are: Do I want the plants to be green throughout the year? Am I willing to be patient and wait the required three years for the plants to fill in and provide a complete cover? Can I afford the cost to purchase sufficient plants to cover my entire site the first year or should I do a patch at a time? Is this a plant that I have seen used successfully in my area as a long-lived, dependable mass planting? Is part of the area that I want to cover in the shade? If so, what plants can tolerate some shade and full sun as well or do I need a combination of plants?

Research or display plantings of ground covers have been done in some states to evaluate their appearance and water requirements over an extended period of time. I visited the display garden at the State Botanical Garden of Georgia in Athens which was installed in 1985 by Classic Groundcovers, Inc., a wholesale nursery that grows varieties from twenty-five plant families. The purpose of the display area is to show low-growing plants that can be used in place of turf in the Southeast and how they appear in massed groups. The site is slightly sloping with mature oaks and chestnuts here and there so that the plants are in filtered shade most of the day but do receive periods of full sun.

The only maintenance of this display had been cutting back the overly vigorous species that threatened to take over the entire area, watering only in the hottest, driest part of the summer, and pulling out the few weeds and tree seedlings that showed up. Unwanted plants were able to sow themselves in the groups that formed a loose cover and in bare spots where a particular species had declined.

Overly vigorous species that had been cut back regularly to keep them in bounds were periwinkle (*Vinca minor*), bigleaf periwinkle (*Vinca major*), and St. John's-wort (*Hypericum calycinum*). These types, which spread by underground rhizomes, would be useful only in large areas where their aggressive habit would be desirable. They would not work in combinations with other ground covers. Wintercreeper (*Euonymus fortunei*) had filled in well and had a neat appearance. This plant spreads by the stems rooting as they trail along the ground. However, naturalists in Illinois have found this plant to be spreading invasively into natural areas and proliferating to such an extent that it crowds out native ground-cover species. They think that the plant is spread by birds who eat the seeds from plants at homesites. Before you select this plant for your yard, check with naturalists in your region to find out if it has become an invader in your state's natural areas.

All of the liriope and mondo grass species in the display looked good. *Liriope muscari*, which spreads slowly by underground rhizomes, had filled in the best. *Liriope muscari* cultivars grow in a clump form and require a layer of mulch between them for weed control. Liriope is evergreen, has straplike leaves, reaches a height of ten to twelve inches, and performs well in southern areas. Mondo grass (*Ophiopogon japonicus*) is similar, but has thinner, more grasslike foliage and grows only six inches high. These evergreen clumping plants spread by underground stolons. A dwarf cultivar (*O. japonicus* 'Nana') which reaches only three inches in height is an especially good alternative to turf.

Two other ground covers that impressed me with their neat appearance and full coverage were carpet bugleweed (*Ajuga reptans*) and *Sedum sarmentosum*.

The use of ground covers and other lawn alternatives is widespread in California, the state that often leads the nation in cultural trends. Seven years of water rationing there, especially in low-elevation areas, has inspired the reduction of "just-for-show" front lawns. Another factor is having a climate that enables people to enjoy being outside throughout the year. Various horticulturists with the University of California extension service have conducted ground-cover trials to evaluate the plants for various characteristics—water requirements, density of coverage, year-round appearance, and resistance to weed invasion. In a trial of twenty-four species near San Francisco, the four top performers were creeping myoporum (*Myoporum parvifolium*), woolly thyme (*Thymus pseudolanuginosus*), dwarf fleece-flower (*Polygonum cuspidatum compactum*), and snow-in-summer (*Cerastium tomentosum*). Ivies (*Hedera* spp.), bugleweed (*Ajuga* spp.), and periwinkle (*Vinca* spp.)—which do well in climates with regular rainfall—required as much water as a bluegrass lawn and thus are not acceptable in dry climates such as the Southwest and California.

According to a San Francisco Bay area guide to ground-cover water use, published by the University of California extension service, some commonly used ground covers that require the least supplemental water are rosemary, myoporum, lantana, dwarf coyote brush (*Baccharis pilularis* 'Twin Peaks'), and low-growing cultivars of ice plant (*Lampranthus* spp.) and African trailing daisy (*Osteospermum* spp.).

Herbs and Creeping Perennials

Single species of herbs or a mixture of ones that complement each other may be used effectively as a lawn substitute in many parts of the country. Single species that work well are mother-of-thyme (*Thymus praecox arcticus*), creeping thyme (*T. serpyllum*), woolly thyme (*T. pseudolanuginosus*), germander (*Teucrium chamaedrys* 'Prostratum' and *T. marjoricum* 'Cossonii'), coast strawberry (*Fragaria chiloensis*), dichondra (*Dichondra micrantha*), yarrow (*Achillea millefolium*), chamomile (*Anthemis nobilis*), and pussytoes (*Antennaria dioica* or *A. neglecta*). Two creeping perennials that spread to create a low carpet are treasure flower (*Gazania rigens*) and snow-in-summer (*Cerastium tomentosum*).

The historic Lummis House near Los Angeles has a thriving yarrow lawn. It is part of a two-acre garden designed by landscape architect Robert Perry of the Department of Landscape Architecture, California Polytechnical Institute, Pomona. The drought-tolerant landscape includes California natives, wildflowers, and plants with origins in climates similar to that of southern California. The yarrow seed was sown in February 1987 and the area was kept moist until it germinated. By May, the fine-textured, ferny foliage of these plants had filled in completely.

The foliage grows only a few inches high and the plant spreads by underground rhizomes. If uncut, the flower (white or red) stalks reach fifteen inches high. Mowing keeps the plants low and forces them to spread out rather than up. The Lummis lawn is mowed four or five times a year and watered twice a week in the hottest part of the summer for about twenty minutes. Volunteers pull weeds twice a year but say that there are not very many. Yarrow's ability to withstand foot traffic has been proven by the hundreds of visitors, especially during special events, who walk across the "lawn."

Yarrow is a widely adapted plant and can be considered for a wild lawn in most parts of the country except for the subtropical tip of Florida, Hawaii, and the coldest zones of the northern parts of the country and Alaska. Because of its adaptability, it is included in all of the ecology lawn mixes developed by Nichols Garden Nursery (see page 112) and can be used alone or blended with other species.

Another low-growing herb that spreads rapidly and can be used successfully as a lawn alternative is snow-in-summer. An aggressive plant that spreads by underground runners, it forms a mat of silvery leaves and is best used alone. This plant will not do well in areas with heat and high humidity combined but, on the other hand, will be overly aggressive in areas with plentiful rainfall and well-drained soil. Shear the plants after blooming and one other time during the year to keep them from looking straggly.

I talked with gardeners in New Mexico, California, and Pennsylvania who have used this plant (also a widely adapted species) as a lawn. In Santa Fe, New Mexico, garden designer Julia Berman used snow-in-summer in a blend with blue grama grass (*Bouteloua gracilis*) accented with several penstemons (*Penstemon pinnifolius*, *P. strictus*, and *P. ambiguus*) and yarrow (*Achillea tageta* 'Moonshine').

Dichondra (*Dichondra micrantha*), sometimes called penny grass, is a prostrate herb with tiny round green leaves that can only be used in the warmest climates of the country—Florida and California. It is important not to confuse this plant with one that has similar, although much larger, leaves and is a pest in Florida called pennywort or dollar weed (*Hydrocotyle sibthorpioides*). A dichondra lawn can be started from seed and once established requires no care. Only two inches tall, it requires no mowing.

Charles Stein, who lives near Pasadena, California, has a garden of ground covers around his home. Besides the dichondra lawn, the other plants massed together in one large expanse include trailing pink verbena (*Verbena peruviana*), blue fescue (*Festuca ovina* 'Blue Finch'), sageleaf rockrose (*Cistus salviifolius*), *Rosmarinus officinalis*, and *Artemisia* 'Powis Castle'. Caraway thyme (*Thymus herba-barona*) is used alone in a large area by the entrance with an interesting small, drought-tolerant, evergreen shrub from New Zealand (*Leptospermum scoparium* 'Ruby Glow') in its midst.

At a home near the coast in Yachats, Oregon, the entire front "lawn" is beach strawberry (*Fragaria chiloensis*), a plant indigenous to the Pacific northwest. The owner, J. W. Gerdemann, explains that this plant just showed up when they moved there twelve years ago. "At first we weeded it out, but then we recognized its attributes and just let it go." The plant requires well-drained soil and does best in full sun. Gerdemann says it creeps underneath shrubs and trees but once the shade becomes too dense, it declines.

In the spring, beach strawberry is covered with white blossoms which are followed by small red strawberries. "The fruit is delicious but just too delicate to pick and keep," says Gerdemann, "so we just pick and enjoy them as we walk through the garden. The birds like them, too." The plant is evergreen and does not require mowing, fertilizer, or water. The only maintenance required is pulling the occasional weeds that show up, but there have been less and less as the years have gone by. This tough, attractive lawn alternative not only withstands foot traffic but actually becomes more dense and compact as a result.

"All I have to do to establish the strawberry plants in a new location," says Gerdemann, "is clear the ground of vegetation by smothering it with heavy mulch or plastic." In a year, it will fill in the area. In the shadiest areas of the property, he used a similar technique to encourage moss. "Removing weeds and unwanted grass gives the moss a chance to spread," he says, "so I have a moss lawn in the shady spots." Two other desirable native plants that have introduced themselves are trout lily (*Erythronium revolutum*) and club moss (a species of *Lycopodium*).

Rita Buchanan, an herb specialist, has created herbal lawns using a combination of low-growing types with grasses. In an article about herbal lawns in *Herb Companion*, she recommends using 50 percent grass and 50 percent herbs, and if you want a neat, flat appearance you can mow them every week or so. The lawns are easy to maintain and withstand foot traffic well. The herbs' fragrance is released when you mow or walk on them.

To begin transforming an existing lawn into an herbal lawn, she says, withhold water and reduce mowing frequency so that more than half of the height of the grass is cut at each mowing. This encourages herbs that commonly exist in lawns in the temperate areas of the United States such as yarrow, clover, and potentilla. You can also remove patches of turf and plug in small herb plants in spring or fall, or whenever the time of most abundant rainfall is in your area. Her recommendations for persistent herbs that can take being mowed at a height of two inches are *Ajuga reptans*, bird's-foot trefoil (*Lotus corniculatus*), Roman chamomile (*Chamaemelum nobile*), dwarf cinquefoil (*Potentilla canadensis* and *P. reptans*), white or Dutch clover (*Trifolium repens*), pearly everlasting (*Anaphalis margaritacea*), pennyroyal (*Mentha pulegium*), pineapple weed (*Matricaria matricarioides*), pussytoes (*Antennaria neglecta*), scarlet pimpernel (*Anagallis arvensis*), speedwell (*Veronica officinalis*), wild strawberry (*Fragaria virginiana* or *F. vesca*), sweet vernal grass (*Anthoxanthum odoratum*), creeping thyme (*Thymus serphyllum*), sweet violet (*Viola odorata*), and yarrow (*Achillea millefolium*).

Three herbs that can be grown as lawn substitutes that do best in mild, damp climates are lavender (*Lavandula spica*), chamomile (*Anthemis nobilis*), and peppermint (*Mentha piperita*).

Herbs that require little water can be combined with one or two ornamental grasses and drought-tolerant perennials in warmer parts of the country to create a front lawn that blooms in succession throughout the season. This approach was used by Dennis Shaw, a landscape designer from Santa Barbara, for a low hillside area adjacent to a home in Montecito, California. He used rosemary (*Rosmarinus officinalis*), gray and green santolina (*Santolina chamaecyparissus* and *S. virens*), French and Spanish lavenders (*Lavandula dentata* and *L. stoechas*), statice (*Limonium* spp.), a native sage (*Salvia clevelandii* 'Alan Chickering'), and fountain grass (*Pennisetum setaceum* 'Rubrum') to provide an overall effect of green and gray. Blue and violet blooms appear in spring, followed by yellow in early summer. The feathery pink plumes of the grass appear in midsummer and become dominant by fall. In winter they are cut back and the garden is green and gray until spring brings on the blooms again. The garden is watered about every three weeks (when there is no rain) to keep it at its best, and plants are trimmed back when blooms have faded.

Heaths and Heathers

These low-growing evergreen shrubs of the *Calluna* and *Erica* genera come from native habitats throughout the British Isles, North Africa, and western parts of Russia. Many of the hardy species are suited to the United States, in fact, there are introduced, naturalized stands along the Atlantic Coast, particularly in Maine and Massachusetts, and along the upper West Coast. By choosing varieties that are cold-tolerant and more adaptable to soil conditions, you can group them together to create a naturalized mass planting in place of a lawn.

Heaths and heathers require full sun and acid, well-drained soil. This means they need to be in sandy soil that has peat moss or compost worked into it. They do not like added nutrients or being overwatered. Select varieties that are low-growing and have a spreading habit. Sketch a plan on paper of how you will arrange them, figuring three plants for every three square feet.

One of the most spectacular features of these plants is the range of foliage color. With good planning, a heather garden can have changing foliage color year round, including green, silvery-gray, yellow, orange, and many shades of red, in addition to the blooming times which come in succession through the seasons.

Although they can be grown as far north as zone 3 and as far south as zone 11, at those extremes, heaths and heathers will require extra care and attention. Since at least part of the purpose of replacing the turfgrass is to create a low-maintenance cover with plants that want to grow in your region and climate, do not consider these plants for this type of use unless you are in zones 4 to 6 and have acid, well-drained soil. Gardeners in zones 7 and 8 where the summers are not long, the soil is well-drained, and the humidity is high would most likely have success as well.

Alice Knight of Heaths & Heathers Nursery in Elma, Washington, reports that many of her customers say they are "digging up more lawn" to plant more heathers. She also says that in her own landscape there is an area that her family has loosely dubbed the "heather lawn." Over the years the heathers have sown themselves there and they mow it regularly. "It is a nice mossylike area," she says, "much like I picture the moors of Scotland after cattle have grazed." She recommends selecting cultivars of *Erica carnea*, *E. tetralix*, and *Calluna vulgaris* to get started because they are some of the most hardy and easy to grow. Of the hundreds of cultivars available, some will tolerate slightly wet or slightly alkaline conditions. Most important, the plants cannot be allowed to dry out at any time; they would not be a good choice as a lawn alternative in places that experience long periods without rainfall.

Calluna vulgaris, the species commonly referred to as heather, includes cultivars from four to twenty inches high and ones that spread two feet or more. Some form hummocks, others are spreading, and some grow in a compact shape. The foliage itself is appealing, not only in varying shades of green, but also yellow, with some that change to orange, red, or bronze in winter. The flowers, which appear in late summer to autumn, may be white, mauve, lavender, lilac-pink, crimson, rose-pink, or salmon. Most cultivars do not require pruning after the first two years but, if needed, it is best done in early spring before new growth begins. The prostrate and low-creeping varieties will not require pruning except to remove branches with winter damage.

Using heathers with some heaths mixed in to replace a lawn has been recommended for years by Kate Herrick of Rock Spray Nursery, Truro, Massachusetts. She suggests blending in a few of the *Erica* species, which have glossy green foliage, as a contrast to the wide range of colored foliage of the *Calluna* species. If plants are placed three per three square feet, within three to five years they will fill in completely. Some of the lower-growing cultivars are: 'Alba Ridgida' (bright green foliage, white flowers); 'Golden Carpet' (yellow-gold to orange-red foliage, light pink flowers); 'Foxhollow Wanderer' (dark green foliage, purple flowers); 'John F. Letts' (gold, red-tipped foliage, lavender flowers); 'Multicolor' (gold foliage, pale mauve flowers); 'Saint Nick' (dark green foliage, lilac pink flowers); 'Sister Anne' (gray-green foliage, pink flowers); and 'White Lawn' (bright green foliage, white flowers).

Spring heath (*Erica carnea*) flowers in winter or very early spring and most cultivars reach about six inches in height. These plants will spread over about a three-foot diameter area in three years, but the more vigorous spreaders may be the best choices to cover a large expanse. Cultivars of that type suggested by Dorothy M. Metheny in her book *Hardy Heather Species* include: 'Springwood Pink', 'Springwood White', 'Foxhollow Fairy', 'Loughrigg', 'Pink Spangles', and 'Sherwoodii' (also called 'Sherwood Creeping').

This group can stand some alkalinity in the soil. The only trimming that may be necessary is to keep a plant in bounds or to renew a very old plant (ten years or more). This must be done at the end of the flowering season because the plants set buds for the next spring during the summer.

Plants in the crossleaf heath group (*Erica tetralix*) can be grown in the usual well-drained acid setting of most heaths and heathers, but will also succeed in wetter locations. Their native habitat is acid soil in bogs, wet heaths, and pine woods. Height ranges from six to twelve inches and the blooms appear from June to October. Most have foliage in shades of gray to gray-green and the flower colors include white, magenta, pink, and salmon.

Planting Heather

Heather can be planted in spring, summer, or fall as long as you pay attention to watering. When you place the plants into the prepared area, unless the soil is moist from a recent rainfall, water them deeply and add a pine bark or pine needle mulch about three inches thick around each one. If the soil is already moist, wait a day or two and water. Then water weekly for the first two months. Always check the soil before you water, especially if it has rained. If it feels cool and moist, wait a few days. Overwatering will kill heather.

Gradually wean the plants from supplemental watering. Once they are well-established, they will tolerant periods of drought. Pull any weeds that show up between the plants and replace the mulch annually.

Young plants, during the first five years, will benefit from annual pruning in early spring to promote bushiness. Cut back the branches just below the old flowers on species of *Calluna vulgaris*. You can cut back farther, if you wish, to improve the shape of the plant. New growth will develop from the point where you cut. The winter-blooming *Erica carnea* species do not have to be pruned at all, unless you want to prevent their spread or to remove branches that have suffered winter injury. If you trim them, do it right after they bloom. Most of the low-growing spreading types will not require pruning. You can use hand pruners or electric hedge shears for pruning, but Kate Herrick, who prunes hundreds of plants each spring, says sheep shears work the best.

In extremely cold climates (zones 3 and 4), young plants may need some protection. Snow cover is ideal but not always reliable. You can place evergreen boughs over plants like a tent. Or, after the ground is frozen, cover the plants with pine needles or straw.

One of the best examples of a heather garden in the United States is that of Jim and Beverly Thompson in northern California.

About ten years ago, Jim ordered a few plants from Heaths & Heathers just to see what they would do. They performed so well in the sandy soil and moist climate of his coastal location that he kept adding more and more. He has tried more than 250 varieties. His collection, planted in mounded raised beds with large groups weaving into each other forming irregular patterns of color, includes more than 100 varieties of *Erica*, *Calluna*, and *Daboecia*. Narrow, mulched footpaths lead through the mosaic of yellows, oranges, reds, greens, and grays.

When he finds a plant that he likes, Jim takes cuttings to increase it. As soon as there are enough, he plants them out to start a new bed or grouping. He spaces them eighteen inches apart or "about three plants per square yard." He mulches around them with wood chips and only has to weed the first year. By the third year they have completely filled in the bed. "The heathers thrive mostly on their own once they are established," Jim says, "and I only water during long dry spells (from May to October) once every three weeks with an overhead sprinkler for one hour.

"My house was built in a development that used to be a meadow, so all that was growing around the house was some straggly grass," says Jim. "The first thing I did was dig shallow trenches for pathways and mound the soil into raised beds." He added compost to them and began planting. He prunes the *Calluna vulgaris* species once a year with electric hedge shears to remove spent blossoms (but not in a straight line; he cuts branches at different lengths to maintain the natural irregular profile of the plant). *Erica carnea* species do not really need to be trimmed unless you want to keep them in bounds, he says.

"Heather is an excellent substitute for a lawn," says Jim, "but there is another plant that works great too—bearberry." He planted bearberry (*Arctostaphylos uva-ursi*) as a ground cover in an area twenty-five by fifty feet. "It is evergreen, will take light foot traffic, and starts easy from cuttings," says Jim.

Heathers for Colder Climes

For gardeners in colder regions, some native plants that are similar to heather might be tried in a massed planting. *Cassiope* and *Phyllodoce*, found in mountain habitats and northern latitudes including Alaska, are low-growing evergreen shrubs with tiny leaves. Often referred to as "mountain heather," *Cassiope* species are dwarf shrubs ranging from one to twelve inches tall. The foliage varies from gray-green to dark green and the blooms, in spring, are usually white. They need to be in a location where they will be covered by snow in winter and the soil will be cool and moist in summer. They require locations with part shade at higher altitudes. Native species are *C. lycopodiodes* and *C. mertensiana*.

Phyllodoce species, referred to as "mountain heath," are also low-growing evergreen shrubs ranging from six to fourteen inches tall. The colors of the flowers, which usually appear in midsummer, may be white, greenish, yellow, rose-pink, or purplish. Native species include *P. aleutica*, *P. caerula*, *P. empetriformis*, and *P. glanduliflora*. Also plants of high altitudes, they require acid, well-drained soil that never dries out. In the mountains these plants may be found in open, sunny areas as well as shady ones. But gardeners who have tried to grow them at lower elevations have learned that part shade is necessary to maintain the soil moisture that they require.

Sedums and Sempervivums

Among the large group of sedums, commonly called stonecrops, and sempervivums (called houseleeks) are numerous low-growing, evergreen cultivars that can be planted together to create a succulent "lawn." Although you will not be able to romp on it, small footpaths winding through will allow you and visitors to your home to enjoy the plants up close. Both plant groups can tolerate cold up to zone 4 and withstand heat through zone 8, but only where they have excellent drainage. They will rot in heavy soil or where they receive too much water. They need gravelly, sandy soil. Plant them in full sun, but in areas where summer temperatures reach 100°F or more, the sempervivums will need some shade in the afternoon. You can start your sedum and sempervivum "lawn" with plants, doing small areas at a time, or with seed.

One of the easiest sedums to grow and the one that most people are familiar with is goldmoss (*Sedum acre*), which is three inches tall, has light green foliage, and forms a dense mat as it creeps over the ground. Beginning in late spring and continuing for a few weeks, the plant is covered with tiny yellow flowers. Stone orphine (*S. reflexum*) also has yellow flowers which appear later in the summer. It is a creeping plant with bluish leaves that reaches six to eight inches in height. Another popular sedum that works well as a ground cover (too well, some people think) is 'Dragon's Blood', a cultivar of two-row stonecrop (*S. spurium*). These plants are about five to six inches tall and spread quickly to eighteen inches wide. The foliage has a purplish bronze cast to it and the flowers are deep red. Two other evergreen species that spread by stolons to form a mat that is two to three inches high are *S. anglicum* and *S. brevifolium*. The first has green foliage, the second gray flushed with red; both have white flowers in summer.

There are three native sedums that will work well for ground-cover use: lance-leaved stonecrop (*Sedum lanceolatum*), covering an area six inches square, with green leaves in summer that turn bronze in fall, and yellow flowers; whorled stonecrop (*S. ternatum*), with a four- by eighteen-inch spread, creeping habit, and white flowers; and *S. spathulifolium*, with a five- by twelve-inch spread, creeping habit, broad blue-green leaves, and yellow flowers. All of the sedums can be increased by taking cuttings in spring or summer, rooting them (takes about two weeks), and then planting them in their new location; or you can just take divisions in spring or summer and plant them in their new location.

The common houseleek (*Sempervivum tectorum*), familiar across the country, is also called hen-and-chicks because tiny replicas (chicks) arise on stolons growing out from the large main rosettes (hens) of the plant. This species has hybridized with many others, producing innumerable named forms and hybrids. The foliage colors are wide-ranging, including silvery white, light green, reds, purples, and pinks. The rosettes range in size from four inches to miniature one-inch ones. According to Micki Crozier of Country Cottage in Sedgwick, Kansas, a small sedum and sempervivum nursery, the little ones are the hardest to grow, as are the cobweb types (*S. arachnoideum*) which form a dense webbing of gray threads from leaf to leaf.

The species that she recommends as "easiest to grow" include many named cultivars of *Sempervivum tectorum*, *S. giuseppi*, and *S. zelebori*, and members of two other succulent groups—*Jovibarba hirta* and *J. sobolifera*, and *Orostachys boehmeri* (sometimes mistakenly sold under the name *O. furusei* or *O. iwarange*) and *O. malacophyllus*. Some of the *Sempervivum tectorum* cultivars include 'Alluring', 'Alpha', 'Cleveland Morgan', 'Dame Arsac', 'Firebird', 'Hot Peppermint', 'King George', 'Old Rose', 'Quintessence', 'Reginald Malby', 'Sanford's Hybrid', and 'Superama'.

All of the houseleeks send up a tall coarse-looking flower stem from the main rosette. Usually the flowering rosette will die, leaving the smaller ones that formed around it to fill in and grow larger. You can increase an area covered by the plants by simply removing the "chicks" and planting them where you want them to spread.

Micki grows more than 650 varieties; most of the ground around her home is covered with raised beds of semps and sedums with grass walkways between them. "Most people that I know who grow these plants in massed groups, use raised beds," she says. "Without the beds, the only place it would work to plant them in an expanse as a substitute for a lawn would be on a site that has sandy, well-drained soil or in a rock garden."

"I started my semp and sedum area by making one raised bed at a time," says Micki, "I created the first beds using cement blocks in long rectangles and filling them with sandy soil from an old chicken house site and topping it with coarse sand." A few years ago when a church near her town replaced their old limestone foundation, she says, "I was lucky enough to get the rocks." These rocks combined with the ones that she "has hauled home for years from the Flint Hills area just east of Wichita," have been used to replace most of the cement blocks around the beds for a more attractive display.

"I believe a whole lawn could be replaced with raised beds," Micki says, using a blend of "rock, bricks, wood, or other interesting local materials" for borders. She says a bed used as a border could be kept low in the front, only a few inches, with a gradual slope up toward the back to about eight inches or so.

Janis Noyes of Squaw Mountain Gardens in Estacada, Oregon, agrees with Micki about the need for raised beds or a rock garden. Her yard is planted with a blend of succulents, grasses, and perennials. The succulents are planted in raised beds and in level areas that have sandy soil. Rocks are used as accents and to ensure good drainage.

"We killed a large part of our mown lawn by applying glyphosate herbicide two times," says Janis, "and then we tilled to a depth of about eight inches." A four-to-six-inch layer of compost was spread and tilled in. "We used rocks to create raised beds and for accents," she continues, "and then planted sedums and sempervivums along with some perennials and small conifers." The featured sedums include *Sedum anglicum*, *S. spurium* 'Bronze Carpet', *S. spurium* 'Pink Jewel', and *S. sexangular* 'Guillomoth'; and sempervivums include 'Red Devil' and 'Frost and Flame.'

Starting a Sedum Lawn

If you have any doubt about whether your soil is sandy and well-drained enough, use raised beds with pathways between them. Sedums are particularly suited to rock garden conditions. They like gravelly, sandy soil, and some of the species like to creep in the niches between stones. For this reason, and for the interesting contrast of texture and color, you may want to add well-placed boulders here and there in your sedum/sempervivum "lawn." Very large ones should be partially buried.

Both sedums and sempervivums can be started indoors from seed. Once they are of transplanting size, move them outdoors after all danger of frost is past. Sedums will take two years to reach flowering size; sempervivums will take three. Since it is so easy to root cuttings or take divisions from both plant groups, you may find it easier to begin by buying enough plants to get started and gradually increasing the area as you have enough new plants to expand.

Space sedums six to eight inches apart; the creeping types will fill in fairly quickly. The beanlike leaves will root in loose, moist soil and form new plants. You can also increase sedums by taking cuttings or divisions in spring or summer and replanting; they will root fairly quickly. Space sempervivums at least six inches from each other or from other sedums or rocks to allow room for the rosettes to form around the main plant. Although they do not spread as quickly as most sedum varieties, they create "baby" plants on stolons around the main rosette. These can be pulled off and replanted where you want the plants to spread.

The only long-term maintenance needed will be to remove weeds that might show up before the plants have completely filled in an area. And, if some of the more vigorous spreaders tend to overtake one part of the garden, you may need to trim off pieces and move them elsewhere or give them to friends.

Front-Yard Gardens

I started to call this section "Cottage Gardens," but decided against it because that wonderful style is truly a British tradition. Although the approach of blending annuals, perennials, bulbs, vegetables, and other flowering plants with a few shrubs and small trees is the same, the appearance is different, especially when the gardener chooses mostly American natives. Although features such as benches, small greenhouses, beehives, or trellises may be part of a true cottage garden, a greensward of any kind would never be. It is this latter characteristic that makes it an alternative to the front lawn, though it is a choice best made only by those who want to be directly involved in gardening everyday.

The examples in this section are unique to the gardener and the site, and reveal the incredible diversity and individuality that is within the reach of every homeowner. This approach is a gift to everyone on the street, but in most cases, it is the one alternative to the front lawn that I discuss which will require daily attention in the beginning and, depending on the plants you choose, could continue to require your involvement at least during the peak growing season. If you like to golf or go boating on the weekends, this would not be the option for you. Creating and taking care of a front garden is for devoted gardeners who enjoy "directing" the display—planting, removing spent blooms, cutting back plants, mulching, tending to bare soil, pruning, and watering (for newly planted annuals, plants that are becoming established, or to remove dust from foliage in dry climates).

The front-yard garden of Trudi Temple of Hinsdale, Illinois, literally stops traffic. A 130-foot-long bed reaching thirty feet back from the curb to the narrow, curved drive in front of the house is filled with blooming perennials and ornamental grasses. An open-work iron fence divides the bed, and the tallest plants are grouped on either side of it. Plants of gradually decreasing height are grouped together to create a descending flow of blooms and foliage down to the low, creeping ones at the front edges along the street and inside by the driveway.

When I visited in August the dominant colors were yellow, soft purple, pink, and white. The gray-green foliage of catmint (*Nepeta* × *faassenii*), various sedums, lavender (*Lavandula angustifolia*), and lamb's-ears (*Stachys byzantina*) was tucked in here and there. The interesting combination included the following natives: yellow prairie coneflower (*Ratibida pinnata*), Indian grass (*Sorghastrum nutans*), yarrow (*Achillea millefolium*), black-eyed Susan (*Rudbeckia hirta*), cupplant (*Silphium perfoliatum*), prairie dropseed (*Sporobolus heterolepis*), columbine (*Aquilegia canadensis*), coreopsis (*Coreopsis lanceolata*), switchgrass (*Panicum virgatum*), butterfly weed (*Asclepias tuberosa*); and well-adapted perennials: garden phlox (*Phlox paniculata*), columbine (*Aquilegia* spp.), blue fescue (*Festuca glauca*), *Verbena bonariensis*, globe thistle (*Echinops ritro*), day-lilies (*Hemerocallis* spp.), *Sedum spectabile* 'Autumn Joy', and woolly thyme (*Thymus pseudolanuginosus*) (between the stones of the walkway). A few annuals used in spots included geraniums, petunias, and nicotiana.

To the left of the front garden was a shady area with all kinds of shade-loving perennials. Along the side of the house was another even larger garden with a small stretch of lawn leading through the middle and curved borders all around. In the back corner was a propagation and nursery area fenced all around and on top to protect young plants and the few vegetables Trudi has growing. She has been gardening here for thirty years and knows how much her garden is enjoyed by others. The front gate is nearly always open for passersby to walk along the paths and see the garden up close.

The home of Cliff and Marilyn Douglas near Phoenix, Arizona, has no lawn and instead is surrounded by a mixture of more than 100 desert trees, shrubs, and low-growing perennials and cactuses. When their home was built on the five-acre undisturbed site more than ten years ago, they worked around and protected the native desert plants that were existing and relocated ones that had to be moved. Native plants and ones from other desert environments were added here and there, chosen not just for their appearance but for their appropriateness to the location and to feed wildlife.

Typical of the way that plants grow in the desert—receiving seven inches or less of annual rainfall—they are spaced far apart on a surface of silver-gray sand. The trees include shoestring acacia (*Acacia stenophylla*), desert willow (*Chilopsis linearis*), blue palo verde (*Cercidium floridum*), foothills palo verde (*C. microphyllum*), desert ironwood (*Olneya tesota*), and Chilean mesquite (a thornless hybrid of *Prosopsis chilensis*). Towering centuries-old saguaro cactus (*Carnegiea gigantea*)—thirty feet high—rise among a layer of brittle bush (*Encelia farinosa*), jojoba (*Simmondsia chinensis*), prickly pear (*Opuntia* spp.), barrel cactus (*Ferocactus* and *Echinocactus* spp.), agave, ocotillo (*Fouquieria spendens*), and chuparosa (*Justicia californica*), which attracts hummingbirds. Other shrubs include creosote (*Larrea divaricata*), bur sage (*Ambrosia deltoidea*), wolfberry (*Lycium fremontii*), and Arizona yellowbells (*Tecoma stans*).

Smaller perennials that bloom at various times during the year are planted closer to the house including verbena (*Verbena bipinnatifida*), penstemon (*Penstemon* spp.), prickly pear (*Opuntia* spp.), autumn sage (*Salvia greggii*), sages (*Salvia* spp.), desert marigold (*Baileya multiradiata*), and other small cactuses. Designed by landscape architect Steve Martino, the only areas that receive regular irrigation are the planting beds close to the house and in back. Douglas says they supply just enough regular water to keep the flowering plants in bloom. The owner of Arid Zone Trees, an important native and desert plant nursery in the Southwest, he says the demand for plants appropriate to the desert environment has continued to grow. "The belief that the desert is an inhospitable place," says Douglas, "which is held not just by newcomers but by some people who have lived here all their lives, and that plants from non-desert habitats should be used instead, is beginning to change."

Although the garden of Eloise Lesan is unique in that it was created along the top and down the slope of a rock ledge, the plants that she selected can be used in other settings as long as the soil is well-drained and acid to neutral, not alkaline. The drama of the site in southern Connecticut is created by the intermingling of the mostly mat-forming sedums, creeping junipers, heaths, heathers, wildflowers, alpine plants, ground covers, and moss. The large gray flat surfaces of buried granite boulders show at ground level between the plants, and moss-covered steps that are cut into the slope and edged with narrow planks to hold the soil lead up to the top of the ledge.

When she moved to the house, Lesan says, "I knew that perennial borders would never work because the soil was not deep and there were just pockets here and there in the rocks for planting." She decided on alpine and rock garden plants, and heaths and heathers. "Because the existing soil was already a woodsy, acid type partly from years of leaves decaying where they fell," says Eloise, "I did not need to add amendments, I just planted right into it." But she did use a mulch of native granite grit to provide good drainage for the alpines and succulents. The heaths and heathers were planted at the top of the ledge in an area that gets full sun. "They like a sandy or peaty, poor soil with good drainage," she says, "but must never dry out." A pine needle mulch is used on these plants and a soaker hose is wound through them so that if there is a long, dry period during the summer she can easily provide the moisture they require.

Most of the planting was done in the beginning, nearly thirty years ago. Since then the plants have spread and little maintenance is required. The chores that remain, such as pulling out weeds that come through the heathers, replenishing mulch, occasional pruning, or adding new plants, are part of enjoying the beauty that this everchanging low-growing garden provides.

Scattered oaks, pines, and cedars grow down one side of the yard, creating filtered shade. Several dogwoods near a path are limbed up to provide more sun to the plants below. "Even though the moss receives a lot of sun," says Eloise, "it is constantly moist and stays green and lush." The steps through this area are bordered by Christmas fern (*Polystichum acrostichoides*), prostrate juniper (*Juniper procumbens*), *Sedum ewersii*, and fire pink (*Silene virginica*). At the top of the ledge is a mixture of heaths including *Erica carnea*, *E. c.* 'Springwood White', *E. darleyensis*, and a heathlike plant called Balkan heath or spike heath (*Bruckenthalia spiculifolium*). All are evergreen and bloom in the early spring, except the last, which blooms in summer. Flowers and bulbs mixed in include muscari, scilla, chionodoxa, *Primula julae* hybrids, and bluets (*Hedyotis caerulea*). Other plants include *Sedum acre* with yellow blooms, *S. ewersii* with pink tiny blooms in summer, *S. album* with red blooms, santolina, ajuga, and the native prostrate shrub, box huckleberry (*Gaylussacia brachycera*).

Susan and Art Ammann of Denver, Colorado, won an award for their water-conserving landscape designed by Alan Rollinger. Only 4 percent of the yard is planted in Kentucky bluegrass, in contrast to typical home landscapes in Denver which have 80 percent. Buffalo grass, which does fine on the fourteen inches of annual precipitation in this part of the country, covers a 1,800-square-foot area. The Ammanns give it a deep irrigation in spring to green it up sooner and another one in fall to postpone its winter dormancy.

Native shrubs and trees such as Gambel oak (*Quercus gambelii*), dwarf rabbit brush (*Chrysothamnus nauseosus*), Rocky Mountain juniper (*Juniperus scopulorum*), and coral berry (*Symphoricarpus orbiculatus*) are clustered throughout the yard. They require little or no irrigation. A hedge of native red-twig dogwood (*Cornus stolonifera*) screens the back patio area and a dry stream bed on the east side captures rainstorm runoff and directs it to plants growing nearby. The plants used at the front of the property near the small patch of bluegrass lawn that require regular irrigation are ajuga, daylilies, and fleeceflower (*Polygonum* 'Border Jewel'). Other plants that provide colorful blooms but do not require as much water are coral bells (*Heuchera* spp.), creeping red penstemon (*Penstemon* spp.), and *Potentilla* 'Gold Drop'. Sweet woodruff (*Galium odoratum*) and pampas grass (*Cortaderia selloana*) are used as ground cover and as accents to the flowering plants. A wood-chip path circulates through the garden, which allows rainwater to penetrate the soil rather than running off.

The Denver Water Department, which gives the Xeriscape Yard Contest awards, says this garden uses 63 percent less water than the typical Denver landscape.

Ann and Dick Bartlett of Lakewood, Colorado, slowly transformed their yard from bluegrass with low junipers around the doorstep to a garden of island beds featuring alpine and drought-tolerant plants. The beds were filled with plants chosen for the areas of shade and sun and the grass was left in the walkway areas. Large, native sandstone boulders were placed here and there in the landscape and some areas were raised to create berms that would improve drainage. The sandstone not only helps with drainage but it adds an interesting contrast to the landscape, says Ann, "and eventually moss will grow on the sides." The soil was also amended to help provide proper drainage for the alpine plants. The amendment was a mixture of one-third gravel, one-third sand, and one-third soil blended with composted animal manure. "Instead of trying to redo the entire yard all at once," says Ann, "we worked on it in stages, hand pulling or hoeing out the grass each time to create a new bed."

A flowering crabapple is a focal point in the front yard. Other plants include *Phlox bifida* 'Betty Blake', *P. subulata* 'Scarlet Flame', *P.* 'Millstream Daphne', columbine (*Aquilegia barnebyi*), buttercup (*Ranunculus montanus* 'Molten Gold'), various sedums, violets (*Viola corsica*), and the small, evergreen shrub, *Daphne oleoides*. Ann and Dick, who are active members of the American Rock Garden Society and photographers, say that more and more people in their area have switched to buffalo grass and many are planting, if not the entire front yard, at least large island beds of drought-tolerant native plants of the prairie and high plains or spring alpines.

California abounds with examples of lawn substitutes. The front garden of Nina Liff, near Santa Barbara, was designed by landscape architect Isabelle Greene. An irregular course of concrete steps with gray-green foliage plants on either side leads down a slope to the entrance. The ground on the left is covered with Australian fuchsia (*Correa pulchella*) with sageleaf rockrose (*Cistus salviifolia*) behind it. To the right are snow-in-summer

(*Cerastium tomentosum*), lamb's-ears (*Stachys byzantina*), and hen-and-chickens (*Echieveria elegans*).

Henrietta Bensussen of San Jose created a more diverse and eclectic blend of plants when she took out the lawn on her forty-by-seventy-foot lot in her urban neighborhood. "The previous owner had laid down a beautiful front lawn without totally eradicating the crab grass underneath," says Henri. "At first I simply mowed it, while planting roses and irises along the edges. Then came a crabapple tree and a lemon tree. And then came my pitchfork." She made the transformation in stages, first digging out the lawn on one side of a sidewalk that led to the front porch.

In place of the lawn, she put in English and French lavender (*Lavandula angustifolia* and *L. dentata*), rosemary, sage, irises, artemisia, and numerous spring bulbs. "We took out the four-foot-wide cement walk that led to the front porch with a sledge hammer and crowbar," explains Henri, "and replaced it with a three-foot-wide brick path, then edged it with thyme and grape hyacinths."

The next year she took out the lawn on the other side and planted more irises, lavender, rosemary, yarrow, and some California native plants. To prepare the ground, she aerated and broke up the soil with a pitchfork, then added redwood compost and leaves from her neighbor's trees. She says the soil is good, just heavy, so the organic matter is needed to improve drainage.

The new front garden "requires less maintenance," says Henri, "only watering deeply once a week in the hottest part of the summer and mulching in the fall. Before, I had to have the sprinkler on every weekend and cut the grass and weed all the time." Now there is no need for mowing or weeding. "My neighbors have not complained," she adds, "they stop by to admire the flowers and ask for plants." Many have been influenced to replace part of their lawn area with beds of flowering plants. "The flower garden we have now is so much more interesting in its varied shapes and colors."

In Palo Alto, all Marge Abel had to do to kill the lawn was to stop watering during the drought of 1990. "We let the lawn die," she says. "In this area lawns need watering once to twice a week. The house came with an irrigation controller that had a maximum four-day cycle!" When they moved into the home, it had been landscaped with a traditional lawn and sheared foundation shrubs. Even the cedar tree was sheared into a "cylinder with a dunce cap shape." The yard was "altogether a crime against plants, boring, and a water hog," says Marge.

The new landscape—installed in three stages from 1991 to 1993—is a mixture of trees, shrubs, perennials, annuals, stone, and ground cover with no lawn. When they were ready to replant the first area, the sod that was left was "removed by hand and by a bobcat scaping it up and removing it." The soil, a clay loam, was loosened but not amended in any way. She had soil tests done to determine that the drainage and pH were fine.

The street trees planted in the area between the street and sidewalk were dying Australian pines *(Casuarina stricta)*; the city gave her permission to remove them. She replaced them with three locust (*Robinia ambigua* 'Purple Robe'), and added two more in other parts of the yard along with a flowering pear (*Pyrus callerayana* 'Aristocrat'). Shrubs include *Pittosporum tobira* 'Variegata', smokebush (*Cotinus coggygria* 'Purpureus'), Pacific wax myrtle (*Myrica californica*), laudanum (*Cistus ladanifer*), and Yedda hawthorne (*Raphiolepis umbellata* 'Minor').

Most of the ground is covered with creeping myoporum (*Myoporum parvifolium* 'Davis'), mulch, and groups of perennials and annuals. "Two inches of mulch is used throughout the yard and some of it will always show," says Marge, "even when the plants are mature, but I don't believe that you have to plant every square inch to have an attractive landscape." A low, decorative stone wall winds through the yard, adding a bold curving shape to the flat plane. The perennials include *Dorycnium hirsutum*, cranesbill (*Geranium sanguineum* and *G. incanum*), swan river daisy (*Brachycome multifida dilatata*), sea pink (*Armeria alliacea*), silvermound (*Artemisia schmidtiana* 'Silver Mound'), *Artemisia* × 'Powis Castle', lamb's-ears (*Stachys byzantina* 'Silver Carpet'), fleabane (*Erigeron karvinskianus*), threadleaf coreopsis (*Coreopsis verticillata* 'Moonbeam'), *Anisodontea* × *hypomadarum*, Russian sage (*Perovskia atriplicifolia*), fortnight lily (*Dietes vegeta*), and society garlic (*Tulbaghia violacea* 'Silver Lace').

Sweet alyssum (*Lobularia maritima*), a perennial that would survive the hot summer if watered, reseeds itself throughout the yard during the wet winter and spring. Marge just removes it when it dries up in summer. Three ornamental grasses that she uses are blue oat grass (*Helichtotrichon sempervirens*), blue fescue (*Festuca ovina* 'Elijah Blue'), and purple-leaved fountain grass (*Pennisetum setaceum* 'Rubrum').

A drip irrigation system was installed by Marge, replacing the traditional lawn sprayer system. "I water new plants every four days to make sure they get established," says Marge, "and every two weeks (when there is no rain) thereafter. Some of the plants would be okay with even less water but I compromise with some—like the myoporum—to get the look that I want. Even so, it is still less than what a lawn would require."

The small front yard of a tract home in Davis, California, was transformed by Michael Glassman, of Greenscapes and Graphics, Sacramento, from a flat surface with struggling grass to a garden of drought-tolerant ground covers and small trees. A six-foot-tall fence was installed ten feet in front of the picture window, fifteen feet from the sidewalk. Trailing pink verbena (*Verbena peruviana*) is the major ground cover with fortnight lilies (*Dietes vegeta*), daylilies (*Hemerocallis* spp.), mugo pines (*Pinus mugo* 'Compacta'), and bonsai Japanese black pines (*Pinus thunbergiana*) planted into it. An overhead trellis provides shade for the interior of the fence where shade-loving plants are featured.

Although lawns are still widespread in Hawaii, Colleen C. Lopez, education coordinator for the Hawaii Plant Conservation Center, National Tropical Botanical Garden, Lawai, Kauai, says "the Honolulu Board of Water Supply has advocated the use of drought-tolerant species for years because of the increasing water demands on Oahu." Bermuda, St. Augustine, zoysia, hilo grass, and centipede are some of the main grasses used for turf and they require the usual high maintenance of mowing, watering, and fertilizing that is typical in the mainland United States.

"Although the use of native Hawaiian plants for landscaping is in its infancy here," says Colleen, "interest is growing." The center was founded in 1989 to collect, propagate, and study the islands' native plants. The HPCC recently published the second edition of a guide to sources for native plants which lists more than sixty nurseries.

The botanical garden installed an exhibit in 1990 to evaluate and display native plants for home landscape use and to educate residents about them. Many of the species were categorized only as "rare" when they were planted, according to the guidebook for the garden. Now the United States Fish and Wildlife Service has recategorized them as "endangered," which demonstrates the "fragile state of our native flora and its accelerating decline in the wild," the booklet says. Limited quantities of native plants, including some endangered ones, have been available for years through commercial enterprises; some of these may be suitable as substitutes for lawn.

Lopez recommends the following native Hawaiian plants for use as low-growing ground covers or shrubs: *Dianella sandwicensis*, flax lily family; *Fimbristylis cymosa*, sedge family; hinahina (*Heliotropium anomalum*), borage family; pohuehue (*Ipomoea pes-caprae*), morning glory family; paʻuohiʻiaka (*Jacquemontia ovalifolia* subsp. *sandwicensis*), morning glory family; nehe (*Lipochaeta* spp.), daisy family; kupukupu (*Nephrolepis cordifolia*), relative of the familiar houseplant Boston fern; ʻulei (*Osteomeles anthyllidifolia*), rose family; ʻala ʻala wai nui (*Peperomia* spp.), same family as another familiar houseplant—peperomia; naupaka (*Scaevola sericea*), goodenia family; ʻilima (*Sida fallax*), mallow family; ʻakia (*Wikstroemia uva-ursi*), akia family; pohinahina (*Vitex rotundifolia*), verbena family.

A little more than ten years ago, Vicki and Ron Nowicki of Downers Grove, Illinois, set out to create a home and a "lawnless" landscape that conserved energy and resources, had the least impact on the environment, and increased their self-reliance. They built a passive solar home, designed by Ron (a landscape architect), with the garage on the north side, which is mostly below a berm (only one small window), and large picture windows on the south to bring in maximum warmth and light in the winter. Deciduous trees such as green ash (*Fraxinus pennsylvanica lanceolata*) and white ash (*Fraxinus americana*) were planted on the south side to provide shade in summer without blocking the sun in winter.

"We chose a location that was close enough to town so that we could walk," says Vicki. "The idea was not only to create a natural landscape and raise some of our own food but to simplify our lives as well." The Nowickis consider the small part of the yard that faces the street as the "back," and the larger south side, the "front." White pine (*Pinus strobus*), white spruce (*Picea glauca*), and Colorado blue spruce (*Picea pungens*) insulate the house and serve as a windbreak on the north side. A small area near the street and one along the left side of the driveway that receive some sun are filled with native wildflowers and grasses. A path covered with a wood-chip mulch winds through the two woodland areas on either side of the house. Some of the native shrubs and wildflowers featured in this shaded location are wild columbine (*Aquilegia canadensis*), Jack-in-the-pulpit (*Arisaema triphyllum*), Jacob's ladder (*Polemonium caeruleum*), violets (*Viola* spp.), and nannyberry (*Viburnum lentago*).

The south side of the lot (not facing the street) contains the vegetable garden of long raised beds, and plantings of berries, grapes, herbs, and dwarf fruit trees. "Live" Christmas trees have been planted each year along the back border. There is also a large composting area at the back of the lot and Vicki leaves the annual flowers that self-sow to use for cut flowers.

In the beginning load after load of wood-chip mulch was brought in to create a foot-deep layer over everything to kill existing weeds and lawn grasses. Trees were planted first, along with ground covers, followed by shrubs, perennials, herbs, and finally, the vegetable garden. The initial years involved a lot of labor, but once established, this natural landscape of mostly native plants has remained low maintenance. Not only that, it provides food and habitat for insects, numerous species of birds, and other wildlife including opossums, raccoons, squirrels, bats, mice, voles, and rabbits. Sitting on the porch with Vicki it seemed as if we were miles from the city.

Since 1990 Ron has been able to specialize in "no-lawn" landscapes, and Vicki, who taught courses in wild edible and useful plants for years, has joined as his partner. They have helped numerous suburban homeowners convert all or part of their yards into plantings of well-adapted and native plants. "Some people get rid of their entire lawn at once," says Vicki, "others do a section at a time." Using a sodcutter is the easiest and most effective way to get rid of the lawn for small-scale projects. "We cut the sod and pile the strips upside down to create berms and mounds," says Vicki, "adding interest to an otherwise flat plane." The mounds are covered with good soil. The mounds, as well as the rest of the bare area, are covered with a ten-to-twelve-inch layer of wood-chip mulch. This prevents weeds from encroaching and holds moisture in the soil. "The mulch gives people a chance to add plants as time and money permit," adds Vicki. Having tried numerous types of edgings for beds that are within a lawn setting, the Nowickis have found that raising the bed up and bordering it with rock or brick is the most effective, or creating an edge with a sharp spade, which has to be renewed every year.

"When people change their yard to a more diverse natural landscape," says Vicki, "they spend more enjoyable time in it. They can interact with nature there rather than going to a park." In their own experience, Ron and Vicki say, "the landscape at times has a mind of its own. We have tried to learn when to interfere and when to stay out of it…our relationship with this landscape is a dynamic, ever-changing adventure."

New Landscaping Ordinances

Some homeowners who have turned their lawns into prairies or meadows have run into legal difficulties as a result of antiquated "weed laws." These are ordinances set by national, state, county, or local governments which regulate the height of and, sometimes, the type of plants that may be grown in their jurisdictional areas. The laws at the three higher levels are usually statutes against noxious weeds that could be harmful to agriculture, fish, and wildlife, or to the public health, for example, ragweed (*Ambrosia artemisiifolia*), Johnsongrass (*Sorghum halepense*), and Canada thistle (*Cirsium arvense*). A few states, such as Illinois and Florida, have added to the list exotic species that encroach on natural areas and overtake them, crowding out the native plants. One example is purple loosestrife (*Lythrum salicaria*); another is punk tree (*Melaleuca quinquenervia*). For others, see the list of noxious and invasive plants on pages 84–87.

Local ordinances, however, were passed more for aesthetic reasons — to enable the local governing body to take action against homeowners who neglect their property by not cutting or managing the vegetation and letting litter and trash pile up that could attract rats or mosquitoes, or cause a fire.

Most of these regulations include a statement that restricts the height of "weeds" to ten or twelve inches.

Another type of local regulation may occur at the private level. Some subdivision developers require anyone who purchases land and builds a home in the development to agree to landscape with specific plants in a specific style. Homeowners who live in those subdivisions know or are able to find out the process necessary to obtain permission to venture from those prescriptions.

Weed Laws

The ordinances are rarely enforced unless a neighbor complains or, for some other reason, the yard is brought to the attention of city officials. In numerous cases across the country, ordinances have been enforced against homeowners who are practicing natural landscaping, specifically planting and taking care of plants instead of traditional lawns. Since natural landscapes and lawn alternatives do not pose a threat to public health or to anyone's safety, the outdated laws have functionally become a tool to force people to comply with a certain aesthetic standard.

Even though many of the popular wildflowers and native grasses grow somewhat taller than twelve inches, they are cultivated plants. The yards in which they grow are a far cry from being "neglected lots": quite the opposite, the planting and first three years of establishment of native plantings require extensive time and labor and, even though maintenance is less after that, it is still required to keep out unwanted invaders that might occur as a result of seeds brought in by birds or the wind.

Once established, native plantings do not require fertilizer or water. They increase the soil's ability to absorb water and thus decrease the amount of urban runoff and nonpoint source pollution. Pollutants may come from a direct source such as factories or cities piping untreated wastes directly into lakes and rivers, or from indirect sources, called "nonpoint" because the contamination is diffuse. For instance, during a storm, water runs off from paved roads, parking lots, construction or mining sites carrying various contaminants with it. Irrigation of farmland, parks, and lawns can also result in contamination of the water supply through seepage into wells or draining off into streams carrying chemical fertilizer and pesticide residues. Natural landscapes not only do not contribute to this problem, but they also provide habitat and food for birds, butterflies, and other wildlife. They increase the health and safety of communities rather than being a threat to them.

Take These Steps

As a result of my many interviews, I advise you to do three things before you begin: draw your plan on paper, inform your neighbors of what you plan to do in a short letter that explains the purpose and benefits, and talk with your local officials to find out if you need to apply for a variance to any regulation. If you have already spoken to local officials before a neighbor complains, says Lorrie Otto, of Wisconsin, they will be able to calm down an irate neighbor and will have the necessary information to explain what is really going on. For instance, they will be able to explain that the plants are native to the area, that some are even protected species, and that they are not "weeds." You can also begin by planting a small island bed rather than doing the whole yard at once.

Many homeowners have found that registering their natural landscapes through the Backyard Wildlife Habitat Program of the National Wildlife Federation or with the National Institute for Urban Wildlife is helpful for two reasons. First, it documents and demonstrates that the plants in their yards serve many positive environmental benefits and are not weeds, and it gives them a way to help educate their neighbors or local officials because they are able to demonstrate their participation in a professional, national program. Craig Tufts, chief naturalist for the Backyard Wildlife Habitat Program, says that some of the members have had trouble with local ordinances and in most cases, a variance has been allowed.

The National Wildlife Federation has encouraged cities to change their weed laws and has become involved in the particular case of Jack Schmidling, Larry Clark, Debra Lynn Petro, and Rich Hyerczyk versus the City of Chicago. This group of citizens filed the case against the city because several of them had been repeatedly prosecuted though not convicted. An unusual irony of the case is that the City of Chicago cultivates a native prairie planting on public property that it manages, and the Chicago Park District and the

Illinois Department of Transportation are both reintroducing prairie plants on public land. Many of the native plants that the officials are using are the same ones that these natural landscapers use in their yards. The plants exceed the height of ten inches and that is the point on which these natural landscapers were cited.

Counsel for the case, Bret Rappaport, has written an excellent article (*The John Marshall Law Review*, summer 1993) which summarizes the background, rationale, and benefits of natural landscaping; the weed laws and why they are a problem; counterarguments to the often-raised complaints of threat of rats, fire, mosquitoes, pollen, and aesthetics; and grounds to oppose the enforcement of weed laws against a natural landscape.

Unfounded Complaints

The first problem cited—attraction of rats—is based on the assumption that naturally vegetated areas will sustain rats. Rats and other animals considered to be vermin require a steady food supply. Natural vegetation does not provide the sort of food in quantities required to sustain a population of vermin. Karen Yaitch, a wildlife biologist for the Arkansas Game and Fish Commission, explained this during a case in Little Rock, Arkansas. She added that other small mammals, such as mice, gophers, and moles do live in grassy areas but do not pose a health threat. Gophers and moles don't enter homes and homeowners can prevent mice from entering the house when the weather starts to turn cold by keeping a two- to three-foot mown strip around it.

The second problem raised is the possibility of fire. Rappaport summarizes comments from David Seaberg, a United States Forest Service expert, who testified in the precedent-setting case of Donald Hagar of Waukesha County, Wisconsin, in 1976 that a grass fire can sustain high heat for only twenty seconds. To ignite wood and sustain a fire potentially damaging to a home, a grass fire would have to burn within four feet of a home for seven-and-a-half minutes. He then refers to comments from John Diekelmann, a noted landscape architect and plant ecologist, who said that most prairie or meadow plantings contain a large portion of green leafy material at ground level during most seasons which does not sustain fire. Again, for appearance and as a firebreak, most people who have prairie or meadow plantings keep a mown area directly adjacent to all sides of the house. In drier parts of the West, prairie plantings are mown more often or burned once a year as part of their management.

The complaint that natural landscaping will lead to the breeding of mosquitoes is incorrect. Here, Rappaport points out that mosquitoes need standing water for ten days in order to complete their life cycle. Prairie and meadow areas absorb water quickly and are less likely than frequently watered lawns to develop small pools of standing water.

And, finally, the problem of pollen. The herbaceous plants that are responsible for most pollen allergens are ragweeds (*Ambrosia* spp.), pigweeds (*Amaranthus* spp.), a few species of goosefoot (*Chenopodium*), and unmown nonindigenous turf and pasture grasses such as Kentucky bluegrass, Bermuda, orchard grass, redtop, and timothy.

Since natural landscapes that contain native and well-adapted species do not cause any of these problems, the more likely reason for complaints against them is an objection to the nonconforming appearance. Peoples' attitudes and willingness to accept natural landscapes have been studied for more than ten years by Joan Nassauer, head of the Department of Landscape Architecture at the University of Minnesota. She says the key factor for most people to accept the more natural and nontraditional look of ecological landscapes is a demonstration of care by the owners.

The prairie or meadow lawns that have been most successful, Nassauer says, "are those where some portion of the turf has been kept since it is a familiar label of care." The mowed part makes it clear to the neighbors that this person cares about their yard and about the community, and the meadow part shows, in a different way, that they care about the ecological health of their region, the environment, wildlife, and helping to preserve the local heritage of native plants.

In an interesting study done by Nassauer's student Susan Magg, office workers at two different corporate headquarters—one had installed a prairie garden ten years ago, the other eighteen months ago—were asked how they perceived it when it was planted and how they perceived it now. Employees at both sites said they found the gardens to be "very attractive." In the beginning they had not found the prairie as attractive as they later did, which led Nassauer to conclude that the adaptation occurred most rapidly between the first and eighteenth month: "It seems that people learn to see and appreciate prairie fairly quickly." In a project to evaluate how receptive people are to alternative landscapes, she showed video simulations of a variety of lawn treatments. Those in the group who were knowledgeable about native plants were very enthusiastic about a slide in which three-fourths of the lawn had been replaced with native plants; those who knew little about native plants did not like it. Everyone disliked a slide that showed a weedy lawn and most disliked one in which 50 percent of the turf had been replaced with only sumac and hazelnut.

Both groups liked the alternative in which 50 percent of the turf was replaced with native herbaceous plants and groups of oak trees and shrubs. This should tell local governments coping with weed ordinances that "there's a landscaping alternative that can win both with people who want to experiment with native plants and with neighbors who don't." She challenges the nursery industry to issue catalogs that go beyond giving hardiness zones for plants and describe the indigenous plant communities that they fit into so that gardeners can select plants that are appropriate to the ecology of their region.

Some cities have responded to the growth of natural landscaping by passing completely new ordinances to permit it, by modifying existing weed laws with setback regulations or variances, or by adopting policies and regulations that promote it.

Natural Landscaping Support

An example of the first type is Madison, Wisconsin. So many homeowners there were interested and already involved in this activity that the city (with the help of some of the experts who lived in the area) devised a Natural Landscaping Ordinance that permits "natural lawns," and published a booklet to guide people through the process, *An Introduction to Naturalized Landscapes: A Guide to Madison's Natural Lawn Ordinance*. The ordinance defines a natural landscape and stipulates maintenance requirements in order to prevent the creation of hazards to adjoining properties or anyone traveling on public ways. If the landscape plan includes grasses that will be allowed to grow to their natural height (exceeding eight inches), then it is necessary to apply for a permit as well.

An example of the second type of local government response grew out of the case of Walter and Nancy Stewart of Rockville, Maryland. They turned six of their seven acres into a meadow and were cited for being in violation of the Montgomery County ordinance which limited lawn height to twelve inches. The Stewarts challenged the ordinance on the grounds that aesthetics cannot be regulated. They also proved in their arguments that the meadow did not attract vermin and did not create a health hazard. After several years, the county changed the ordinance and now allows meadows on certain conditions. A fifteen-foot buffer zone has to be maintained around the property in which plants are twelve inches or less, noxious species must be controlled, and dead vegetation near a structure must be kept cleared to prevent fire hazards.

Another example is Boone County, Illinois. Three years ago, some residents replaced their lawns with plantings of native grasses and wildflowers that were indigenous to the area and a few of the neighbors complained, says William Hatfield, the environmental director for the county. "The conflict created enough of a stir that the county board struck down the weed ordinance altogether," says Hatfield, "saying that this is a rural area where many of the native plants remain and if someone is planting them in their yard, they belong there." The smallest county in Illinois, it is mostly agricultural and has a population of about 30,000. In recent years, some new subdivisions have been developed and the people who have moved out from more urban areas not only have complained about natural landscapes but also about the combines making too much dust. The city of Harvard in McHenry County, also in Illinois, passed an ordinance that protects natural landscapers from prosecution by allowing exceptions to the weed law for "native plantings, wildlife plantings, and other environmentally beneficial landscapes."

Two examples of innovative programs are Long Grove, Illinois, and Fort Collins, Colorado. Long Grove has no law restricting the height of plants. Instead, a law requires developers to provide 100-foot scenic easements along roadways in subdivisions that include native plants, wildflowers, and grasses. They also cannot build on natural areas but can include that land as backyards or "parks" for the subdivision. The village sells native plants and seed mixes to residents and employs a naturalist on staff to advise developers and homeowners.

What is unusual about Long Grove's policy is that unlike other communities, "it did not arise from conflicts between neighbors or between a homeowner and village officials," says Cal Doughty, village manager for sixteen years. "When the area was developed in the 1950s it was a 'far' suburb of the Chicago metropolitan area and still had a rural setting," he continues. The founders wanted to be sure that the rural atmosphere was maintained, and they wanted to protect the abundant lakes, wetlands, woodlands, and open prairie areas with the existing natural vegetation.

"They realized that if developments occurred with homes lined up on one-acre lots with mowed lawns," says Doughty, "the rural atmosphere and natural areas would be destroyed." Zoning regulations set lot sizes at one, two, and three acres with none less than one acre. The management of natural areas requires periodic burning and, in some places, installing native plants or seeds to restore an area. The village has an ongoing education program that teaches its residents about native plants, how to burn safely, and what nonnative species to remove. Doughty said the only one that is a problem in the area is ragweed and after two burns it disappears.

"Many people who have natural areas on the property when they arrive eventually begin expanding those areas," says Doughty, "often allowing most of their front yard to become a prairie planting." To let an area go natural, he recommends mowing high in late fall for two years in a row and burning the third year. "The fourth year the planting is mostly natives and the changing display of flowers and grasses through the seasons is spectacular," says Doughty, whose own yard contains an open prairie area, a wooded area, and a woods/prairie edge. He still mows an area near the house.

Fort Collins has a ten-acre nature preserve in the center of the downtown area, and they have a program to certify the backyards of homeowners who landscape for wildlife. The program is modeled after national ones, and applicants are required to fill out a form including a list of all the plants in their yard and what methods they use to provide water and shelter. Edith Felky, who coordinates the program, says it grew out of a general interest: "Our entire community is environmentally oriented." The city still has strict weed ordinances on the books but homeowners who create a wildlife habitat or natural landscape and have it certified will not be cited.

Some Legal Battles

Situations in which homeowners have taken their case to court and been forced to eradicate a natural planting are rare, according to Rappaport, who has studied and followed the natural landscaping legal battles for years. The classic example—much publicized at the time—happened in New York: Kenmore Village Court versus Stephen Kenney. He had planted a wildflower meadow in his front yard including oxeye daisies, black-eyed Susans, coneflowers, and bachelor's buttons. He was fined $50 for every day that the flowers remained standing, despite expert testimony that the plants were not harmful and did not create a health hazard. A New York appeals court reduced the fine to $500 but due to continual harassment from his neighbors, including threats, vandalism, and shots taken at his cat, he moved. At his new home in Rensselaer, New York, he has been able to grow his natural landscape.

In Little Rock, Arkansas, Lyndae Allison turned her yard into a natural landscape and was cited by the city. A state biologist, Karen L. Yaich, with the Arkansas Game and Fish Commission, testified that the yard provided a natural wildlife area. Allison won her case and was allowed to keep her yard.

The Davises of Boynton Beach, Florida, built their home on a three-and-a-half-acre site in the midst of a native pine woods. Instead of clearing the site, they built around the plants, removing only seven of the 300 trees. Most of the plants were slash pine, saw palmetto, and gallberry. This canopy created a self-mulching yard with pine needles as the ground layer. In 1985 the county filed a complaint under the lot-clearing ordinance and demanded that all "uncultivated vegetation" be removed. The Davises appealed to the Environmental Control Hearing Board and, with the aid of the Florida Native Plant Society, Audubon Society, and twelve neighbors, saved the habitat. The ordinance was rewritten to exclude native vegetation.

In another Florida town, Dunedin, Alice Earle stopped mowing the area around the lake on her two-acre property more than six years ago to let the native plants reclaim the bank. She wanted to provide food and cover for turtles, water birds, opossums, and other local fauna. In the summer of 1989, city officials sent a maintenance crew and cut it down (based on a grass-height ordinance) and charged her for it. She refused to pay and started to work on having the local ordinance changed.

The conflict between her and the neighbors was brought to national attention by reporter Pamela Sebastian in the *Wall Street Journal*. Earle's daughter, biologist Sylvia Earle, encouraged her mother to reestablish the native plants to create a nature preserve. The law was amended to allow uncut grass as part of a "nature preserve" that had been planned and was taken care of by its owners.

When the conflict began, the Earles had invited all of the neighbors to take part in restoring the native vegetation. They asked everyone to stop mowing up to the lake's edge. The neighbors wanted the plants on the lake bank cut down. After the city cut the area, the Earles put up a four-foot picket fence around the lake with six-foot panels between their land and the neighbors next door. The native plants that have returned include holly, bulrushes, sour grass, and palmetto.

The Sierra Club and the National Wildflower Research Center are also involved in helping change weed laws that stand in the way of individuals who are installing natural landscapes or trying to restore native habitats in their yards. The effort has to be carried out at the local level, town by town, region by region. In Appendix III, you'll find sample ordinances and guidelines to use in helping to modify your community's existing weed laws or to create wholly new landscape laws that promote and encourage the natural approach.

Water Conservation and Reduced Lawn Area Incentives

In many parts of the United States, the freshwater supply is vulnerable to climatic conditions, particularly drought. Water sources, such as lakes, rivers, and groundwater and aquifer beds, are dwindling as a result of industrial, hydroelectric, agricultural, and municipal uses and are being degraded as a result of point and nonpoint pollution. Point-source pollution was the main target of legislation in the 1970s when factories and cities were still piping untreated wastes into lakes and rivers. With some of these problems partly curbed, the remaining and more-difficult-to-remedy situation involves nonpoint sources such as runoff from agricultural fields (chemical fertilizer and pesticides), cities (storm water often carrying pollutants from yards maintained with chemicals by homeowners), construction sites, and mining operations.

Conserving and protecting our water supply is a complicated issue. Outdoor water use by homeowners is very high during summer months, reaching 40 to 60 percent of the overall amount supplied by a utility during that time, but it is still a fractional amount of the billions of gallons used by industry, agriculture, and thermoelectric power plants. But individuals have influenced and can continue to influence the water supply directly. Besides water-saving measures inside the home, we can use native and well-adapted plant species in our yards that are used to the levels of rainfall and other climatic factors in our specific regions. This not only reduces the amount of water needed for outdoor use but also provides a landscape that survives temperature fluctuations, does not depend on chemical pesticides and fertilizer, and benefits wildlife populations as well.

Two cities are now offering customers cash rebates for removing all or part of their turfgrass and replacing it with drought-tolerant, water-conserving plants. John Olaf Nelson, general manager of the North Marin Water District just north of San Francisco, California, is the brain behind the innovative water conservation program which began there eight years ago.

The district serves a population of about 53,000, and residential use accounts for most of the water consumption. Most of the residences are single-family dwellings. An analysis of water consumption showed that outside water use accounted for 40 percent of all use (peaking at 65 percent in July) and that 75 to 90 percent of outside water use was applied to turf. The district was hit hard by the drought in the 1970s and had to cut water use between 30 and 65 percent to avoid running out.

Thus, in 1989 the district started a pilot program that offered a rebate for removing turf and replacing it with water-conserving plant materials. People who expressed interest received a packet of information about Xeriscaping, including suggested plants, and a list of California nurseries where they could be found. After filling out an application and completing the landscape changes, an inspection was performed by the district to ensure that all requirements were met and the rebate was sent.

The pilot program ended in July 1990, but was reinstated as a permanent program in March 1992. The rebate is $35 per 100 square feet up to a set amount, for example, $200 for single-family homes. "Even though the rebate does not cover the costs of replacing the entire lawn," says Nelson, "many of the participants do." The district also offers a credit on the water connection charge to new users who reduce the use of turf in the landscape — to the developer if the landscaping is done before purchase, to the home buyer if it is done after purchase.

Through 1992, 47 percent of all new landscapes since 1986 (1,823) participated in the credit/rebate program for installing water-conserving landscapes on new sites. Fifty-five residents have received "cash for grass" rebates for replacing turf with other plant materials. The district expects to reduce annual demand by 12 percent.

The city of Glendale, Arizona, pays $100 to homeowners who convert 50 percent of their yards to nonturf and $35 to those who install automatic timers on drip irrigation systems. The program is tied to a landscape design review service so that the site is visited before changes begin and revisited afterwards. The visits are important since many of the new residents are from out of state and have little or no knowledge of plants for a desert environment. They often overwater the new drought-tolerant plants, sometimes to the point of killing them. More than 1,700 residents have received the rebate for turf reduction and 600 have received it for the timers.

Appendices

Appendix I

Sources for Seeds, Plants, and Equipment

Prairies/Meadows/Grasses

Appalachian Wildflower Nursery
Rt. 1, Box 275A
Reedsville, PA 17084
(717) 667-6998   catalog $2

    Wildflower plants

Applewood Seed Co., Inc.
P.O. Box 10761
Edgemont Station
Golden, CO 80401
(303) 431-6283   catalog free

    Wildflower seed

Bamert Seed Co.
Rt. 3, Box 1120
Muleshoe, TX 79347
(800) 262-9892   catalog free

Native Texan and southern Great Plains grass seed

Kurt Bluemel, Inc.
2740 Greene Lane
Baldwin, MD 21013-9523
(410) 557-7229   catalog $3

Ornamental grass plants

Ernst Crownvetch Farms
R.D. 5, Box 806
Meadville, PA 16335
(800) 873-3321   catalog free

Pennsylvania and Northeast native grass seed, wetland plants, wildflower seed mix

Greenlee Nursery
301 E. Franklin Ave.
Pomona, CA 91766
(714) 629-9045   catalog $5

Native and ornamental grass plants

High Altitude Gardens
P.O. Box 419
Ketchum, ID 83340
(800) 874-7333   catalog $2

Northwestern wildflower and grass seeds and plants

J. L. Hudson, Seedsman
P.O. Box 1058
Redwood City, CA 94064   catalog $1

    California wildflower and grass seeds and plants

Limerock Ornamental Grasses
R.D. 1, Box 111C
Port Matilda, PA 16870
(814) 692-2272   catalog $2.50

    Native and ornamental grass plants

Niche Gardens
1111 Dawson Road
Chapel Hill, NC 27516
(919) 967-0078   catalog $3

    Native wildflowers, grasses, shrubs, and trees

Plants of the Southwest
Aqua Fria, Rt. 6, Box 11-A
Santa Fe, NM 87501
(505) 471-2212   catalog free

    Wildflower and native grass seed, meadow mixes, native lawn grass blends, native shrubs

Prairie Nursery
Rt. 1, Box 365
Westfield, WI 53964
(608) 296-3679   catalog $3

    Wildflower and native grass seeds and plants

Prairie Restorations, Inc.
P.O. Box 327
Princeton, MN 55371
(612) 389-4342   catalog free

Wildflower and native grass plants

Prairie Ridge Nursery
R.R. 2 973B Overland Road
Mt. Horeb, WI 53572-2832
(608) 437-5245   catalog $1

Wildflower and native grass seeds and plants

Rocky Mountain Rare Plants
P.O. Box 20483
Denver, CO 80220-0483   catalog $1

Alpine and other drought-tolerant plants and seeds

Shooting Star Nursery
444 Bates Road
Frankfort, KY 40601
(502) 223-1679   catalog free

Prairie/meadow seed mixes, native grass and wildflower seed, consulting services available

Siskiyou Rare Plant Nursery
2825 Cummings Road
Medford, OR 97501
(503) 772-6846   catalog $2 (refundable with first order)

Specializes in low-growing wildflower, and alpine and rock garden plants

Vermont Wildflower Farm
Rt. 7, Box 5
Charlotte, VT 05445-0005
(802) 425-3931   catalog free

Wildflower seed and meadow mixes

Wildseed Farms, Inc.
1101 Campo Rosa Road, P.O. Box 308
Eagle Lake, TX 77434
(800) 848-0078   catalog $2

Wildflower seed and meadow mixes

Heaths/Heathers

Heather Acres/Heaths and Heathers
1199 Monte-Elma Road
Elma, WA 98541
(206) 482-3258   For a catalog, send a business-size, self-addressed, stamped envelope.

Extensive list of *Calluna vulgaris*, *Erica*, and *Daboecia* species

Rock Spray Nursery
Box 693
Truro, MA 02666
(508) 349-6769   catalog free

A diverse selection of *Calluna vulgaris* and *Erica* plants. Catalog has helpful cultural information.

Sedums/Sempervivums

Country Cottage
Rt. 2, Box 130
Sedgwick, KS 67135
(316) 976-0496   For a catalog, send a first-class stamp.

Plants

Perpetual Perennials
1111 Upper Valley Pike
Springfield, OH 45504
(513) 325-2451   catalog free

Plants

Squaw Mountain Gardens
36212 S.E. Squaw Mountain Road
Estacada, OR 97023
(503) 630-5458   catalog free

Plants

Thompson and Morgan
Box 1308
Jackson, NJ 08527
(908) 363-9356   catalog free

Seed

Ground Covers

Gilson Gardens
P.O. Box 277
Perry, OH 44081
(216) 259-4845   catalog free

Plants

Nichols Garden Nursery
1190 North Pacific Highway
Albany, OR 97321-4598
(503) 928-9280   catalog free

> Herb and ground-cover seed and plants, ecology lawn mixes

Andre Viette Farm & Nursery
State Route 608
Rt. 1, Box 16
Fishersville, VA 22939
(703) 943-2315   catalog $3

> Plants

Equipment

Langenbach
P.O. Box 453
Blairstown, NJ 07825-0453
(800) 362-1991   catalog free

> Primus spot weeder, a small torch fueled with a propane cylinder that can be used to kill young weeds in a meadow planting, between bricks, on gravel paths, around trees and shrubs, and so forth

New Tribe
5517 Riverbanks Road
Grants Pass, OR 97527
(503) 476-9492   For a brochure, send a self-addressed, stamped envelope.

> Weed wrench, used for pulling up woody plants by the roots, comes in four sizes based on jaw capacity for 1-inch up to $2\frac{1}{2}$-inch stem

Appendix II

Organizations

The American Floral Meadow Society
c/o John M. Krouse
University of Maryland
Cherry Hill Turf Research Facility
3120 Gracefield Road
Silver Spring, MD 20904
(301) 572-7247

> Quarterly newsletter, annual conference, published proceedings from the conference, annual membership $35.

Arizona Native Plant Society
P.O. Box 41206, Sun Station
Tucson, AZ 85717

> Publishes pamphlets on desert accent plants, wildflowers, ground covers, shrubs, and trees. Forthcoming: native grasses.

Association of Florida Native Nurseries
P.O. Box 1045, Dept. D92
San Antonio, FL 33576
(904) 588-3687

>   Publishes *Assn. of Florida Native Nurseries Plant and Service Directory*,
> $2.50 plus $1 postage to order, and *Xeric Landscaping with Florida
>   Native Plants*, $10 plus $2.50 postage.

Backyard Wildlife Habitat Program
National Wildlife Federation
1400 16th St. N.W.
Washington, D.C. 20036
(202) 797-6800 or (800) 432-6564

>   When the application is completed and approved, the homeowner
>   receives a certificate recognizing the yard as an official Backyard
>   Wildlife Habitat. A booklet comes with the application. The fee is
> $15. You do not have to join the Federation to have your yard
>   certified but if you are interested, the annual membership is $16.00
>   and includes the bimonthly *National Wildlife* or *International Wildlife*.
>   If you wish to receive both magazines, the membership is $22.
>   Members may participate in camps sponsored by the organization.

California Native Grass Association
Box 566
Dixon, CA 95620

>   Membership $35. Information packets, seed sources, and periodic
>   workshops available.

California Native Plant Society
Growing Natives
Box 489
Berkeley, CA 94701

>   To join and subscribe to this bimonthly newsletter, send $30.

Colorado Native Plant Society
P.O. Box 200
Fort Collins, CO 80522

Annual membership, $12 individual, $15 family, includes newsletter published six times a year. Field trips and workshops sponsored by local chapters and statewide. *Step-by-Step Guide to Creating a Shortgrass Prairie Garden* (1991) by Rick Brune available for $3.

Connecticut College Arboretum
270 Mohegan Ave.
Connecticut College
New London, CT 06320
(203) 439-2140

Membership $25, includes notices of lectures and tours and 40 percent discount on arboretum publications. The arboretum has promoted the use of native plants and the reduction of lawn area for more than forty years. Two naturalistic landscape demonstration areas were established in the 1950s with native and well-adapted grasses, wildflowers, and shrubs. Three helpful publications are: No. 21, "Energy Conservation on the Home Grounds—The Role of Naturalistic Landscaping," $1; No. 30, "Native Shrubs for Land-scaping," $5; and Warren Kenfield, *The Wild Gardener in the Wild Landscape: The Art of Naturalistic Landscaping*, $25.95 (plus $1.65 postage and handling).

Florida Native Plant Society
P.O. Box 680008
Orlando, FL 32868
(407) 299-1472

Membership $20, includes subscription to quarterly newsletter. Numerous local chapters throughout the state.

Hawaii Plant Conservation Center
National Tropical Botanical Garden
Box 340, Lawai
Kauai, HI 96765
(808) 332-7324

> Publishes *Directory of Sources for Native Hawaiian Plants*, $5. The booklet lists growers who offer native plants and support services, illustrations of selected species, and a key to Hawaiian names for the plants.

National Wildflower Research Center
2600 FM 973 North
Austin, TX 78725
(512) 929-3600

> Memberships begin at $25, include newsletter published six times a year and journal published twice a year as well as free brochures on recommended species for your region and sources of native seeds and plants.

Native Prairies Association of Texas
301 Nature Center Drive
Austin, TX 78746
(512) 327-8181

> Quarterly publication, workshops, and field trips; annual membership $15, individual; $25 family.

Natural Areas Association
180 Fox St.
Mukwonago, WI 53149
(414) 363-5500

> Quarterly publication and annual conference, annual membership $25.

New England Wild Flower Society
Garden in the Woods
Hemenway Road
Framingham, MA 01701
(617) 237-4924

> Brochures and booklets on meadow gardening; *Meadows and Meadow Gardening*, a special issue of their publication called *Wild Flower Notes*, is especially helpful. Send $5.50. Individual memberships, $35. They also publish a source list of native plant nurseries, $2.95.

Urban Wildlife Sanctuary Program
National Institute for Urban Wildlife
10921 Trotting Ridge Way
Columbia, MD 21044
(301) 596-3311

> When the application is completed and approved, the property owner receives a certificate designating the property as an Urban Wildlife Sanctuary. The fee is $25 and includes the booklet *A Guide to Urban Wildlife Management*, the first ten issues of the *Urban Wildlife Manager's Notebook*, complimentary one-year subscription to *Urban Wildlife News*, and access to a hot line number to ask questions about managing land for wildlife. Annual membership, $25 a year, includes the benefits mentioned above as well as a discount on publications and activities.

The Wild Ones
P.O. Box 23576
Milwaukee, WI 53223-0576
(414) 242-2723

> Membership $15, includes a newsletter published six times a year.

Appendix III

Sample Natural Landscape Ordinances

Encouraging your own community to adopt an ordinance that allows the environmental alternative of natural landscaping is a positive way to prevent the conflicts that occur when someone changes their landscape and outdated plant-height restriction laws are still in place.

The National Wildflower Research Center and the Milwaukee Audubon Society have both written sample ordinances which can be adapted and revised to fit your local situation.

MILWAUKEE AUDUBON SOCIETY MODEL NATURAL LANDSCAPE ORDINANCE

WHEREAS it is the role of local government to provide for appropriate solid waste management and disposal as well as protect the health, safety, and welfare of its residents;

WHEREAS the current, predominant method of landscaping residential property involves the use of a lawn, the maintenance of which necessitates periodic mowing, watering, fertilizing, and applying of pesticides. Such maintenance produces large quantities of yard waste, creates air and noise pollution, consumes significant amounts of water, exposes residents and their pets to fertilizers and pesticides, and reduces populations of songbirds and butterflies;

WHEREAS the State of Wisconsin has prohibited the disposal of yard waste in any solid waste disposal facility in this state after January 3, 1993. W.S.A. 159.07(2). It is also a policy of the State of Wisconsin to encourage solid waste reduction. W.S.A. 159.05(2);

WHEREAS it is in the public interest to promote activities which reduce air and noise pollution and conserve water supplies;

WHEREAS there are people and animals which are sensitive to exposure to fertilizers and pesticides, as applied to lawns, and experience acute effects as a result of such exposure, including, but not limited to, severe reactions;

WHEREAS there exist alternative methods of landscaping, other than the use of lawns, which produce little or no yard waste, do not necessitate the use of lawn mowing machines, need only small amounts of water, and require no fertilizers or pesticides. These alternative methods are not less visually pleasing than lawns, and they promote an appreciation for the diversity of plant life and serve as reminders of our natural heritage;

NOW, THEREFORE, be it ordained:

Section 1. Natural heritage and ornamental gardens. Notwithstanding any provision of any other ordinance, an owner or occupier, who has written authorization of the owner, of residential property may establish and maintain a natural heritage or ornamental garden, provided that:

(a) Such a garden, or any portion thereof, does not encroach property ownership line or public right-of-way; and

(b) The owner or occupier complies with the notice provisions of Section 2.

Section 2. Notice. If any natural heritage or ornamental garden, or the combination thereof, occupies an area in excess of fifty percent (50%) of the surface area of the property, not otherwise occupied by buildings, structures, or improvements, the owner or occupier shall file a notice with _____. Such notice shall contain:

(a) The name and address of the owner or occupier filing the notice;

(b) A drawing or sketch that depicts the area of the garden relative to all property ownership lines, public rights-of-way, buildings, structures, and improvements located on or immediately adjacent to the property. This drawing need not be to scale; and

(c) In the case of a natural heritage garden, the drawing shall identify the type of natural community which is intended to be simulated. If more than one natural community is intended, the different locations for the different intended natural communities should be identified. In the case of an ornamental garden, the drawing shall indicate the relative location, within the garden area, of the various plantings.

Section 3. Garden Advisory Board. There is created a Garden Advisory Board composed of ___ members, appointed by _____, for ____ years. Garden Advisory Board members shall have knowledge, expertise, or experience in the field of natural or ornamental botany, or native plant ecology, or in the design, construction, or maintenance of natural heritage or ornamental gardens. Upon the request of any person who wishes to establish and maintain a natural heritage or ornamental garden to which the notice provisions of Section 2 of this ordinance would be applicable, the Garden Advisory Board shall provide advice and consultation to that person so as to encourage the development of a garden design, including the use of plant species and plant associations, that would be appropiate for and sensitive to the physical attributes of the garden location as well as the visual and botanic character of the surrounding area.

Section 4. Definitions.

Natural heritage garden: An area that: is managed with the intention of simulating a natural community or communities native to the State of Wisconsin, such as a prairie, meadow, or woodland; contains only plants that are identified by Curtis, John T., *Vegetation of Wisconsin*, University of Wisconsin Press (1959), which is hereby incorporated by reference, as components of the particular natural community or communities intended to be simulated; and does not contain any plant which is defined as a "nuisance weed" pursuant to W.S.A. 66.955 or a "noxious weed" pursuant to W.S.A. 66.96.

Ornamental garden: An area that is managed for the visual display of a variety of plants, including, but not limited to, trees, shrubs, ferns, flowers, grasses, ground cover, mosses, and that does not contain any plant which is defined as a "nuisance weed" pursuant to W.S.A. 66.955 or a "noxious weed" pursuant to W.S.A. 66.96.

Section 5. Severability.

If any provision of this ordinance is held to be invalid or invalid as applied, its invalidity shall not affect the validity or applicability of the other provisions of this ordinance, and for this purpose, the provisions of this ordinance are hereby declared to be severable.

Reprinted by permission of Fred Sweet, President,
Milwaukee Audubon Society, Mequon, Wisconsin.

NOTE: For the new version of this sample ordinance,
which was adopted as this book went to press, write to
the Milwaukee Audobon Society,
12248 Farmdale Road 99 W, Mequon, WI 53902.

NATIONAL WILDFLOWER RESEARCH CENTER SAMPLE NATURAL LANDSCAPE ORDINANCE

An ordinance to promote the use of native vegetation, including native grasses, in planned landscapes and to allow the use of such plants in the preservation or restoration of natural plant communities.

Legislative Purpose

The use of wildflowers and other native plants in managed landscape design can be economical, low-maintenance, effective in soil and water conservation, and may preclude the excessive use of pesticides, herbicides, and fertilizers. Furthermore, native vegetation and native plant communities, on a worldwide basis, are disappearing at an alarmingly rapid rate. The legislature recognizes the desirability of permitting and encouraging the managed preservation and restoration of natural plant communities in urban, suburban, and rural areas while maintaining public health and safety. It is not the intent of this legislation to allow vegetated areas to be unmanaged or overgrown when such growth provides demonstrated health hazards or prevents detection of accumulated trash and refuse that constitutes either a direct health hazard or provides a breeding ground for fauna known to create a safety or health hazard. The legislature recognizes that a limited number of species may be serious agricultural pests or may adversely affect human health or safety. In such instances, the legislature has provided a remedy by specifically defining plants recognized to be a threat to the agricultural economy or to human health and safety.

Natural Landscaping Defined and Protected

"Preservation" means to keep intact desirable components of the existing vegetation at a building or construction site.

"Restoration" means to replant a building or construction site with vegetation native to the region, including grasses, forbs, shrubs, and trees.

Noxious Weeds Identified

The following plant species are defined as noxious weeds:
(This list should be made appropriate for the area and should be minimally restrictive. The state list of noxious weeds may be helpful.)

A list for central Texas would include *Amaranthus palmeri* (Palmer amaranth), *A. retroflexus* (redroot pigweed), *Ambrosia artemisiifolia* (ragweed), *A. psilostachya* (ragweed), *A. trifida* (ragweed), *Sonchus asper* (sowthistle), and *Sorghum halepense* (Johnsongrass).

It shall be lawful to grow native plants, including ferns, grasses, forbs, shrubs, and trees, in a managed landscape design when said plants were not obtained in violation of local, state, or federal laws. No commissioner or other agent of the [town, city, village, county, etc.] may undertake to damage, remove, burn, or cut vegetation on a preservation or restoration project or in any other landscape incorporting native plants, except those specifically prohibited herein, and except on order of a court of record following a hearing at which it is established (1) that noxious weeds specifically named in the weed ordinance exist in such preservation or restoration projects and that a condition creating a clear and present hazard to public health or safety has arisen or (2) that the project is a threat to the agricultural economy. An action for a court order under this subsection shall be maintained as an action to enjoin a public nuisance. A court order under this subsection shall provide that the destruction, cutting, or removal of vegetation shall be selective unless general cutting, destruction, or removal is necessary to eliminate the offending condition.

*Reprinted by permission of the National Wildflower
Research Center, Austin, Texas.*

Appendix IV

Bibliography

Brown, Lauren. *Grasses: An Identification Guide* (New York: Houghton Mifflin, 1979).

DeWolf, Gordon P., Jr. (ed.). *Taylor's Guide to Ground Covers, Vines, and Grasses* (New York: Houghton Mifflin, 1987).

** Diekelman, John, and Robert Schuster. *Natural Landscaping: Designing with Native Plant Communities* (New York: McGraw Hill, 1982).

Druse, Ken. *The Natural Habitat Garden* (New York: Clarkson Potter, 1994).

Ellefson, Connie, Tom Stephens, and Doug Welsh. *Xeriscape Gardening: Water Conservation for the American Landscape* (New York: Macmillan, 1989).

* Gleason, Henry A., and Arthur Cronquist. "The Floristic Provinces of the Continental United States and Canada," *The National Geography of Plants* (New York: Columbia University Press, 1964).

Greenlee, John. *The Encyclopedia of Ornamental Grasses* (Emmaus, Pa.: Rodale Press, 1992).

** Harker, Donald, Sherri Evans, Marc Evans, and Kay Harker. *Landscape Restoration Handbook* (Boca Raton, Fla.: Lewis Publishers, 1993).

Hitchcock, A. S. *Manual of the Grasses of the United States* (revised by Agnes Chase, 2nd ed.; New York: Dover Publications, 1971), 2 volumes.

Holmes, Roger (ed.). *Taylor's Guide to Natural Gardening* (New York: Houghton Mifflin, 1993).

Jones, Samuel B., and Leonard E. Foote. *Gardening with Native Wild Flowers* (Portland, Ore.: Timber Press, 1990).

Kenfield, Warren G. *The Wild Gardener in the Wild Landscape* (New London, Conn.: Connecticut College Arboretum, 1991; orig. ed., 1966).

Knopf, Jim. *The Xeriscape Flower Gardener: A Waterwise Guide for the Rocky Mountain Region* (Boulder, Colo.: Johnson Books, 1991).

* Kuchler, A. W., "Potential Natural Vegetation of the Coterminous United States." *Goode's World Atlas* (Chicago: Rand McNally & Co., 1974, 14th ed.).

Martin, Laura C. *The Wildflower Meadow Book* (Chester, Conn.: Globe Pequot, 1990, 2nd ed.).

McIntyre, Kipp, and Lynne Randolph. "A Guide to Mosses and Moss Gardening" (Stockbridge, Ga., 1991). For a copy of this small brochure, send $6.50 to Mostly Moss, 130 Sandy Drive, Dept. A., Stockbridge, GA 30281.

Metheny, D. *Hardy Heather Species* (Seaside, Ore.: Frontier Publishing, 1991).

Pauly, Wayne R. "How to Manage Small Prairie Fires" (Madison, Wis.: 1988). Send $3 to Dane County Park Commission, 4318 Robertson Road, Madison, WI 53714, or call (608) 246-3896.

* Pirkle, E. C., W. H. Yoho, and J. A. Henry, "Dominant Vegetation Types." *Natural Landscapes of the United States* (Dubuque, Iowa: Kendall/Hunt Publishing Co., 1985, 4th ed.).

Robinson, William. *The Wild Garden* (reprint ed., London: Scolar Press, 1977; orig. ed. 1894).

Scott, Jane. *Field and Forest: A Guide to Native Landscapes for Gardeners and Naturalists* (New York: Walker and Company, 1984).

Sears, Paul B. *Lands Beyond the Forest* (Englewood Cliffs, N.J.: Prentice-Hall, Inc., 1969).

"Sources of Native Seeds and Plants," a brochure published by the Soil and Water Conservation Society, 7515 Northeast Ankeny Road, Ankeny, IA 50021; (515) 289-2331. $3 postpaid.

Stein, Sara. *Noah's Garden: Restoring the Ecology of Our Own Back Yards* (New York: Houghton Mifflin, 1993).

U.S. Department of Agriculture, Forest Service. *Land Areas of the National Forest System* (Washington, D.C., 1993). Map with listings of remaining acres of national grasslands and forests. Call (202) 205-1248 to order a copy.

Wasowski, Sally, with Andy Wasowski. *Requiem for a Lawnmower: And Other Essays on Easy Gardening with Native Plants* (Dallas, Tex.: Taylor Publishing, 1992).

Weaver, J. E. *North American Prairie* (Lincoln, Nebr.: Johnsen Publishing, 1954).

Wildland Home Fire Risk Meter (National Wildfire Coordinating Group, 1990). Developed by Dennis G. Simmerman and William C. Fischer, USDA Intermountain Research Station. Available from your local forest service in the Western states.

Wilson, Jim. *Landscaping with Wildflowers: An Environmental Approach to Gardening* (New York: Houghton Mifflin, 1992).

Wilson, William H. W. *Landscaping with Wildflowers and Native Plants* (San Ramon, Calif.: Ortho Books, 1984).

* *The general native plant communities map on page 21 is based on the work of Gleason (and Cronquist), Kuchler, and Pirkle (Yoho and Henry).*

** *These books provide detailed information about small, localized native plant communities and the species that are indigenous to them.*

Index

euonymus (*Euonymus*), 86, 147
Eupatorium, 91, 141
   E. maculatum, 91, 99, 100
Euphorbia, 85, 92, 96
evening primrose, 30, 107, 131, 141
evergreen blueberry, 31
everlasting, pearly, 151

Fagus grandifolia, 22, 136, 137
fairy bells, 32, 137
fairy duster, 30
fairy trumpet, 33
Fallugia paradoxa, 29, 141–42
false indigo, 99, 104
   blue, 91, 101, 125
false lily-of-the-valley, 22, 23, 55
false Solomon's-seal, 32
false sunflower (oxeye sunflower), 91, 96
feather reed grass, 13
fennel, bronze, 129
fern(s), 25, 32, 125, 138, 143
   Christmas, 23, 137, 163
   in coastal plain, 24
   in eastern woodlands, 23
   hay-scented, 125, 138
   mountain wood, 22, 32
   in northern conifer forest, 22
   in Pacific forest, 32
fernbush, 27
Ferocactus, 31, 161
fertilizer blends, organic, 72
fescue (*Festuca*), 12, 42, 112, 113, 124, 131, 132, 142
   blue (*F. ovina, F. cinerea, F. glauca*), 41, 124, 149, 161, 166
   California (*F. californica*), 41, 132
   fine-leaved (*F. tenuifolia*), 42, 112
   red (*F. rubra*), 112, 119
   sheep's, 112, 124
   tall (*F. arundianacea*), 113, 127
fetterbush, 136
field bindweed, 85
field pussytoes, 25
Filipendula rubra, 91, 96, 97, 125
Fimbristylis cymosa, 168
fir, 20, 27, 31
fire, 174–75
   reducing risk of, 80–81
   see also burning
fire pink, 137, 163
flax, blue, 124
flax lily, 168

fleabane, 29, 166
fleeceflower, 48, 163
Florida bluestem, 25
Florida gama grass, 108, 109
Florida thatch palm, 24
flowering currant, 28
flowering dogwood, 22, 125
flowering raspberry, 136
flowering spurge, 92, 96
flowers, *see* wildflowers
foamflower, 23, 137, 138
Foeniculum vulgare, 129
forest:
   northern conifer, 20–22
   Pacific, 21, 31–32
   Rocky Mountain, 21, 26–29
   tropical, 21, 24–25
   see also trees; woodlands
Forestiera neomexicana, 29
fortnight lily, 166, 167
fountain grass, 151, 166
Fouquieria splendens, 30, 161
foxglove, wild, 94
Fragaria, 52, 148, 150, 151
   F. virginiana, 52, 92, 129, 131, 143, 151
Fraxinus, 168
fringed puccoon, 107
fringed sage, 48, 114
fringetree, white, 24
front-yard gardens, 159–69
   see also photo 10
frostweed, 141
fuchsia, 164
   California, 63, 132–33
fumewort, 137

gaillardia (*Gaillardia*), 130
   G. aristata, 118, 127, 130
   G. pulchella, 94, 130, 141
Galanthus, 79
galax (*Galax*), 52
Galium odoratum, 137, 164
gama grass, Florida, 109
Gambel's oak, 29, 163
gardens, xii, 159–69
garlic, society, 166
garlic chives, 129, 130
garlic mustard, 85, 99, 138, 143
Gaultheria procumbens, 23, 52
gaura (*Gaura*), 107, 130, 141
gayfeather, 13, 25, 94, 107
Gaylussacia, 53, 125, 163
Gazania rigens, 148
gentian (*Gentiana*), 98
geranium (*Geranium*), 161, 166
   wild (*G. maculatum*), 125, 130
germander, 60, 148

Geum triflorum, 28, 91, 97, 99
giant reed, 83
Gilia, 33
gill-over-the-ground, 143
ginger, wild, 27, 32, 49, 138, 143
Glecoma hederacea, 143
globe amaranth, 130
globe thistle, 161
glory-of-the-snow, 79
glossy buckthorn, 87
golden alexander, 97
golden banner, 33
goldenrod, 22, 94, 96, 101, 108, 125, 127, 141
   stiff, 91, 98, 100, 125
golden smoke, 33
goldenstar, 137
goldmoss, 156
gold poppy, 30
Gomphrena, 130
goodenia, 168
goosefoot, 175
gopher apple, 25, 54
grama, 93, 141
   blue, 26, 28, 29, 37, 90, 96, 104, 114, 115, 128, 149
   sideoats, 26, 29, 37, 90, 93, 96, 97, 99, 103, 104, 114, 115, 121, 122, 124, 128, 141
Gramineae, 12, 34
grape, wild, 123
grape hyacinth, 79, 165
grasses, 12–15, 67
   in chaparral, 33
   in coastal plain, 24
   in eastern woodlands, 23
   invasive, table of, 84
   native, 89–115
   in Pacific forest, 32
   planting of, 73–75
   in prairie, 25–26
   in Rocky Mountain forest, 26, 27–29
   in Sonoran Desert area, 30–31
   sources for seeds and plants, 185–89
   table of, 34–45
   in tropical forest, 25
   in western desert/great basin, 29–30
   wildflowers with, 17, 119–22
   see also ground covers; meadow; prairie
gray birch, 125
gray goldenrod, 125
Grayia spinosa, 28

the WILD LAWN handbook